TEACHING FOR DEMOCRACY IN AN AGE OF ECONOMIC DISPARITY

Teaching for Democracy in an Age of Economic Disparity addresses the intersections between democratic education and economic inequality in American society. Drawing upon well-established theoretical constructs in the literature on democratic citizenship as well as recent events, this volume outlines the ways in which students can not only be educated about democracy, but become actively engaged in the social issues of their time.

The collection begins with an examination of how the confluence of capitalism and education has problematized the current model of democratic education, before transitioning into discussions of how teachers can confront economic disparity both economically and civically in the classroom. The authors then introduce a variety of ways in which teachers can engage and empower students' civic action at all grade levels. As a final component, the volume explores new avenues for civic action, including the use of social media for democratic engagement in schools and opportunities for critical reflection and cross-cultural dialogue. This book is a valuable resource both for scholars interested in the research on democratic education and practicing teachers wishing to turn their students into critical, active citizens.

Cory Wright-Maley is Assistant Professor of Education at St. Mary's University, where he teaches elementary curriculum, instruction, and assessment, specializing in social studies education.

Trent Davis is Associate Professor of Education at St. Mary's University, where he teaches the philosophical and historical foundations of education.

TEACHING FOR DEMOCRACY IN AN AGE OF ECONOMIC DISPARITY

Edited by Cory Wright-Maley and Trent Davis

Routledge
Taylor & Francis Group

NEW YORK AND LONDON

First published 2017
by Routledge
711 Third Avenue, New York, NY 10017

and by Routledge
2 Park Square, Milton Park, Abingdon, Oxon, OX14 4RN

Routledge is an imprint of the Taylor & Francis Group, an informa business

© 2017 Taylor & Francis

Library of Congress Cataloging in Publication Data
Names: Wright-Maley, Cory, editor. | Davis, Trent, editor.
Title: Teaching for democracy in an age of economic disparity / edited by
    Cory Wright-Maley and Trent Davis.
Description: New York, NY : Routledge, 2016. | Includes bibliographical
    references and index.
Identifiers: LCCN 2016003843| ISBN 9781138933415 (hardback) |
    ISBN 9781138933422 (pbk.) | ISBN 9781315678603 (e-book)
Subjects: LCSH: Democracy and education—United States. |
    Democracy—Study and teaching—United States. | Citizenship—Study
    and teaching—United States. | Social justice—Study and teaching—
    United States. | Income distribution—United States.
Classification: LCC LC89 .T43 2016 | DDC 379—dc23
LC record available at https://lccn.loc.gov/2016003843

ISBN: 978-1-138-93341-5 (hbk)
ISBN: 978-1-138-93342-2 (pbk)
ISBN: 978-1-315-67860-3 (ebk)

Typeset in Bembo
by Swales & Willis Ltd, Exeter, Devon, UK

Printed and bound in the United States of America by Publishers Graphics,
LLC on sustainably sourced paper.

CONTENTS

ACKNOWLEDGMENTS

No collection like this one is published without help. We would like to thank the many contributors who crafted such strong essays and unfailingly responded to our repeated requests with exemplary grace. We would also like to formally recognize the many reviewers who gave of their time and expertise to offer substantive and focused feedback that made each piece better. Our warmest thanks go to Jodi Benenson, Stephen Brookfield, Margaret Brower, Shauna Butterwick, Stephen Caliendo, Antonio Castro, Shira Eve Epstein, Ron Evans, Rich Gibson, Eric Gordon, Tim Harvey, Reinhold Hedtke, Mark Helmsing, Nathalia Jaramillo, Ray La Raja, Michael MacLeod, Meg Monaghan, Judith Pace, Walter Parker, Julie Pennington, Greg Queen, Wayne Ross, Beth Rubin, Edda Sant, Sandra J. Schmidt, David Schoem, and Jennifer Tupper. Finally, we would like to express our gratitude to our editor at Routledge, Catherine Bernard, for her advice and support. On a more personal note, we would like to thank our St. Mary's colleagues and friends for their kind support. Trent would like to thank his sister Tanya and his parents. Additionally, Cory would like to thank his partner, Jenn, and children, Aulden and Eli, for their outsized patience for many late nights and moments of distraction.

INTRODUCTION

Cory Wright-Maley and Trent Davis

Situating Economic Disparity

Preparing students to participate in democracy is one of the central charges of today's schools. Thomas Jefferson (1784/1954) argued that education was "essentially necessary" to help ensure that the people were prepared to participate in government, and to guard against the corruptions of wealth, privilege, and the degeneracies of human weakness inherent in all human constructs. He believed that the "people themselves" were the republic's "only safe depositories" (para. 1).

This word *republic* is an important one to keep in mind. Thomas Paine (1789/2011) explained how the radical shift of power away from the monarchy and toward the people elevates "the public good" (p. 134). We have positioned this text as one that aligns fundamentally with the ideals and principles of this "public good" within our liberal democracy, albeit one that is, as Giroux points out in Chapter 1, "under siege." However, it is important to note that we don't believe there ever was a halcyon period to which we must return. The participatory ideal, towards which democracy strives, is ever in process and in various stages of imperfection (Derrida, 2006). This is true, too, of how we prepare our students to be engaged citizens.

Currently much of what constitutes democratic education takes place in civics classes, where students learn about the functions of government and their potential roles as citizens. Throughout the social studies curriculum students are pressed to think critically, learn the tools and dispositions of social discourse, and involve themselves in the mainstream political process. Although such preparation constitutes important components of civic education, it is embedded within a political landscape that is increasingly informed by a neoliberal ideology with an overriding emphasis on enhancing the power of corporations and wealthy individuals, or, as Jefferson called them, the "artificial aristocracy" (as cited in Hartmann, 2010, p. 91).

Obviously, Jefferson's insight that economic disparity would undermine democratic life was not revelatory. Numerous political thinkers from across the political spectrum have expressed a similar concern throughout the modern period. At its inception Jean-Jacques Rousseau (1755/1984), for example, effectively demonstrated that, as France's overall wealth grew, the inequality between its citizens proceeded apace. Early in the past century Carl Schmitt warned that it would be impossible to keep economic interests from ultimately co-opting the armature of political power (Schmitt, 1938/1996), with democracy itself becoming "only a poor façade concealing the dominance of parties and economic interests" (1923/1988, p. 20). Over 40 years ago John Rawls (1971) with his influential "two principles of justice" tried to admit inequalities in his ideal polity only if they could be demonstrated to benefit the least advantaged.

Most recently, two prominent political theorists, Michael J. Sandel and Sheldon S. Wolin, both offered diagnoses of the current problem of economic inequality in the United States. Sandel (2012) pointed out that "the reach of markets, and market-oriented thinking, into aspects of life traditionally governed by non-market norms is one of the most significant developments of our time" (p. 7). He then offered two connected reasons why we should be alarmed by this development: First, over the past several decades there has been a growing disparity in terms of a widening gap between rich and poor that compromises—if not outright betrays—any commitment to equal opportunity for all. Second, when increasingly everything is subject to market forces, there is a corresponding increase in the "corrosive tendency of markets" to change the way people feel about the good being exchanged (p. 9). To illustrate this point, Sandel provided the example of paying children to read in school, demonstrating how it alienated students from their desire to read as an end in itself.

In a similar vein, Wolin (2008) pointed out that within liberal democracy life has become "managed" through collusion between corporate and political actors. As this collusion gets tighter and tighter the grave threat of nothing less than "inverted totalitarianism" grows ever more likely (p. 57). As Wolin explained, this is a peculiar variation of totalitarianism suited to the complex reality of neoliberalism in which more and more power is concentrated in the hands of fewer people through the deliberate manipulation of the levers of media, politics, and finance.

Tellingly neither Sandel nor Wolin believe that there is an easy remedy in sight, and, while they both offer some measured hope that democratic life can still be rejuvenated, neither has anything novel to recommend. For his part, Wolin (2008) insisted that, "if democracy is about participating in self-government, its first requirement is a supportive culture, a complex of beliefs, values, and practices that nurture equality, cooperation, and freedom" (pp. 260–261). Neither, however, is naïve to the enormous difficulties that reanimating such a "culture" would involve.

Incredibly, even politicians from across the political spectrum are echoing these concerns. Republican Vance McAllister, former House representative from Louisiana, outlined the ways in which the contributions of wealthy individuals are treated as a quid pro quo in the decision making of elected representatives (MacNeal, 2014). Bernie Sanders's (2016) political platform explicitly states: "In the year 2015, with a political campaign finance system that is corrupt and increasingly controlled by billionaires and special interests, I fear very much that, in fact, government of the people, by the people, and for the people is beginning to perish in the United States of America" (para. 2). And even Ron Paul (2013), on the libertarian right, has suggested that one of the problems with ceding power to governments is that corporations just end up seizing it from the American people, who ultimately have little control over how that power is wielded, and yet bear the consequences of sequestered policy.

Economists and economic scholars, too, have pointed out the disparities in the capitalist system and its corrosive impacts on both economic development and democracy (e.g., Chakrabortty, 2016; OECD, 2015; Piketty, 2014; Stiglitz, 2013, 2015; Taibbi, 2015). Economic disparity in America has manifold, interwoven consequences. In the richest country on the planet, more than 43 million people live below the poverty line, and perhaps as many as half of all Americans are but one paycheck away from falling below it (Kotler, 2015). Roughly 3.5 million people are homeless (Caliendo, 2015) or cannot afford access to housing in safe neighborhoods near available work, even though they would like to find both (Kotler, 2015). These neighborhoods are frequently subject to regular violence, causing Taibbi (2015) to note that it is "literally dangerous to be poor" in America (p. 343). In part, this is because the educational opportunities are themselves unequal (e.g., Kozol, 1991, 2005); and thus the education performance differential between rich and poor students is dramatic, having risen 40 percent over the last quarter century ("True progressivism," 2012).

Overall people have less leisure time, are less happy, and report declining societal well-being (Anielski, 2013). In addition to these personal and social consequences of economic disparity, the influence of corporations and wealthy interests erodes public trust, leading citizens to stop participating because they see politicians catering to the interests of the wealthy. This magnifies the influence of wealth in politics, and ultimately diminishes the health both of Americans (Wilkinson and Pickett, 2009) and of American democracy (Reich, 2014; Stiglitz, 2013). It is little wonder then that President Barack Obama (2013) called economic disparity the "defining challenge of our time" (para. 6).

Purposes

Thomas Piketty's (2014) book motivated us to really consider how our traditional civics curricula fail to address the ways in which economic disparity undermines democracy and the public good in America. Piketty effectively exposed the ideological lie that in the twentieth century unfettered capitalism benefited everyone equitably. He revealed for us two key conclusions. First, the market has "no natural, spontaneous process to prevent destabilizing, inegalitarian forces from prevailing permanently" (p. 21), which means "top earners can quickly separate themselves from the rest by a wide margin" (p. 23). Second, Piketty argued that "the history of inequality is shaped by the way economic, social, and political actors view what is just and what is not, as well as by the relative power of those actors and the collective choices of that result" (p. 20). In other words, human-driven political policies matter, and the ways in which we frame economic and democratic justice and equity determine the degree to which economic disparity exists in our society. Further, how we choose to make decisions about democracy and economic equity in the future can ameliorate or even reverse the present circumstances (Kotler, 2015; Reich, 2014; Stelzner, 2015; Stiglitz, 2013, 2015).

The process must, we believe, begin with how we educate students to engage in democratic practices in spite of democracy's contemporary woes. We recognize that we are picking up the mantle of other educators before us, Bowles and Gintis (1976/2011) foremost among them. They articulated the existence of inequality and the myriad problems that grew out of this reality 40 years ago. Nevertheless, we also recognize that, unlike the case in 1976, this concern has now become part of the zeitgeist.

We share the view that Bowles and Gintis (1976/2011) articulated in the revised introduction they included in their recent reissue of *Schooling in Capitalist America*: that the ways in which we prepare students to influence their government and contribute civically matter. We also believe, however, that our methods for doing so are outmoded. We live within a political milieu that undermines the traditional message that all of our students' voices matter within the political process. It is not our goal to frame this volume pessimistically or cynically. On the contrary, we wish to call educators to action to address the troubling context in which the traditional means of preparing students for civic life no longer provide them with the tools to engage effectively in our democracy. Just as the nature of democracy is ever evolving, democratic education, too, must be a sphere of practices that are constantly renegotiated based on the needs of the people and circumstances they are meant to serve (Torres, 1998).

As we conceptualized this book, we sought to initiate conversations that would help attend to two central questions. First, in an age of economic disparity, how can we use democratic education to meaningfully promote effective citizen engagement that in turn substantively impacts the ways the nation is governed? Second, how do we prepare students to counter the fundamental imbalances generated by economic inequality that corrupt and weaken the democratic ethos of the American people and the institutions of democracy under which we operate? We are therefore immensely grateful to the many smart and engaged scholars who produced high quality chapters for this volume. They are both timely and provocative in the way they stimulate discussion about the role of democratic education today. After considering various organizational approaches we divided the 14 chapters into four sections. Our intention was to find an arrangement that encouraged similar themes to resonate within each section, as well as for the collection as a whole to provide a coherent development of thought on the topic of democratic education in today's environment of economic disparity. To the extent that we have succeeded, it is our hope that this volume will play a role in the ongoing effort to confront economic disparity and the challenges it presents for democracy and democratic education.

A Preview of Chapters

Section I, "Setting the Context," aims to describe in broad yet arresting terms how the confluence of crony capitalism and education has made problematic the ways we have attempted to prepare students for democratic life. Henry A. Giroux gets things rolling with a pointed and thorough analysis of how democratic education is struggling under neoliberalism. Joseph R. Nichols, Jr. then helps us understand how the construct of the "economic citizen" has grown ascendant in recent years, and that this troubling trend undermines civic education. In his contribution Mark Edward Johnson offers readers the historical development of two predominant approaches to social studies education, the "emancipatory" and the "pluralist." Using these frameworks, he offers two different ways that teachers may likely approach issues of economic disparity. This section helps situate the reader in terms of the current context of education and its intersections with economic philosophy, as well as the historical trends that have emerged in citizenship and democratic education.

Section II, "Confronting Economic Disparity," aims to build upon the framework of Section I by looking at different ways to approach democratic education in this neoliberal age. John Rogers and Joel Westheimer share insights from their research on the extent to which teachers from a range of backgrounds address economic disparity in their classrooms. Tamara L. Sober examines how we ought to frame economics and teach about economic inequity in schools. She provides clear insights into why fresh thinking is so important here. Wayne Journell, Brett L. M. Levy, and James M. M. Hartwick offer reflections on how to teach students about the seminal topic of campaign finance, which has become a clarion call for many individuals and organizations across the political spectrum concerned with the influence of money in politics. They offer multiple avenues through which the current state of campaign finance might be reformed. Together these chapters help to reveal current practices and approaches, while offering theoretical avenues for confronting economic inequality.

In Section III, "Building Spaces to Nurture Student Action," the authors attend more specifically to how teachers can best be prepared to engage and empower student civic action at all levels: primary, secondary, and during preservice teacher education. This is the largest section, and each chapter offers a sustained and helpful analysis of how teachers can think more concretely about democratic education. Kathryn E. Engebretson and Alexandria Hollett look at student empowerment in education through feminist pedagogy and the challenges inherent in creating new pedagogical spaces for civic empowerment for all students. The essential role of literacy is the topic of Jennifer E. Dolan and Douglas Kaufman's chapter, which imaginatively links the best literacy pedagogy with the cultivation of student voice. Their chapter reveals the means through which we can come to appreciate the challenges and support preservice teachers to foster students in a democratic society through literature and literacy. Drawing on Paulo Freire's pedagogical vision, Ryan Colwell describes an approach to empowering elementary students to learn about social issues through the lens of homelessness. In this chapter he provides an illustrative approach to incorporating civic involvement over the course of a unit on the topic. Karon LeCompte and Brooke Blevins explain how citizenship can be enhanced through the dynamics of "action civics" by way of positive youth development programs. They describe the ways in which students are engaged in community projects and how they can be leveraged into powerful opportunities for civic engagement. Finally in this section, Emma Kornfeld, Jill Bass, and Brett L. M. Levy discuss the Mikva Challenge as another form of action civics, in which the synthesis of democratic classroom practices and opportunities to engage in democratic processes in the real world is of central importance. They illustrate the ways in which this program contributes to the development of youth community leaders and enables students to find their civic voices. These chapters help to illuminate promising civic practices to meaningfully engage students of all ages in the process of civic engagement at the intersections of economic disparity and democracy.

In Section IV, "New Fronts in the Fight for Democracy," the authors explore recent cultural developments and elucidate fresh possibilities that can invigorate sites of civic learning. Lauren Arend and Alexander Cuenca discuss the lessons we can learn from the Mike Brown tragedy in terms of imagining new possibilities of democratic engagement and expression. Their chapter challenges readers to reconsider what counts as civic engagement and by whose reckoning. They provide multiple forms of civic action that challenge both the structural inequities and the traditional conceptions of democratic participation. Tara Hyland-Russell and Corinne Syrnyk, colleagues of ours at St. Mary's University, describe their social justice approach to Humanities 101 and how an attention to narrative through the liberal arts can open possibilities for democratic education. Their careful attention to the needs of marginalized adults helps to accentuate the inherent possibility that exists within all of us to blossom intellectually and civically when provided the space and supports to do so. Finally, Daniel G. Krutka and Jeffrey P. Carpenter look at social media and how it is changing our sense of democratic communication, agency, and pedagogy. They offer readers the chance to consider both the affordances and the challenges associated with social media, as well as insights into the promise that social media may hold for future democratic engagement even in an unequal economic landscape. Although addressing very different challenges, each chapter in this section helps to illustrate the constantly evolving nature of meaningful democratic action, revealing that, even in the face of economic disparity, pedagogical possibilities for vibrant democratic practice continue to emerge to confront the challenges that the current context presents.

Final Thoughts

This collection was initially informed by our deeply held conviction that *teaching matters*. Of course, this is not a novel insight: committed and effective educators have realized for a long time that better teaching leads to better learning. Notwithstanding this belief, there is no denying that teaching about and for democracy in an age of economic disparity may seem a daunting, even insurmountable, task. It is vital that educators not succumb to a debilitating sense of futility. Almost 50 years ago Albert Camus (1968) captured this sentiment; he reminded us that "the first thing is not to despair" (p. 135).

Adam Phillips (2005) recommended that our culture needed to recover the notion of "sanity." What would a sane pedagogy for democracy look like? If "insanity" means being out of touch with an equitably shared social reality, then according to Phillips "sanity is lived according to acknowledgements" (p. 231). We would like to highlight three key points that educators should acknowledge if they are to keep exploring possibilities for democratic education within the context of a "rigged" game (Warren, 2014).

First, although we should appreciate the importance of the local struggles that define our responsibilities as educators, we must also never lose sight of the *broader context* in which we work. Feeling isolated and alone is a sure recipe for frustration and burnout; we cannot confront economic disparity alone. We must seek camaraderie situated within a broader perspective to build solidarity and keep us going. Although our own pedagogical decisions might seem small and even insignificant at times, small coordinated changes add up. The work of teachers is the planting of seeds, which we may not be around to see grow to fruition; the impact of our teaching extends beyond the classroom to the community, the country, and even the world. It is therefore of the utmost urgency that we advance a civic education that reflects the contemporary challenges facing our democracy.

Second, teaching is inevitably and invariably a *political act*. Virtually all aspects of teaching and learning are infused with values and judgments that are not universally shared. This is not something to be lamented, but celebrated. Although it can seem as though our professional autonomy is hedged in by a monolithic and hegemonic system, we must not hesitate to exercise our pedagogical freedom; indeed it is imperative that we do so. It is through conscious and deliberate action that teachers can begin to reclaim the pedagogical autonomy to truly act as agents of transformation (Giroux, 2013). As the chapters contained within this volume powerfully demonstrate, despite the givens of our teaching lives in terms of curricula, testing, and other formalities of schooling, there almost always remain openings where democratic possibilities can flourish.

Finally, *hope* remains essential. Since succumbing to fatalism leads inevitably to exhaustion and acquiescence, it is important to maintain a sense of hopefulness that things can get better. But, as Noel Pearson (2009) points out, hope must be based in one's faith in one's ability to act: "hope founded on mere optimism is not serious, and a serious person is not readily gulled into hope, especially not by his or her own wishful thinking" (pp. xi–xii). We therefore call teachers to action to build upon the ideas presented here to work toward a vision of democracy that enables a radical hope, one that insinuates the practices of insurgent pedagogies to empower serious people determined to work in solidarity to achieve that vision. We recognize that our book only scratches the surface; our volume does not explicitly address the important aspects of labor education, indigeneity, the environment, or the global nature of many of the challenges discussed herein. It is our wish, however, that this book will help to generate a discussion and subsequent actions that will, in turn, begin to address these fundamental issues.

Every generation must struggle to keep democracy alive, and ours is no different. To borrow from some of our authors, democracy is an ongoing process, a "verb" if you will; its health—now and in the future—is contingent upon how we act to nurse it today. As many authors in this book have noted, the economic disparity that benefits so few, and harms so many, is not inevitable. And we, as educators, have a key role to play in effectuating change. We believe that it is not hubristic to claim that future generations of Americans will judge us by how we confront economic disparity now, for our choices today will determine the conditions under which they live.

References

Anielski, M. (2013). *The economics of happiness: Building genuine wealth*. Gabriola Island, BC: New Society.

Bowles, S., and Gintis, H. (2011). *Schooling in capitalist America: Educational reform and the contradictions of economic life*. Chicago, IL: Haymarket Books. (Original work published 1976.)

Caliendo, S. M. (2015). *Inequality in America: Race, poverty, and fulfilling democracy's promise*. Boulder, CO: Westview Press.

Camus, Albert. (1968). *Lyrical and critical essays*. New York: Alfred A. Knopf.

Chakrabortty, A. (2016, May 31). You're witnessing the death of neoliberalism – from within: IMF economists have published a remarkable paper admitting that the ideology was oversold. *The Guardian*. Accessed from http://www.theguardian.com/commentis free/2016/may/31/witnessing-death-neoliberalism-imf-economists?CMP=share_ btn_link

Derrida, J. (2006). *Specters of Marx: The state of the debt, the work of mourning and the new international*. New York: Routledge Classics.

Giroux, H. A. (2013). Teachers as transformative intellectuals. In A. Canestrari and B. Marlowe (Eds.), *Educational foundations: An anthology of critical readings* (pp. 189–198). Thousand Oaks, CA: Sage.

Hartmann, T. (2010). *Unequal protection: How corporations became "people"—and how you can fight back* (2nd ed.). San Francisco, CA: Berrett-Koehler.

Jefferson, T. (1954). Notes on the State of Virginia. In *The Founders' Constitution* (vol. 1, ch. 18, doc. 16). Chapel Hill: University of North Carolina Press for the Institute of Early American History and Culture. Retrieved from http://press-pubs.uchicago.edu/founders/documents/v1ch18s16.html. (Original work published 1784.)

Kotler, P. (2015). *Confronting capitalism: Real solutions for a troubled economic system*. New York: Amacom.

Kozol, J. (1991). *Savage inequalities: Children in America's schools*. New York: Crown.

Kozol, J. (2005). *The shame of a nation: The return of apartheid schooling in America*. New York: Crown.

MacNeal, C. (2014, June 9). GOP rep. acknowledges that members expect donations for votes. *TPM LiveWire*. Retrieved from http://talkingpointsmemo.com/livewire/mcallister-contributions-votes.

Obama, B. (2013). *Remarks by the President on economic mobility*. Washington, DC: White House. Retrieved from https://www.whitehouse.gov/the-press-office/2013/12/04/remarks-president-economic-mobility.

OECD. (2015). *In it together: Why less inequality benefits all*. Paris: OECD Publishing.

Paine, T. (2011). *Rights of man*. Buffalo, NY: Broadview Press. (Original work published 1789.)

Paul, R. (2013, September 19). Ron Paul defines libertarianism—Charlie Rose interview. Retrieved from https://www.youtube.com/watch?v=tfYBvIcAtko.

Pearson, N. (2009). Radical hope: Education and equality in Australia. *Quarterly Essays, 35,* 1–106.

Phillips, Adam. (2005). *Going sane: Maps of happiness*. London: Penguin.

Piketty, T. (2014). *Capital in the twenty-first century* (trans. A. Goldhammer). Cambridge, MA: Belknap Press.

Rawls, J. (1971). *A theory of justice*. Cambridge, MA: Belknap Press.

Reich, R. (2014, May 12). How to shrink inequality. [Blog]. Retrieved from http://robertreich.org/post/85532751265.

Rousseau, J.-J. (1984). *A discourse on inequality*. New York: Penguin. (Original work published 1755.)

Sandel, M. J. (2012). *What money can't buy: The moral limits of markets*. New York: Farrar, Straus and Giroux.

Sanders, B. (2016). Getting big money out of politics and restoring democracy. Retrieved from https://berniesanders.com/issues/money-in-politics/.

Schmitt, C. (1988). *The crisis of parliamentary democracy*. Cambridge, MA: MIT Press. (Original work published 1923.)

Schmitt, C. (1996). *The Leviathan in the state theory of Thomas Hobbes: Meaning and failure of a political symbol*. Westport, CT: Greenwood. (Original work published 1938.)

Stelzner, M. (2015). *Economic inequality and policy control in the United States*. New York: Palgrave Macmillan.

Stiglitz, J. E. (2013). *The price of inequality: How today's divided society endangers our future*. New York: W. W. Norton.

Stiglitz, J. E. (2015). *The great divide: Unequal societies and what we can do about them*. New York: W. W. Norton.

Taibbi, M. (2015). *The divide: American injustice in the age of the wealth gap.* New York: Spiegel & Grau.

Torres, C. T. (1998). Democracy, education, and multiculturalism: Dilemmas of citizenship in a global world. *Comparative Education Review, 42*(4), 421–447.

"True progressivism." (2012, October 13). *Economist.* Retrieved from http://www.economist.com/node/21564556.

Warren, E. (2014). *A fighting chance.* New York: Metropolitan Books.

Wilkinson, R., and Pickett, K. (2009). *The spirit level: Why greater equality makes societies stronger.* New York: Bloomsbury Press.

Wolin, S. S. (2008). *Democracy Inc.: Managed democracy and the specter of inverted totalitarianism.* Princeton, NJ: Princeton University Press.

SECTION I
Setting the Context

1

DEMOCRATIC EDUCATION UNDER SIEGE IN A NEOLIBERAL SOCIETY[1]

Henry A. Giroux

Public education is under assault by a host of religious, economic, ideological, and political fundamentalists. The most serious attack is being waged by advocates of neoliberalism, whose reform efforts focus narrowly on high-stakes testing, traditional texts, and memorization drills. At the heart of this approach is an aggressive attempt to disinvest in public schools, replace them with charter schools, and remove state and federal governments completely from public education in order to allow education to be organized and administered by market-driven forces (e.g., Ferguson, 2012; Giroux, 2010; Madrick, 2011).

It would be an understatement to suggest that there is something very wrong with American public education. For a start, this counter-revolution is giving rise to punitive evaluation schemes, harsh disciplinary measures, and the ongoing deskilling of otherwise excellent educators. Additionally, as more and more wealth is distributed to the richest Americans and corporations, states are drained of resources and are shifting the burden of such deficits on to public schools and other vital public services. With 40 percent of wealth going to the top 1 percent, public services are drying up from lack of revenue, and more and more young people find themselves locked out of the dream of getting a decent education or a job, while being robbed of any hope for the future.

As the nation's schools and infrastructure suffer from a lack of resources, right-wing politicians enact policies that lower taxes for the rich and mega-corporations. For the elite, taxes constitute a form of state coercion and class warfare waged by the state against the rich. What is ironic in this argument is the startling fact that not only are the rich not taxed fairly, but they also receive over $92 billion in corporate subsidies. This poisonous mix of wealth, politics, and power translates into an array of anti-democratic practices that by virtually every major metric creates an unhealthy society—as Wright-Maley and Davis point out in the Introduction (see Sandel, 2012; Stiglitz, 2013).

Money no longer simply controls elections; it also controls policies that shape public education. One indicator of such corruption is that hedge fund managers now sit on school boards across the country doing everything in their power to eliminate public schools and punish unionized teachers who do not support charter schools. In New Jersey, hundreds of teachers have been sacked because of alleged budget deficits. Not only is Governor Christie using the deficit argument to fire teachers; he also uses it to break unions and balance the budget on the backs of students and teachers. How else to explain Christie's refusal to oppose reinstituting the "millionaires taxes," or his craven support for lowering taxes for the top 25 hedge fund officers, who in 2009 raked in $25 billion, enough to fund 658,000 entry-level teachers (Leopold, 2010)? In this conservative right-wing reform culture, the role of public education, if we are to believe the Heritage Foundation and the likes of Bill Gates-type billionaires, is to produce students who laud conformity, believe job training is more important than education, and view public values as irrelevant. Students in this view are no longer educated for democratic citizenship.

On the contrary, students are now being trained to fulfill the need for human capital (Glenn, 2010). What is lost in this approach to schooling is what Noam Chomsky (2011) called "creating creative and independent thought and inquiry, challenging perceived beliefs, exploring new horizons and forgetting external constraints" (para. 13). Not only are the lines between the corporate world and public education blurring, but public schooling is being reduced to what Peter Seybold (2008) called a "corporate service station," in which the democratic ideals at the heart of public education are now up for sale (pp. 115–116). At the heart of this crisis of education are larger questions about the formative culture necessary for a democracy to survive, the nature of civic education, the role of educators as transformative civic intellectuals, and what it means to understand the purpose and meaning of education as a site of individual and collective empowerment.

At work here is a pedagogy that displaces, infantilizes, and depoliticizes both students and large segments of the American public. Under neoliberalism, schools have been transformed into a private right rather than a public good. Students are now being educated to become consumers rather than thoughtful, critical citizens (see Nichols, Chapter 2). Increasingly as public schools are put in the hands of for-profit corporations, hedge fund elites, and other market-driven sources, their value is derived by their ability to produce profits and compliant students eager to join the workforce (Hass, 2009).

This blight of conformity and instrumentalism is turning public education into a repressive site of containment, a site devoid of poetry, critical learning, and soaring acts of curiosity and imagination. As Diane Ravitch (2012) has pointed out, what is driving the current school reform movement is a profoundly anti-intellectual project that promotes "more privately managed schools, more testing, merit pay, longer school hours" (para. 4) as well as systems that are set up for "mass firings and [school] closure" (para. 8). There are no powerful and profound intellectual dramas in this view of schooling, just the muted rush to make schools another source of profit for finance capital with its growing legion of bankers and billionaires.

One consequence is that many public schools, especially those occupied by poor minority youth, have become the new factories for dumbing down the curricula and turning teachers into what amounts to machine parts. At the same time, such schools have become increasingly militarized and provide a direct route for many youth into the prison–industrial complex or what is called the school-to-prison pipeline (see American Civil Liberties Union, n.d.; Giroux, 2009; Walshe, 2012). What is buried in the wake of the educational rhetoric of hedge fund and casino capitalism is the ideal of offering public school students a civic education that provides the capacities, knowledge, and skills that enable students to speak, write, and act from a position of agency and empowerment.

Crucial to any viable reform movement is the need to understand the historical context in which public education has been transformed into an adjunct of corporate power as well as the ways in which current right-wing reform operates within a broader play of power, ideology, and other social forces that bear down in anti-democratic ways on the purpose of schooling and the practice of teaching itself. Making power visible is important, but only as a first step in understanding how it works and how it might be challenged. But recognizing such a challenge is not the same thing as overcoming it. Part of this task necessitates that educators anchor their own work in classrooms, however diverse, in projects that engage the promise of an unrealized democracy against its existing, often repressive forms.

Schools should be viewed as crucial to any viable notion of democracy, while the pedagogical practices they employ should be consistent with the ideal of the good society. This means teaching more than the knowledge of traditional canons. In fact, teachers and students need to recognize that, as a moral and political practice, pedagogy is about the struggle over identity just as much as it is a struggle over what counts as knowledge. At a time when censorship is running amok in public schools, the debate over whether we should view schools as political institutions seems not only moot, but irrelevant. Pedagogy is a mode of critical intervention, one that rests on the premise that teachers have a responsibility to prepare students not merely for jobs, but for being in the world in ways that allow them to influence the larger political, ideological, and economic forces that bear down on their lives. Schooling is an eminently political and moral practice, both because it is directive and because it actively legitimates what counts as knowledge, sanctions particular values, and constructs particular forms of agency.

One of the most notable features of the contemporary conservative reform effort is the way in which it increasingly positions teachers as liabilities, and in doing so aligns them with modes of education that are as demeaning as they are deskilling. These reforms are not innocent and often promote failure in the classroom. And, when successful, they open the door for more public school closures, provide opportunities to bust unions, and allow such schools to be taken over by private and corporate interests. Under the influence of market-based pedagogies, teachers are the new welfare queens; they are repeatedly subjected to what can only be described as repressive disciplinary measures in the school and an increasing chorus of verbal humiliation from politicians outside of the classroom. Teachers are not only on the defensive in the neoliberal war on schools; they are also increasingly pressured to assume more instrumental and mercenary roles. Such approaches leave them with no time to be creative, use their imagination, work with other teachers, or develop classroom practices that are not wedded to teaching for the test and other demeaning empirical measures.

Fighting for democracy as an educational project means encouraging a culture of questioning in classrooms, one that explores both the strengths and the weaknesses of the current era. Bauman (2002) is right in arguing that, "if there is no room for the idea of *a wrong* society, there is hardly much chance for the idea of a good society to be born, let alone make waves" (p. 170). At stake here is the question: What kind of future do our teachings presuppose? What forms of literacy and agency do we make available to our students through our pedagogical practices? This broader project of addressing democratization as a pedagogical practice should be central to any worthwhile attempt to engage in classroom teaching. And this is a political project.

As educators, we have to begin with a vision of schooling as a democratic public sphere, and then we have to figure out what the ideological, political, and social impediments are to such goals and organize collectively to derail them. In other words, educators need to start with a project, not a method. They need to view themselves through the lens of civic responsibility and address what it means to educate students in the best of those traditions and knowledge forms we have inherited from the past, and also in terms of what it means to prepare them to be in the world as critically engaged agents.

Educators need to be more forceful, if not committed, to linking their overall investment in democracy to modes of critique and collective action that address the presupposition that democratic societies are never too just or just enough. Moreover, such a commitment suggests that a viable democratic society must constantly nurture the possibilities for self-critique, collective agency, and forms of citizenship in which teachers and students play a fundamental role. Rather than being forced to participate in a pedagogy designed to increase test scores and undermine forms of critical thinking, students must be involved pedagogically in critically discussing, administrating, and shaping the material relations of power and ideological forces that form their everyday lives.

Central to such an educational project is the ongoing struggle by teachers to connect their pedagogical practices to building an inclusive and just democracy that should be open to many forms, offers no political guarantees, and provides an important normative dimension to politics as an ongoing process. Such a project is based on the realization that a democracy open to exchange, question, and self-criticism never reaches the limits of justice; it is never just enough and never finished. It is precisely the open-ended and normative nature of such a project that provides a common ground for educators to share their resources with a diverse range of intellectual pursuits, while refusing to believe that such struggles in schools ever come to an end.

In order to connect teaching with the larger world so as to make pedagogy meaningful, critical, and transformative, educators will have to focus their work on important social issues that connect what is learned in the classroom to the larger society and the lives of their students. Such issues might include the ongoing destruction of the ecological biosphere, the current war against youth, the hegemony of neoliberal globalization, the widespread attack by corporate culture on public schools, the dangerous growth of the prison–industrial complex, the ongoing attack on the welfare system, the increasing rates of incarceration of people of color, the rise of a generation of students who are laboring under the burden of debt and the increasing spread of war globally, or the increasing gap between the rich and the poor.

But educators need to do more than create the conditions for critical learning for their students; they also need to responsibly assume the role of civic educators willing to share their ideas with other educators and the wider public by writing for a variety of public audiences in a number of new media sites. This suggests using opportunities offered by a host of public means of expression including the lecture circuit, radio, Internet, interview, alternative magazines, and the church pulpit, to name only a few. Such writing needs to become public by crossing over into spheres and avenues of expression that speak to more general audiences in a language that is clear but not theoretically simplistic. Capitalizing on their role as intellectuals, educators can address the challenge of combining scholarship and commitment through the use of a vocabulary that is neither dull nor obtuse, while seeking to speak to a broad audience. More importantly, as teachers organize to assert the importance of their role and that of public schooling in a democracy, they can forge new alliances and connections to develop social movements that include and also expand beyond working with unions.

Educators also need to be more specific about what it would mean to be both self-critical and attentive to learning how to work collectively with other educators through a vast array of networks across a number of public spheres. This might mean sharing resources with educators in a variety of fields and sites, extending from other teachers to community workers and artists outside of the school. At the very least, they could make clear to a befuddled American public that the deficit theory regarding school cutbacks is a fraud. There is plenty of money to provide quality education to every student in the United States. As Babones (2012) points out, the issue is not about the absence of funds as much as it is about where funds are being invested and how more revenue can be raised to support public education in the United States.

Surely, this country's military budget could be trimmed appropriately to divert much-needed funds to education, given that a nation's highest priority should be investing in its children rather than in the production of organized violence. As capital, finance, trade, and culture become extraterritorial and increasingly removed from traditional political constraints, it becomes all the more pressing to put global networks and political organizations into play to contend with the reach and power of neoliberal globalization. Engaging in intellectual practices that offer the possibility of alliances and new forms of solidarity among public school teachers and cultural workers such as artists, writers, journalists, academics, and others who engage in forms of public pedagogy grounded in a democratic project represents a small, but important, step in addressing the massive and unprecedented reach of global capitalism.

Educators also need to register and make visible their own subjective involvement in what they teach, how they shape classroom social relations, and how they defend their positions within institutions that often legitimate educational processes based on narrow ideological interests and political exclusions. This suggests making one's authority and classroom work the subject of critical analysis with students, but taken up in terms that move beyond the rhetoric of method, psychology, or private interests. Pedagogy in this instance can be addressed as a moral and political discourse in which students are able to connect learning to social change, scholarship to commitment, and classroom knowledge to public life. Such a pedagogical task suggests that educators define intellectual practice "as part of an intricate web of morality, rigor and responsibility" that enables them to speak with conviction, enter the public sphere in order to address important social problems, and demonstrate alternative models for what it means to bridge the gap between public education and the broader society (Roy, 2001, p. 6).

One useful approach to embracing the classroom as a political site, but at the same time eschewing any form of indoctrination, is for educators to think through the distinction between a *politicizing pedagogy*, which insists wrongly that students think as we do, and a *political pedagogy*, which teaches students by example and through dialogue about the importance of power, social responsibility, and the importance of taking a stand (without standing still), while rigorously engaging with the full range of ideas about an issue.

Political pedagogy offers the promise of nurturing students to think critically about their understanding of classroom knowledge and its relationship to the issue of social responsibility. Yet it would also invoke the challenge of educating students not only to engage with the world critically, but also to be responsible enough to fight for those political and economic conditions that make democratic participation both in schools and in the larger society viable. This pedagogy affirms social experiences and the obligations they evoke regarding questions of responsibility and transformation. In part, it does this by opening up for students important questions about power, knowledge, and what it might mean for them to critically engage with the conditions under which life is presented to them. In addition, a pedagogy of freedom (Freire, 1998) would provide students with the knowledge and skills to analyze and work to overcome those social relations of oppression that make living unbearable for those who are poor, hungry, unemployed, deprived of adequate social services, and viewed largely as disposable under the aegis of neoliberalism. What is important about this type of critical pedagogy is the issue of responsibility as both a normative issue and a strategic act. Responsibility highlights the performative nature of pedagogy by raising questions about not only the relationship that teachers have to students, but also the relationship that students have to themselves and others.

Of central importance for educators is to encourage students to reflect on what it would mean for them to connect knowledge, criticism, and self-reflection as part of a wider effort to become critical and informed social agents motivated by a profound desire to overcome injustice on a wide variety of fronts. Political education teaches students to take risks and challenge those with power, and encourages them to be reflexive about how power is used in the classroom. Political education proposes that the role of the teacher as public intellectual is not to consolidate authority but to question and interrogate it; and further that teachers and students should temper any reverence for authority with a sense of critical awareness and an acute willingness to hold it accountable for its actions and their consequences. Moreover, political education foregrounds education not within the imperatives of specialization and professionalization, but within a project designed to expand the possibilities of democracy by linking education to modes of political agency that promote critical citizenship and address the ethical imperative to alleviate human suffering.

In contrast, politicizing education silences in the name of orthodoxy and imposes itself on students while undermining dialogue, deliberation, and critical engagement. Politicizing education is often grounded in a combination of self-righteousness and ideological purity that silences students as it enacts "correct" positions. Authority in this perspective rarely opens itself to self-criticism or for that matter to any criticism, especially from students. Politicizing education cannot decipher the distinction between critical teaching and pedagogical terrorism, because its advocates have no sense of the difference between encouraging human agency and social responsibility and molding students according to the imperatives of an unquestioned ideological position. Politicizing education is more religious than secular and more about training than educating; it harbors a great dislike for complicating issues, promoting critical dialogue, and generating a culture of questioning.

If teachers are truly concerned about how education operates as a crucial site of power in the modern world, they will have to take more seriously how pedagogy functions on local and global levels to secure and challenge the ways in which power is deployed, affirmed, and resisted within and outside traditional discourses and cultural spheres. In this instance, pedagogy becomes an important theoretical tool for understanding the institutional conditions that place constraints on the production of knowledge, learning, and academic labor itself. Pedagogy also provides a discourse for engaging with and challenging the production of social hierarchies, identities, and ideologies as they traverse local and national borders. In addition, pedagogy as a form of production and critique offers a discourse of possibility, a way of providing students with the opportunity to link meaning to commitment and understanding to social transformation—and to do so in the interest of the greatest possible justice. Unlike traditional vanguardists or elitist notions of the intellectual, critical pedagogy and education should embrace the notion of rooting the vocation of intellectuals in pedagogical and political work tempered by humility, a moral focus on suffering, and the need to produce alternative visions and policies that go beyond a language of sheer critique (see Hyland-Russell and Syrnyk, Chapter 13 as an example of this work).

Implications

I now want to shift my frame to focus on the implications of the concerns I have addressed thus far, including how they might be connected to developing an academic agenda for teachers as public intellectuals, particularly at a time when neoliberal agendas increasingly guide social policy.

Teachers as Public Intellectuals

Defending education at all levels of learning as a vital public sphere and public good, rather than merely a private good, is necessary to develop and nourish the proper balance between democratic public spheres and commercial power, between identities founded on democratic principles and identities steeped in forms of competitive, self-interested individualism that celebrate selfishness, profit-making, and greed. This view suggests that public education be defended through intellectual work that self-consciously recalls the tension between the democratic imperatives and possibilities of public institutions and their everyday realization within a society dominated by market principles. If public education is to remain a site of critical thinking, collective work, and thoughtful dialogue, educators need to expand and resolutely defend how they view the meaning and purpose of their work with young people.

As I have stressed repeatedly, academics, teachers, students, parents, community activists, and other socially concerned groups must provide the first line of defense in protecting public education as a resource vital to the moral life of the nation, and open to people and communities whose resources, knowledge, and skills have often been viewed as marginal. This demands not only a new revolutionary educational idea and concrete analysis of the neoliberal and other reactionary forces at work in dismantling public education, but also the desire to build a powerful social movement as a precondition to real change and free quality education for everyone.

Such a project suggests that educators develop a more inclusive vocabulary for aligning politics and the task of leadership. In part, this means providing students with the language, knowledge, and social relations to engage in the "art of translating individual problems into public issues, and common interests into individual rights and duties" (Bauman, 2002, p. 70). Leadership demands a politics and pedagogy that refuse to separate individual problems and experience from public issues and social considerations. Within such a perspective, leadership displaces cynicism with hope, challenges the neoliberal notion that there are no alternatives with visions of a better society, and develops a pedagogy of commitment that puts into place modes of critical literacy in which competency and interpretation provide the basis and impetus to intervene substantially in the world. Leadership invokes the demand that pedagogy become more political by linking critical thought to collective action, human agency to social responsibility, and knowledge and power to a profound impatience with a status quo founded upon deep inequalities and injustices.

Teachers in Opposition to Neoliberalism

There is a lot of talk among educators and the general public about the death of democratic schooling and the institutional support it provides for critical dialogue, nurturing the imagination, and creating a space of inclusiveness and critical teaching. Given that educators and others now live in a democracy emptied of any principled meaning, the ability of human beings to imagine a more equitable and just world becomes more difficult. I would hope educators, of all groups, would be the most vocal and militant in challenging this assumption by making clear that at the heart of any notion of a substantive liberal democracy is the assumption that learning should be directed toward the public good, by both creating a culture of questioning and promoting democratic social change.

Of the crucial challenges faced by educators, one is rejecting the neoliberal collapse of the public into the private, the rendering of all social problems as biographical in nature. The neoliberal obsession with the private not only furthers a market-based politics—which reduces all relationships to the exchange of money and the accumulation of capital—but also depoliticizes politics itself and reduces public activity to the realm of utterly privatized practices and utopias, underscored by the reduction of citizenship to the act of buying and purchasing goods (see Nichols, Chapter 2). Within this discourse all forms of solidarity, social agency, and collective resistance disappear into the murky waters of a politics in which the demands of privatized pleasures and ready-made individual choices are organized on the basis of marketplace interests, values, and desires that cancel out all modes of social responsibility, commitment, and action.

The second such challenge now facing educators, especially in light of the current neoliberal attack on public workers, is to reclaim the language of the social, agency, solidarity, democracy, and public life as the basis for rethinking how to name, theorize, and strategize a new kind of education, as well as more emancipatory notions of individual and social agency, and collective struggle. This challenge suggests, in part, positing new forms of social citizenship and civic education that have a purchase on people's everyday lives and struggles.

Teachers bear an enormous responsibility in opposing neoliberalism—the most dangerous ideology of our time—by bringing democratic political culture back to life. Part of this effort demands creating new locations of struggle, to question what it is they have become within existing institutional and social formations, to develop vocabularies and values that allow people in a wide variety of public spheres to become more than they are now, and "to give some thought to their experiences so that they can transform their relations of subordination and oppression" (Worsham and Olson, 1999, p. 178). As Mark Edward Johnson points out in Chapter 3, teachers can approach this issue from different directions. But any attempt to give new life to a substantive democratic politics must address the issue of how people learn to be political agents. Moreover it needs also to cultivate ways to recognize what kinds of educational work are necessary within what kinds of public spaces to enable people to use their full intellectual resources to provide a profound critique of existing institutions and to undertake a struggle to make the operation of freedom and autonomy achievable for as many people as possible in a wide variety of spheres. In this way, individual and social agency—both political and pedagogical—become meaningful as part of the willingness to think in oppositional, if not utopian, terms working towards a more humane future (Chomsky, 2000) and toward the unfinished promise of liberal democracy (Derrida, 2006).

Teachers as Agents of Hope

Hope is the affective and intellectual precondition for individual and social struggle, the mark of courage on the part of intellectuals in and out of the academy who use the resources of theory to address pressing social problems. But hope is also a referent for civic courage, which translates as a political practice and begins when one's life can no longer be taken for granted, making concrete the possibility for transforming politics into an ethical space and a public act that confronts the flow of everyday experience and the weight of social suffering with the force of individual and collective resistance and the unending project of democratic social transformation.

Under such circumstances, knowledge can be used for amplifying human freedom and promoting social justice, and not for simply creating profits. The diverse terrains of critical education and critical pedagogy offer some insights for addressing these issues, and we would do well to learn as much as possible from them in order to expand the meaning of political education and revitalize the pedagogical possibilities of cultural politics and democratic struggle.

The late Pierre Bourdieu argued that intellectuals need to create new ways for doing politics by investing in political struggles through a permanent critique of the abuses of authority and power, especially under the reign of neoliberalism. Bourdieu (2000) wanted educators to "enter into sustained and vigorous exchange with the outside world (especially with unions, grassroots organizations and issue-oriented activist groups)" rather than "being content with waging the 'political' battles" in the confines of their own classrooms and scholarly circles (p. 44).

At a time when our civil liberties are being destroyed and public institutions and goods all over the globe are under assault by the forces of a rapacious global capitalism, there is a concrete urgency on the horizon that demands not only the most engaged forms of political opposition on the part of teachers, but new modes of resistance and collective struggle buttressed by rigorous intellectual work, social responsibility, and political courage. The time has come for educators to distinguish caution from cowardice and recognize the need for addressing the dire crisis public education is now facing. As Derrida (2006) reminded us, democracy is always referred to as yet "to come" (p. 81). It is, therefore, of the utmost urgency that we pursue the project of closing the gap between the "infinite promise" of liberal democracy's ideal and the "necessarily inadequate forms [it takes] . . . to be measured against this promise" (p. 81). We have seen glimpses of such a promise among those brave students and workers who have demonstrated in Montreal, Paris, Athens, Toronto, New York, and many other cities across the globe.

Assuming the role of public intellectual suggests being a provocateur in the classroom; it means asking hard questions, listening carefully to what students have to say, and promoting teaching against the grain. But it also means stepping out of the classroom and working with others to create public spaces where it becomes possible not only to "shift the way people think about the moment, but potentially to energize them to do something differently in that moment," to link one's critical imagination with the possibility of activism in the public sphere (Smith and Guinier, 2001, pp. 34–35). This is, of course, a small step, but, if we do not want to repeat the present as the future or, even worse, become complicit in the workings of dominant power, it is time for educators to collectively mobilize their energies by breaking down the illusion of unanimity that dominant power propagates while working diligently, tirelessly, and collectively to reclaim the promises of a truly global, democratic future.

Note

1 A version of this chapter was published previously as Giroux, H. A. (2012, October 16). Can democratic education survive in a neoliberal society? *Truthout*. Retrieved from http://www.truth-out.org/opinion/item/12126-can-democratic-education-survive-in-a-neoliberal-society.

References

American Civil Liberties Union (ACLU). (n.d.). What is the school to prison pipeline? Retrieved from https://www.aclu.org/fact-sheet/what-school-prison-pipeline.

Babones, S. (2012, August 21). To end the jobs recession, invest an extra $20 billion in public education. *Truthout*. Retrieved from http://www.truth-out.org/opinion/item/11031-to-end-the-jobs-recession-invest-an-extra-$20-billion-in-public-education.

Bauman, Z. (2002). *Society under siege*. Malden, MA: Blackwell.

Bourdieu, P. (2000). For a scholarship of commitment. *Profession*, 40–45.

Chomsky, N. (2000). Paths taken, tasks ahead. *Profession*, 32–39.

Chomsky, N. (2011). Chomsky: Public education under massive corporate assault—what's next? *AlterNet*. Retrieved from http://www.alternet.org/story/151921/chomsky%3A_public_education_under_massive_corporate_assault_%E2%80%94_what's_next.

Derrida, J. (2006). *Specters of Marx: The state of the debt, the work of mourning and the new international* (trans. P. Kamuf). New York: Routledge Classics.

Ferguson, C. (2012). *Predator nation*. New York: Crown Business.

Freire, P. (1998). *Pedagogy of freedom: Ethics, democracy, and civic courage*. New York: Rowman & Littlefield.

Giroux, H. A. (2009). *Youth in a suspect society*. New York: Palgrave.

Giroux, H. A. (2010). *Zombie politics in the age of casino capitalism*. New York: Peter Lang.

Glenn, D. (2010, September 2). Public higher education is "eroding from all sides," warn political scientists. *Chronicle of Higher Education*. Retrieved from http://chronicle.com/article/Public-Higher-Education-Is-/124292/.

Hass, N. (2009, December 6). Scholarly investments. *New York Times*, p. ST1 10.

Leopold, L. (2010, May 4). "Hey dad, why does this country protect billionaires, and not teachers?" *AlterNet*. Retrieved from http://www.alternet.org/story/146738/%22hey_dad,_why_does_this_country_protect_billionaires,_and_not_teachers%22.

Madrick, J. (2011). *Age of greed: The triumph of finance and the decline of America, 1970 to the present*. New York: Vintage.

Ravitch, D. (2012, September 14). Two visions for Chicago's schools. *Common Dreams*. Retrieved from http://www.commondreams.org/views/2012/09/14/two-visions-chicagos-schools.

Roy, A. (2001). *Power politics*. Cambridge, MA: South End Press.

Sandel, M. (2012). *What money can't buy*. New York: FSG.

Seybold, P. (2008). The struggle against the corporate takeover of the university. *Socialism and Democracy, 22*(1), 115–125.

Smith, A. D., and Guinier, L. (2001). Rethinking power, rethinking theater: A conversation between Lani Guinier and Anna Deavere Smith. *Theater, 31*(3), 31–45.

Stiglitz, J. E. (2013). *The price of inequality*. New York: W. W. Norton.

Walshe, S. (2012, August 31). US education orientation for minorities: The school-to-prison pipeline. *Guardian*. Retrieved from http://www.theguardian.com/commentisfree/2012/aug/31/us-education-orientation-minorities.

Worsham, L., and Olson, G. A. (1999). Rethinking political community: Chantal Mouffe's liberal socialism. *Journal of Composition Theory, 19*(2), 163–199.

2

THE ECONOMIC CITIZEN

Civic Education and Its Discontents

Joseph R. Nichols, Jr.

Corruption is a fitting word to start this chapter, because corruption is how we got here. The act of corruption involves the action of making someone or something morally depraved—it involves debasement. And, even though corruption can be found in many forms, the corruption I discuss here stems from the general and erroneous assumption that the economic market is the natural state of affairs for human life. Its emphasis on productivity and profit has manipulated our ability to empathize with each other. Jean-Jacques Rousseau (1755/1984) argued that wealth inequality corrupts humankind's natural inclinations and replaces natural inequalities with moral ones. In this sense, the economic market debases humankind for material wealth, thereby perverting our better human natures.

When I think further about this corruption, I think about how we have used market forces and the concept of profit to organize our lives. The human experience has a long history of treating people like commodities rather than living, breathing beings who share life together. Thus this corruption is not new— economically powerful groups have profited from the economically disenfranchised for as long as human society has existed. In the American context, the economic obsession with market thinking has turned real people with real lives into dollar signs and commodities.

For example, shortly after President Barack Obama signed legislation to extend healthcare coverage to the uninsured in the United States, the rhetoric around how changes in the law would affect people focused almost exclusively on the economic sphere of their lives.[1] In one stark case, Governor Nathan Deal (2013) of Georgia—who was opposed to the law—argued that providing healthcare outside the market would simply cost too much. Governor Deal pointed out that "these costs stand to hurt our state's private sector. Because as all businessmen and women know, the higher your input costs, the lower your profits; the lower your profits, the less you operate, expand or employ" (para. 22). From this perspective, people are dehumanized, treated merely as inputs that lead to or take away from profits. By forcing businesses to provide people with access to affordable healthcare, the change in law increased the input cost of people and, thus, reduced how much one can profit from them.

Under the assumption that the market is the natural state of affairs, the same corruption that frames people as economic units also creates a common-sense logic that propagates individualistic behavior toward economic ends. No area of life is safe from such influence and, as a result, policy decisions that shape how our society is organized are justified by economic means and ends above other considerations. And, because schooling plays an important socializing role in how societies are constructed and perpetuated, this corruption is especially influential in the development of school policy and curricula.

The marketization of public schooling and the corporatization of the curriculum have created the environment necessary for individualistic, economically focused citizens to grow and flourish. This influence is troubling for those who are concerned with democratic ideals, particularly because democracy is the product of associated living (Parker, 1996). If left unchecked, the continued rise of the economic citizen will lead to more economic inequality and further contribute to civic education's discontent over the decline of democratic society. The following historical narrative about schooling for economic purposes, as illustrated by educational policies in Georgia, has led me to conceptualize the economic citizen.

What Is the Purpose of Schooling in the United States?

Schools in the United States have a long history of chasing contradictory purposes. In the early stages of the republic, the new government required new ways of engagement with civic life; this context helped define what schools should do. For example, Pennsylvanian Benjamin Rush (1786/2006) pointed out that the newly created national government needed an education system that would "lay the foundations for nurseries of wise and good men, to adapt our modes of teaching to the peculiar form of our government" (p. 58). For his part, Thomas Jefferson envisioned a nation of agrarian yeomen who would control their own lives and think about how to organize society. In a letter to diplomat William Jarvis, Jefferson (1820/2009b) wrote that he saw "no safe depository of the ultimate powers of the society but the people themselves; and if we think them not enlightened enough to exercise their control with a wholesome discretion, the remedy is not to take it from them, but to inform their discretion by education" (p. 163). Jefferson was so committed to the civic mission of schooling that he attempted—albeit unsuccessfully—to push a public school plan through the Virginia General Assembly.

Though the school conversation in the founding period focused on creating citizens who could uphold the new republic (Labaree, 1997), the ideas that drove universal schooling were not free of inequity. Writing to political leader and educationalist Peter Carr, Jefferson (1814/2009a) noted that his school plan would educate every citizen "portioned to the condition and pursuits of his life," and that, "at the discharging of the pupils from elementary schools, the two classes separate" (p. 589). It is not without irony that the early school plans like Jefferson's, though civically oriented, were designed to maintain the aristocratic structures he claimed to deplore which also reinforced racism, slavery, patriarchy, and economic division. Accordingly, the political mission of schooling in early America was to fashion citizens who would maintain the power and privileging structures that defined the American founding period.

With the acceleration of immigration in the early 1800s, the American aristocracy turned to schooling to mitigate cultural pluralism, while, at the same time, Jefferson's agrarian society of independent yeomen was being supplanted by the consolidation and urbanization of labor around factories. The economic transformation that took place in the mid- to late nineteenth and early twentieth centuries corresponded with a xenophobic concern with what immigrants—especially Irish and German Catholics—might do to the American way of life. The convergence of these events resulted in a common school movement, the purpose of which was "to move people from a rural and agricultural economy to urban and industrial ones, while constructing a national culture out of local, linguistic, immigrant or colonial populations" (Feinberg, 2008, p. 91).

Coded language about economic production made its way into how school leaders talked about schools. For example, in a report of the Massachusetts School Board, Horace Mann (1848/2006)—leader of the common school movement—wrote that schools were the "grand machinery by which the 'raw material' of human nature can be worked into inventors and discoverers, into skilled artisans and scientific farmers, into scholars and jurists, into the founders of benevolent institutions, and the great expounders of ethical and theological science" (para. 1). Mann believed schools could serve an important economic role, and were a means of fighting inequality by alleviating poverty and securing abundance for all. Common schools, as articulated by Mann, were the welfare tools that would make individuals responsible for their own economic destiny. Mann argued on behalf of the board that each person was responsible for himself and that the "necessaries and conveniences [food, shelter, etc.] of life should be obtained by each individual himself, or by each family for themselves, rather than accepted from the hand of charity, or extorted by poor-laws" (p. 63). Even in its earliest development, the production language in his school reports illustrates the power capital has had over the creation of American public schools.

Cuban (2004) pointed out that business-directed education reform occurred within two periods: the 1890s to 1930s and the 1970s to the present. During the first reform movement educationalists were concerned with systems of efficiency.

By the time widespread industrialization took hold in the United States, the political arguments shaping the founding period had settled into the operational details of a functioning republic. This transition made it easier for industrial forces to shape the expanding public school system around business needs. Though schools in the United States started as civic institutions, the common school movement schools ensured they now had a decidedly economic role to play.

The class structures embedded within the civic arguments of early school promoters such as Jefferson provided the foundation for an economic rationale for schooling. The urbanization of the workforce and the demands of factory production necessitated a supposed remedy for inequality if capitalism was to survive. Following the logic of Mann, capitalists found their solution in the idea that public schools provided an equal opportunity, thereby placing the onus of individuals' economic success on themselves, rather than finding fault in the social structures of the time. Schooling, in this sense, provided the capital class an easy explanation for economic inequality, bolstered by the ideologies of laissez-faire capitalism and social Darwinism (Wyllie, 1959).

During this time, the school reform movement was dominated by proponents of scientific management who appropriated business principles and applied them to schools. For example, Edward L. Thorndike (1903)—an advocate of scientific management and school reform leader in the early 1900s—argued that: "Education agencies are a great system of means not only of making men good and intelligent and efficient, but also of picking out and labeling those who for any reason are good intelligent and efficient. . . . They help to put the right men in the right places" (p. 94). Thorndike's logic for schooling was straight out of the scientific management playbook. His focus was social efficiency and emphasizing quantifiable and measurable behaviors of students, in much the same way that this approach was applied to industrial work (e.g., Taylor, 1915). According to this philosophy, schools were conceived of as assembly lines that sorted students into their proper places in society.

The educationalists who promoted scientific management in the early 1900s set the foundation for a series of measurement and evaluation reforms that took hold in schools over the next several decades. The advent of World War I accelerated these social efficiency policies. In response to the need to mobilize large groups of troops quickly, the United States Army developed a testing mechanism—the Army Alpha—to determine which soldiers they would deploy to the front lines. The success of Army Alpha for sorting troops and the American victory in World War I had profound implications for schools. According to Hanson (1993), "the war changed the image of tests and of the tested. . . . [The tests] were now legitimate means of making decisions about the achievements and aptitudes of normal people" (p. 212). Testing created a currency for broader corporate influence over American schools.

The system efficiencies put into place during the early 1900s created the landscape necessary for the second period of business-directed reform, which began in the 1970s with the publication of Lewis Powell's (1971) famous memo *Attack on American Free Enterprise System*. Writing to the chairperson of the United States Chamber of Commerce, Powell argued that the business community had been too apathetic to the public pushback against the market system. The business community, according to Powell, needed to do more to support the American market system, including engaging directly in school policy.

The 1970s and 1980s saw a series of corporate reform movements, the energies of which were directed at the public school system. For example, the Business Roundtable—formed in the early 1970s shortly after Lewis Powell wrote his memo—acted, and still acts, as one of the microphones for business-directed school reform in the United States (Evans, 2015). And, even though myriad policy documents and organizations have turned the market lens toward schools, the publication of *A Nation at Risk* (National Commission on Excellence in Education (NCEE), 1983) was one of the most important impetuses in the corporatization of American schools.

As I have argued, schools have shifted from a political to a market rationale. With this shift, school policy in the United States has become more and more concerned with the economic role schools should play in our society. This shift in how we define the purpose of schooling that started during the common school movement has accelerated toward the economic since the publication of *A Nation at Risk* and the policies the report made possible (Mehta, 2013a).

The Economic Is Crowned the King of Schooling

Mehta (2013b) pointed out that policy arguments are won and lost at the level of policy definition. This characteristic of the policy process means that "the way a problem is framed has significant impact for the types of policy solutions that will seem desirable" (p. 291). From this perspective, *A Nation at Risk* (NCEE, 1983) did more than any other federal policy document to elevate the economic as the overarching logic of schools and schooling; the economy is king. With its bellicose language, promoted through the megaphone of President Ronald Reagan's ideology of laissez-faire economics, *A Nation at Risk* articulated a policy of schooling for economic purposes to the exclusion of all others. The report pointed out that schools are economic instruments through which "all children by *virtue of their own efforts*, competently guided, can hope to attain the mature and informed judgment needed to *secure gainful employment and to manage their own lives*, thereby serving not only *their own interests* but also the *progress of society* itself" (p. 8, emphasis added). Echoing Mann's argument that people are responsible for their own plight, *A Nation at Risk* positioned schooling as the tool that would enable children to determine their own destiny. The logic outlined in *A Nation at Risk*, and underlined in the quoted text, is clear. One's own efforts lead to gainful employment, which allows one to advance one's own interests, which is how society moves forward. The economic logic of *A Nation at Risk* assumed that society can progress only through individualistic economic pursuits. Thus the credentialing role schooling plays in our capitalist society now places the burden of economic performance on the backs of schools and in the hands of individuals, reifying the myth of meritocracy that undergirds the prevailing common sense of what American society represents. When schools and individuals within schools are labeled as "failing," politicians, media, and everyday people blame the schools, teachers, or the individuals themselves (see Giroux, Chapter 1). In this sense, "the myth of individualism may be the most disruptive and unsettling in the way it legitimates social isolation and contributes to an increasingly alienated lifestyle" (Callero, 2009, p. 34).

A Nation at Risk manufactured political tropes that identified scapegoats to be readily targeted for failure that aligned neatly with neoliberal ideological positions. The public bureaucracy was to blame because it exists outside of the market's logic and the common-sense perspective that markets are humankind's natural organizing tool. Individuals were at fault for the decisions that created their failure. From this perspective, the capitalist system maintained the cover it needed to continue the corruption of expanding inequality.

The economic purpose of schooling established in *A Nation at Risk* (NCEE, 1983) also set the foundation for a curricular intervention that would serve to foster the development of the economic citizen in schools. For example, the report argued that:

> The people of the United States need to know that individuals in our society who do not possess the levels of skill, literacy, and training essential to this new era will be effectively disenfranchised, not simply from the material rewards that accompany competent performance, but also from the chance to participate fully in our national life.
>
> *(p. 7)*

By connecting skills, literacy, and training to disenfranchisement, the rhetoric of *A Nation at Risk* connected the economic role of schools to an economically defined citizenship. The argument in the report was that good citizens create and access the "material rewards that accompany competent performance" (p. 7), whereas those who cannot create or access such material wealth also fail to perform in their role as citizens.

The economic citizenship model outlined in *A Nation at Risk* was only the beginning. Organizations such as the Business Roundtable, the Heritage Foundation, and the American Legislative Exchange Council, combined with groups such as the National Governors' Association, acted in tandem to push corporate reforms into schools (Cuban, 2004; Evans, 2015). Because the policy-making process is bound up in sociopolitical culture and its "taken-for-granted paradigms constrain the range of policies that policy makers are likely to consider" (Campbell, 2002, p. 23), no one should be surprised that American schools have been further poisoned by the capitalist elixir over the last 30 years. School policy in the United States assumes that schooling is the social welfare tool that fosters individualism, creates meritocracy, and serves the production needs of capital. Within this context, the economic king creates the market of schooling it needs to rule.

The King Creates the Market

A Nation at Risk laid the foundation for the economic purpose of schooling and ushered in a wave of reforms. From Goals 2000 to No Child Left Behind (NCLB) to Race To The Top (RTTT), the policy landscape in the United States reified the economic purpose of schooling in concrete ways that continue to play out operationally in teaching practice. For example, the academic standards movement, which started as a suggestion in Goals 2000 and was solidified as a requirement in NCLB, was built on the history of 1850s–1930s reform. This process created the information and currency framework needed by capitalism to make manifest the economic purpose of schooling. Value cues—like those expressed through pricing—are vital to capitalism; the standards movement created such a system of cues through which the marketization of schools can take place. Policies such as Goals 2000 and NCLB created mechanisms that policymakers use to control the production of information and generate the currency of schooling.

By connecting standards to high-stakes assessments, policymakers can measure student, teacher, and school performance against the production needs of capitalism. This system provides economists with the tools they need to make arguments about the human capital role of education and the value-added function schooling plays in the economy (e.g., Chetty et al., 2011; Hanushek, 2011). The standards and high-stakes assessment system in the United States contributes to the meritocracy myth that drives our society—it hides the real problems under the proverbial rug. As Wayne Au (2013) has pointed out, "socio-economic factors simply have an overwhelming effect on education achievement, and this reality is effectively masked by the ideology of meritocracy embedded in high-stakes testing" (p. 14). In other words, student achievement, measured and reported, perpetuates a system set up to meet the needs of capitalist production, not student learning.

RTTT takes the economic purpose of schooling a step further by encouraging states to adopt additional policy prescriptions around four broad areas: (1) standards and assessments; (2) data systems that will illustrate to parents, schools, and other shareholders how students are progressing against the standards; (3) programs for teacher and leader improvement; and (4) school turnaround efforts to help ensure that schools and students meet the standards outlined in the state-level policies. RTTT appears innocuous in its support of student achievement and improvement of student learning; however, the RTTT initiative raises several questions. For example, how do RTTT states define student achievement?

Toward what ends is student achievement directed? And who and what does the improvement of student learning serve?

A close examination of individual states' RTTT applications provides a good sense of how state education policy is defined by capitalism. On the heels of Goals 2000 and NCLB, RTTT solidifies the information and currency framework needed for capitalist production in schools. Like *A Nation at Risk*, RTTT propagates the school–economy connection demanded by American capitalism. At the time this chapter was written, the webpage for President Obama's RTTT initiative advertised the heading "Knowledge and Skills for the Jobs of the Future" (White House, 2015, n.p.) as the purpose of the program.

The Economic Citizen

The remainder of this chapter illustrates how RTTT and state curricular reforms encourage policy prescriptions for schools around the economic. I use the state of Georgia as a case study for this argument because Georgia is representative of the United States' obsession with climbing the economic ladder. Georgia policymakers have used RTTT monies to support a statewide longitudinal data system to measure the economic outcomes of Georgia's public schools. At the same time, the Georgia Department of Education has implemented a college and career clusters/pathways program in its high schools, thus explicitly corporatizing the curricula in Georgia schools. These policy changes are just one more example of how "schooling has been a crucial tool for perpetuating the [American] capitalist system amid rapid economic change" (Tyack, 1976, pp. 384–385). The valorization of the economic in schools—like the reforms in Georgia—fosters an economic citizenship that supports the corruption of democracy, by way of inequity, that is the focus of this book.

Schooling that is defined as an economic tool gives rise to a civic education that defines good citizenship in economic terms. Because schooling in the United States acts as a credentialing mechanism for the capitalist economy, the school is situated as the avenue through which individuals are moved into areas of production. In this sense, schooling in the United States "works to justify economic inequality and to produce a labor force whose capacities, credentials, and consciousness are dictated in substantial measure by the requirements of profitable employment in a capitalistic economy" (Bowles and Gintis, 1976, p. 151). Education policy in Georgia connects schooling to economic citizenship in two ways. One is through the creation of a statewide longitudinal data system that measures the economic outcomes of Georgia's public schools. The other is through a curricular program that connects schooling to specific economic pursuits. These programs were developed after the 2008 financial crash and were regarded by policymakers in the state as ways through which Georgia's citizens could solve their economic woes. They both value the American obsession with economic outcomes and extend capital's corruption of schools, thereby perverting the civic "form of life" promoted by these schools (Wittgenstein, 1953/2009; see also Wright-Maley, 2015).

Georgia's RTTT-Funded Longitudinal Data System

Georgia applied for and was awarded a $400 million RTTT grant in 2010. A major component of this grant was funding focused on bolstering the state's longitudinal data system. The purpose of this system is to quantify the value-added metric of a Georgia public school education in a way that connects that value to the capitalist production needs of the state. The assumption here is that schooling is the welfare and social policy tool the state extends to individuals to make their way in capitalist society.

According to a recent report by Greg Bluestein and Janel Davis of the *Atlanta Journal-Constitution* (2014), Georgia employers cannot find qualified workers to fill the labor market needs of their industries. Instead of viewing this human capital issue as a problem of labor market incentives or the unfair allocation of economic power created by capitalism, policymakers in Georgia and throughout the United States blamed the schools. The problem—building off the language of *A Nation at Risk* (NCEE, 1983)—is thought to be the direct result of inadequate schooling.

The solution to this perceived problem is to further connect the business community to the public school system. The Georgia Partnership for Excellence in Education (GPEE) (2015)—a think-tank focused on the economic role of schooling—has noted that only "two out of every 10 [businesses throughout the country] are using strategic partnerships with education institutions, helping design curriculum, and sponsoring courses and prospects to address workforce gaps" (p. 33). Thus GPEE promotes and lobbies for systems that cement Georgia businesses to Georgia's public schools so they can better meet industry needs.

The statewide longitudinal data system Georgia has developed via RTTT grant monies provides the technical support Georgia businesses need to partner with education institutions, design the curriculum and implement it in schools, and sponsor specific courses and programs aimed at their workforce needs. According to the Workforce Data Quality Campaign (2014), Georgia's data system is designed to track students from schools into the workforce. The state has achieved, has mostly achieved, or is in the process of creating school/workforce measurements that:

- Establish metrics for career pathways: These metrics connect the curriculum in Georgia's public schools to specific career pathways targeting specific industries (which I discuss further in the next section).
- Track graduate employment rates: These data provide the state with information on how various academic programs in Georgia's public schools and colleges or universities fulfill the employment needs of the state.

- Measure industry-based skills gaps: These measures connect student data to labor market information so that the state can compare labor market demands with academic programming.
- Create scorecards for students and workers: The scorecards rate various academic programs across the state on how well they align with industry needs so that prospective students of those programs can make decisions before investing time and money in a course of study.
- Provide dashboards for policymakers: This component of the data system articulates school to workforce data to policymakers so they can create education policy around economic needs.

Through its statewide longitudinal data system, Georgia can extend capitalism's rationalizing logic to the schools in ways that were not possible before the technological revolution of the last two decades. The economic data this system produces can provide policymakers with the information and the currency they need to further shape Georgia's public schools. As Hill and Kumar (2009) pointed out, "business wants education fit for business—to make schooling and higher education subordinate to the personality, ideological, and economic requirements of capital, and to make sure schools produce compliant, ideologically indoctrinated, procapitalist, effective workers" (p. 21). The statewide longitudinal data system Georgia has, and is putting into place, allows policymakers to better create capitalist-indoctrinated schooling.

The citizenship experience students have in Georgia's public schools focuses on how they can use the system to meet their own personal economic goals as well as the production needs of the state's business community. This system, mediated by economic disparity, is likely to further promulgate the corruption of democracy. It positions the capitalist-identified scapegoat of schooling in ways that allow for the blaming of schools and individuals for the economic failures of society.

College and Career Clusters/Pathways Program

Along with Georgia's longitudinal data system, the economic purpose of schooling is solidified in the curriculum of Georgia's public high schools through the college and career clusters/pathways program. At the start of their freshman year, students in Georgia's public schools are required to select a career pathway they will complete as they matriculate through high school. The program, of course, is focused on several capitalistic goals and is predicted to produce myriad workforce dividends for the state. According to Lynn Plunkett of the Georgia Department of Education, "one [of those rewards] certainly is to offer opportunities for our students to have good jobs and bright futures . . . [and] building and creating a very sustainable workforce in our state is certainly a benefit of it as well" (Dalton, 2013, para. 5). From this perspective, the college and career clusters/pathways program is the curricular scheme that gives individual students the ability to navigate the path of economic citizenship laid out by corporate capitalism.

This program in Georgia is governed by House Bill 186 (Georgia General Assembly, 2011), which legislates the purpose of schooling. In the bill, the Georgia General Assembly found that "[Georgia's] long-term prosperity depends on supporting an education system that is designed to prepare students for a global economy" (p. 1), and it created a curricular system to support that contention. Specifically, the bill outlines two key steps Georgia's public high schools must take to help ensure their curriculum aligns with the workforce needs of the state.

First, Georgia House Bill 186 mandates curricular reform around the labor market. The bill notes that "local school systems must provide every student with choices that are academically rigorous and aligned to opportunities in high-demand, high-skill, high-wage career fields and to post-secondary career and technical pathways leading to advanced credentials or degrees" (p. 2). Thus the Georgia Department of Education, working with the Georgia Chamber of Commerce, created career clusters/pathways focused on the biggest industries in the state. These pathways include career cultures in the following areas: agriculture, food, and natural resources; architecture and construction; arts, audio-visual/technology, and communications; business, management, and administration; education and training; energy; finance; government and public administration; health services; information technology; law, public safety, corrections, and security; manufacturing; marketing; science, technology, engineering, and mathematics; and transportation, distribution, and logistics.

Each career cluster is broken into several job areas that the Georgia Department of Education and Chamber of Commerce have identified as important for the labor market needs of the state. To support these career pathways, the state Department of Education has created a series of courses for each pathway, as well as curriculum guides explaining the economic opportunities students will gain by choosing a specific pathway, and has even developed materials for students and parents outlining the monetary and employment benefits and consequences of specific pathways. The purpose here is to focus student and family decisions about the curriculum on the economic gains students can expect from the decisions they make about schooling.

At the same time, the career pathways are rigged toward a corporatist interpretation of specific industries. For example, the energy career cluster does nothing to promote job opportunities in renewal and green energy industries. Three of the four job areas outlined in the government and public administration career pathway are military related. The other job area—public administration—legitimizes specific forms of governance in that it targets urban and regional planners, administration of the state court system, postal services, and community managers (e.g., city manager, county manager). In this sense, students in Georgia's public schools are forced into curricula defined by the capital needs of the state.

Second, the Georgia General Assembly called on Georgia's business community to partner with Georgia's public high schools around the college and career clusters/pathways initiative. House Bill 186 warranted that "Georgia's strategic industries must be partners in our public education system (secondary and post-secondary) so that they are assured that our high school graduates are prepared for success in the workforce" (Georgia General Assembly, 2011, p. 2). The bill gives the Georgia business community legislative authority to design and implement an industry-related curriculum in Georgia's public high schools while mandating that the schools comply with those demands. The Georgia Department of Education (2013) student guide articulates possible outcomes of such collaboration by noting that the college and career clusters/pathways program will accomplish the following goals:

> development of a highly-skilled and educated workforce that contributes to economic prosperity for the individual and workforce needs of the region/ state/nation/world ... increased awareness of the connection between education and work ... increased number of students receiving a national industry-recognized credential ... better and more informed educational and career planning decision-making for students and their families.
>
> *(p. 4)*

The assumption behind this logic is that the college and career clusters/pathways program will create a synergistic relationship between the business community and schooling. According to the capitalist logic driving these reforms, the connection produced by this relationship will result in an education experience that will lead to economic prosperity for individual students and, thus, the economy as a whole. By connecting the statewide longitudinal database to specific curricular programs in Georgia's public high schools, policymakers can forge an economic citizenship model around the needs of capital. Educational reforms such as these follow the market logic outlined in *A Nation at Risk* (NCEE, 1983), and are made possible through the policy history of Goals 2000, NCLB, and RTTT. Furthermore, these policy prescriptions make clear to students that schooling is an economic enterprise—that the outcome of their school choices should be economic.

The logic here is laid out very clearly by capitalistic assumptions that remain tainted by the ghosts of social Darwinism. Schools today are conceived as the economic pipeline through which individuals can access material wealth. Students enter schools which provide the curriculum needed to maximize economic gain, and they make choices that lead them to access, or prevent them from accessing, material wealth. In the event individuals cannot access material wealth or the economy produces unequal distribution of economic spoils, this capitalistic logic places the blame on the individuals and the schools. Thus capitalist schooling makes true Horace Mann's erroneous argument that schools are a means of fighting inequality by acting as the social welfare tool that alleviates poverty and secures abundance for all.

Conclusion

The economic is the king of the American school system. The business-focused obsession with producing workers to meet the needs of capital and further market expansion pervades policy talk about what schools in the United States should do and how they should be viewed: both "for liberals and conservatives, nearly everything is justified through two economic promises: the possibility of upward economic mobility and the necessity of global economic competition" (Saltman, 2013, p. 67). These two promises capture the essence of the longitudinal database and the college and career cultures/pathways program in Georgia. By creating educational pathways and measurement systems that corporatize the curriculum, Georgia school policy individualizes economic success and failure.

Education policy that defines the economic, especially in terms of failure, as an individual construct is not unique to Georgia. Katz (2013) argued that Americans view poverty and economic disparity as a problem of people. The way in which schooling has defined citizenship as an individualistic, economic pursuit is the manifestation of a capitalist paternalism—the notion that the market knows best and that it alone should hand out economic rewards and punishments (Soss et al., 2011). In this sense, economic citizenship "promotes personal responsibility through individual choice within markets" (Hursh, 2007, p. 496). The economic citizen is at home in an environment defined by the market, and the contemporary elevation of this version of citizenship has fomented civic education's winter of discontent by atomizing and disabling the traditionally social means by which citizens have influenced government.

Capitalism's corruption is not only a political or economic problem; it is also a spiritual problem. The corruption erodes the very nature of who we are as a people. According to Glass (2000), humanness can only flourish "in an educational process in which people come to understand themselves as precisely the kind of creatures who have the ability and need to produce culture and history" (p. 280). Corporate education reform assumes that culture and history have already been created by the evolution of capital. The market, in this kind of education, *is* the culture, and the accumulation of capital *is* what drives the history. Schooling entrapped in this context strips human beings of their humanness. Education that produces economic citizens also contributes to the commodification of human life. Instead of seeing living, breathing beings who share a human experience, this capitalist form of corruption creates a social system that sees only commodities. Through corporate-defined education, we might profit and become materially wealthy, but we risk chasing profit to the neglect of our humanity and that of others. Schooling that produces an economic citizenry forces us to choose between giving in to the corruption and fighting futilely against it as atomized and isolated individuals. Either way we will not be at peace.

Corruption is how we got here, but corruption is not where we have to end. In an age of economic disparity, it may seem that capital has been elevated to such a supreme status that it cannot be undone. Yet, regardless of how irredeemable this corrupted system may seem and how pervasive its instruments may appear, pockets of resistance have sprung up throughout the country. The Occupy Education movement is one example of how we can reclaim public schools in the United States from corporate reformers ("Occupy education," 2012). And, even though the movement has addressed a number of structural changes such as school privatization and high-stakes testing brought about by business-led reform, the central concern in this chapter is the corporate curriculum.

Reclaiming the curriculum was highlighted in a *Rethinking Schools* editorial that argued that "it is equally urgent that we bring this occupy spirit to the struggle to reclaim classrooms and schools from the imposition of scripted, standardized, corporate-produced curriculum" ("Occupy education," 2012, para. 11). Through curriculum initiatives like the college and careers clusters/pathways program in Georgia, capitalism rationalizes schooling in ways that further link education to the needs of corporations and, thus, creates more inequality as wealth evaporates toward the 1 percent (Sleeter, 2014). In this sense, the capitalist school system creates a pipeline whereby citizen-as-worker students are the wealth-generating pawns that enrich the wealthy.

Reclaiming the curriculum is hard work. Though the corporate assault on schools has created curricular structures that advantage the capitalist agenda, Sleeter (2008) has shown that teachers who teach strategically can accomplish democratic goals. The key is to teach children how to think critically about questions of power, privilege, and justice so that they can create a more humane world in which to live, in much the same way as Giroux describes in Chapter 1. Curriculum initiatives such as RadicalMath (2007), the Zinn Education Project (2015), and UCLA Center X (2015) all provide powerful examples of the kinds of teaching frameworks teachers can use to teach democratic concepts that confront the corporately defined, standards-based learning environments that pervade American public schools.

In conjunction with teaching strategically, we must use our political agency to effect change in our school communities and claim the public square of schooling for democratic purposes. Because schooling helps fashion citizens and plays a role in constructing society, we must view public schools as the space where the manifestations of capitalism and democratic values compete for legitimacy. Tienken (2013) has called for teachers, parents, and students concerned about corporate-based education reform to "refuse to play in the corporate boardroom" (p. 312). Paying attention to this corruption is important. Fighting against the corruption revealed to us by critics like Rousseau (1755/1984) and even Adam Smith himself (1759/2010) is our moral obligation—indeed it is a moral imperative—because, in the words of Thich Nhat Hanh (1987), "letting people profit from human suffering or the suffering of other beings is something we cannot do" (p. 102). The way in which we fashion citizens determines the kinds of societies we create. Unjust societies profit from human suffering; just societies alleviate it. By corporatizing citizenship, schools act as peddlers of injustice. If we do, indeed, value justice, then we cannot continue to perpetuate economic citizenship and all that it represents.

Note

1 In this chapter, I will refer to the economic spheres of people's lives and the economic purposes and arguments about schooling simply as "the economic."

References

Au, W. (2013). Hiding behind high-stakes testing: Meritocracy, objectivity, and inequality in U.S. education. *International Education Journal: Comparative Perspectives, 12*(2), 7–19.

Bluestein, G., and Davis, J. (2014, December 10). Georgia's employers can't find qualified workers in key fields. [Report]. *Atlanta Journal-Constitution*. Retrieved from http://www.myajc.com/news/news/state-regional-govt-politics/report-georgias-employers-cant-find-qualified-work/njQDf/.

Bowles, S., and Gintis, H. (1976). *Schooling in capitalist America: Educational reform and the contradictions of economic life.* New York: Basic Books.

Callero, P. L. (2009). *The myth of individualism: How social forces shape our lives.* Lanham, MD: Rowman & Littlefield.

Campbell, J. L. (2002). Ideas, politics, and public policy. *Annual Review of Sociology, 28*, 21–38.

Chetty, R., Friedman, J. N., and Rockoff, J. E. (2011). *The long-term impacts of teachers: Teacher value-added and student outcomes in adulthood* (No. w17699). Cambridge, MA: National Bureau of Economic Research.

Cuban, L. (2004). *The blackboard and the bottom line: Why schools can't be like businesses.* Cambridge, MA: Harvard University Press.

Dalton, M. (2013, August 14). Georgia freshmen begin career pathways program. *90.1 WABE: Atlanta's NPR station.* Retrieved from http://wabe.org/post/georgia-freshmen-begin-career-pathways-program.

Deal, N. (2013, January 16). *"Free" health care will cause a crunch.* Retrieved from https://gov.georgia.gov/press-releases/2013-01-17/deal-speech-free-health-care-will-cause-crunch.

Evans, R. W. (2015). *Schooling corporate citizens: How accountability reform has damaged civic education and undermined democracy.* New York: Routledge.

Feinberg, W. (2008). Culture and the common school. In M. Halstead and G. Haydon (Eds.), *The common school and the comprehensive idea: A defense by Richard Pring with complementary essays* (pp. 91–107). Malden, MA: Wiley-Blackwell.

Georgia Department of Education. (2013). *College and career clusters/pathways student plan of study guidance* (Rev. 1). Retrieved from https://www.gadoe.org/ Curriculum-Instruction-and-Assessment/CTAE/Documents/Student-Plan-of-Study-Guidance.pdf.

Georgia General Assembly. (2011). *House Bill 186 (as passed by the House and Senate)*. Retrieved from http://www.legis.ga.gov/Legislation/20112012/116702.pdf.

Georgia Partnership for Excellence in Education (GPEE). (2015). *Top ten issues to watch in 2015* (11th ed.). Atlanta: GPEE.

Glass, R. D. (2000). Education and the ethics of democratic citizenship. *Studies in Philosophy and Education, 19*(3), 275–296.

Hanh, T. N. (1987). *Being peace*. Berkeley, CA: Parallax Press.

Hanson, F. A. (1993). *Testing, testing: Social consequences of the examined life*. Berkeley: University of California Press.

Hanushek, E. A. (2011). The economic value of higher teacher quality. *Economics of Education Review, 30*(3), 466–479.

Hill, D., and Kumar, R. (2009). Neoliberalism and its impacts. In D. Hill and R. Kumar (Eds.), *Global neoliberalism and education and its consequences* (pp. 12–29). New York: Routledge.

Hursh, D. (2007). Assessing No Child Left Behind and the rise of neoliberal education policies. *American Educational Research Journal, 44*(3), 493–518.

Jefferson, T. (2009a). Letter to Peter Carr (1814). In *The life and selected writings of Thomas Jefferson* (ed. A. Koch and W. Peden). New York: Modern Library. (Original work published 1814.)

Jefferson, T. (2009b). Letter to William Jarvis (1820). In *The works of Thomas Jefferson* (ed. P. L. Ford, vol. 12, pp. 161–164). New York: Cosimo. (Original work published 1820.)

Katz, M. B. (2013). *The undeserving poor: America's enduring confrontation with poverty* (2nd ed.). New York: Oxford University Press.

Labaree, D. F. (1997). Public goods, private goods: The American struggle over educational goals. *American Educational Research Journal, 34*(1), 39–81.

Mann, H. (2006). Selection from Report No. 12 of the Massachusetts School Board. In E. F. Provenzo, Jr. (Ed.), *Critical issues in education: An anthology of readings* (pp. 58–60). Thousand Oaks, CA: Sage. (Original work published 1848.)

Mehta, J. (2013a). *The allure of order: High hopes, dashed expectations, and the troubled quest to remake American schooling*. New York: Oxford University Press.

Mehta, J. (2013b). How paradigms create politics: The transformation of American educational policy, 1980–2001. *American Educational Research Journal, 50*(2), 285–324.

National Commission on Excellence in Education (NCEE). (1983). *A nation at risk: The imperative for educational reform*. [Report to the nation and Secretary of Education, United States Department of Education]. Washington, DC: Government Printing Office.

"Occupy education." (2012). *Rethinking Schools, 26*(3). Retrieved from http://www.rethinkingschools.org/archive/26_03/edit263.shtml.

Parker, W. C. (1996). "Advanced" ideas about democracy: Toward a pluralist conception of citizen education. *Teachers College Record, 98*(1), 104–125.

Powell, L. F. (1971, August 23). *Attack on American free enterprise system*. Retrieved from http://law2.wlu.edu/powellarchives/page.asp?pageid=1251.

RadicalMath. (2007). Retrieved from http://www.radicalmath.org/main.php?id=about.

Rousseau, J.-J. (1984). *A discourse on inequality*. New York: Penguin. (Original work published 1755.)

Rush, B. (2006). Thoughts upon the mode of education proper in a republic. In E. F. Provenzo, Jr. (Ed.), *Critical issues in education: An anthology of readings* (pp. 58–60). Thousand Oaks, CA: Sage. (Original work published 1786.)

Saltman, K. J. (2013). The new market bureaucracy in U.S. public schools. In J. Gorlewski and B. Porfilio (Eds.), *Left behind in the race to the top: Realities of school reform* (pp. 65–84). Charlotte, NC: Information Age.

Sleeter, C. E. (2008). Teaching for democracy in an age of corporatocracy. *Teachers College Record, 110*(1), 139–159.

Sleeter, C. E. (2014). Multiculturalism and education for citizenship in a context of neo-liberalism. *Intercultural Education, 25*(2), 85–94.

Smith, A. (2010). *The theory of moral sentiments*. New York: Penguin. (Original work published 1759.)

Soss, J., Fording, R. C., and Schram, S. F. (2011). *Disciplining the poor: Neoliberal paternalism and the persistent power of race*. Chicago, IL: University of Chicago Press.

Taylor, F. W. (1915). *The principles of scientific management*. New York: Harper and Brothers.

Thorndike, E. L. (1903). *Educational psychology*. New York: Science Press.

Tienken, C. H. (2013). Neoliberalism, social Darwinism, and consumerism masquerading as school reform. *Interchange, 43*(4), 295–316.

Tyack, D. B. (1976). Ways of seeing: An essay on the history of compulsory schooling. *Harvard Educational Review, 46*(3), 355–389.

UCLA Center X. (2015). Retrieved from https://centerx.gseis.ucla.edu/.

White House. (2015). *Race to the Top*. Retrieved from https://www.whitehouse.gov/issues/education/k-12/race-to-the-top.

Wittgenstein, L. (2009). *Philosophical investigations*. Chichester, UK: Wiley-Blackwell. (Original work published 1953.)

Workforce Data Quality Campaign. (2014). *Mastering the blueprint: State progress on workforce data*. Retrieved from http://www.workforcedqc.org/resources-events/resources/mastering-blueprint-state-progress-workforce-data.

Wright-Maley, C. (2015). Beyond the "Babel problem": Defining simulations for the social studies. *Journal of Social Studies Research, 39*(2), 63–77.

Wyllie, I. G. (1959). Social Darwinism and the businessman. *Proceedings of the American Philosophical Society, 103*(5), 629–635.

Zinn Education Project. (2015). Teaching a people's history. *Rethinking Schools and Teaching for Change*. Retrieved from http://zinnedproject.org/.

3

EMANCIPATORY AND PLURALIST PERSPECTIVES ON DEMOCRACY AND ECONOMIC INEQUALITY IN SOCIAL STUDIES AND CITIZENSHIP EDUCATION

Mark Edward Johnson

For the last several decades, much of the scholarship on democracy and citizenship education has been informed by the different, but not mutually exclusive, emancipatory and pluralist perspectives. Teachers concerned about income inequality can identify as pluralist or emancipatory, and both perspectives are used to address economic inequality. Despite their shared concern with the effects of an increasing income and wealth gap, the approaches and ultimate goals of emancipatory and pluralist theorists differ. As presented here, emancipatory scholars and educators maintain that the purpose of education is to improve society by making it more equitable and just. The justice orientation generally begins with the premise that economic inequality is a moral issue that should be addressed. In this view, a primary purpose of education is to improve society. As such, emancipatory scholars generally desire to move beyond discussing ideas and theories and seek to encourage social action that makes the world a better place. Citing a moral imperative, emancipatory educators have at times been critical of pluralist approaches on the grounds they are relativistic, linger too long in academic discussion, and fail to move students to actually do something about inequality.

One need not be an emancipatory educator, however, to be concerned about the recent increase in wealth and income inequality. Pluralist educators, identified here as those who maintain that the ultimate purpose of education is to promote intellectual freedom and rational agency, are also sometimes compelled to address inequality. Pluralists maintain in contrast, however, that addressing inequality in classroom settings should be restrained by the more fundamental educational goal of developing rational agency. Pluralist educators seek to provide students with the cognitive tools to address income inequality if and how they choose.

The following historical and theoretical examination of the two perspectives is intended to help clarify these established approaches and make us more cognizant of the interpretations of and solutions to inequality that are made readily available by these perspectives. In order to provide some historical context for the two leading approaches for addressing social issues in social studies and citizenship education, a concise intellectual history of the connections and differences between the pluralist and emancipatory perspectives will be provided initially. This broad history is followed by a more focused discussion of examples of emancipatory and pluralist approaches drawn from the last 40 years of scholarship on citizenship education. The chapter closes with a brief description of how I address economic inequality in my courses.

A Concise History of Ideas

Kant's (1784/1970) famous essay "An Answer to the Question: 'What Is Enlightenment?'" serves as a familiar and effective starting point for a history of the actual and desired function of education in modernity. Speaking on behalf of the Enlightenment, Kant suggested that the point of education should be to provide persons with the courage to think for themselves (*sapere aude*) rather than accept as true and binding the pronouncements made by those in positions of authority. By claiming that all people have access to reason and should use it to think for themselves rather than accept the self-incurred tutelage that comes from deferring thinking to sources of traditional authority, Kant linked emancipation to rational agency. This link between education and agency connects the contemporary pluralist and emancipatory perspectives and separates them from conservative perspectives on education that emphasize authority, continuity, and accepted conventions. Pluralist and emancipatory educators, following Kant, insist that students be exposed to the causes and effects of established understandings and be allowed to explore the limitations as well as the benefits of sanctioned ideas, conventions, and institutions. To the extent that pluralist and emancipatory educators desire to endow students with the tools to examine and possibly critique the status quo, both share a lineage that includes Kant.

A second thinker to consider in the development of pluralist and emancipatory approaches to economic inequality is G. W. Hegel (1837/1952). Like Kant, Hegel was a German thinker strongly influenced by the Protestant worldview associated with Pietism. Hegel discussed social evolution and development more than Kant, and he also understood reason differently. Hegel's historicism postulated that reason becomes manifest more perfectly over time as humans increase self-awareness and social equality. Thus, whereas a Kantian model of education would help students *access* an unchanging universal reason, a Hegelian model of education would emphasize the *development* of communal reason in accordance with the historical telos of human equality. Because reason becomes fully manifested only in connection with increased equality, teaching (even if the goal is the development of rational agency) would demand a concern with political, social, and economic equality. The pluralist project is thereby subsumed within an equality-focused, emancipatory program. Thus scholars and educators who maintain that the development of rational agency is an end that cannot be achieved without a corresponding development in social and economic equality are likely to find support and inspiration in Hegel's historical dialectic.

Karl Marx (1867/1990) developed Hegel's philosophy and is generally considered emancipatory education's most influential theorist. Like Hegel, Marx and colleague Friedrich Engels (Marx and Engels, 1978) argued that we need not posit a guiding world-spirit, or reason, to explain the evolution of human societies. We should instead seek to understand how those in power attempt to retain and enhance their authority by controlling resources and the means of production, because these determine the organization and norms of society. According to Marx, however, understanding is not enough. The point of philosophy, and by extension education, is to change the existing, material world.[1] With Marx, then, the educational goal of developing an individual's rational agency is largely displaced by the aim of developing political and social consciousness for the sake of economic and social change. Marx thus provides a direct theoretical ground for transformative educators who wish to use the classroom to address the structural causes of systemic inequality.

It is likely helpful to pause at this point and briefly reflect on the binary used to distinguish between pluralist and emancipatory scholars. As with all binaries, this one oversimplifies the issue, but it also serves as a delineating marker that helps to organize thinking: whereas the primary goal of pluralist educators is to promote rational agency (Kant), emancipatory educators seek to promote economic equality (Marx). The discussion does not end here, however, as there has been a century and a half of scholarship since Marx. In fact, the educative roles ascribed to Marx's dialectical materialism and to Kant's universal reason were both diminished by Max Weber.

Weber (1905/2002) suggested that neither the socioeconomic order nor the direction of history was determined by material factors alone; both were also influenced by nonmaterial stimuli such as culture and tradition. Weber observed that society evolves in unintended ways that produce unexpected consequences and that the application of reason to social issues (whether for the sake of preserving power or to make the world a better place) does not, as a matter of course, lead to equality or liberty. Weber's examination of the rationalization of Europe's religious, economic, and governing systems found reason to be a cold, instrumental force that tends to trap citizens in metaphorical *iron cages* that regulate daily life and tightly bind opportunities to expectations associated with prevailing social and economic stations. Weber's analysis of the social use of reason called into question attempts to emancipate individuals through rational agency and groups through social change. Weber brought to attention the invasive, creeping nature of instrumental reason and led scholars, educators, and students to consider which forms of social and interpersonal relationships should be nurtured in contemporary society.

Kant, Hegel, Marx, and Weber each influenced the theorists identified with the Frankfurt School. Scholars such as Horkheimer and Adorno (1944/1997) were sympathetic to Weber's contention that scientific rationality did not provide an unimpeded path to emancipation or social progress. The troubling events of the early twentieth century led to theorists retracing the evolution of reason from its Enlightenment promise to its use in the twentieth century as an instrument of state and corporate exploitation. Horkheimer and Adorno, drawing from Kant's (1781/1996) *Critique of Pure Reason* and Weber's (1905/2002) "The Protestant Ethic and the 'Spirit' of Capitalism," developed a revised, historical critique of reason: specifically of instrumental, means–end, and technical rationality. By presenting an evolution of reason removed from Hegel's (1807/1977) narrative of unfolding destiny, Horkheimer and Adorno helped to revitalize the discussion of values and purposes: topics largely pushed aside during the nearly unchecked reign of instrumental reason.

Likely the most influential member of the Frankfurt School for social studies theorists writing in the last several decades has been Jürgen Habermas. Like Weber, Horkheimer, and Adorno, Habermas (1984) believed that, although scientific rationality led to technical and bureaucratic advances, increasingly efficient means of exploitation had not ushered in unequivocal progress in all areas of human coexistence. Following Kant (1781/1996), Habermas organized the application of reason into a tripartite division of human interests: productive/technical, communicative/practical, and reflective/emancipatory.

Habermas (1984) used this model of knowledge/interests to explain that, in the past, the semi-independent spheres of rationality formed a complementary whole that served human interests, but that, with the ascendance of the market system as the organizational core of governance, this began to change. European republics allowed policy to be subject to public reason. These societies came to rely upon instrumental rationality and market structures to such an extent, however, that the public discourse the republican forms were intended to evoke was, over time, eviscerated and replaced by a bureaucratic decision-making process. This bureaucracy excluded questions about human life that were not answered in terms of increasing the efficient exploitation of resources—including, of course, human resources. If rationality is understood primarily in association with the efficient exploitation of labor and resources, conversations about what is meaningful are delegitimized or absent altogether from the forum of rational, public deliberation. In such an arrangement, discussions of economic inequality, for example, tend to focus narrowly on the efficient exploitation of labor and resources, and come to be understood as an economic problem that can be solved solely through market mechanisms, thereby precluding the use of communicative and reflective forms of rationality, understood by Habermas to be better suited for addressing how we wish to live together.

Pluralist educators moved by this line of thinking are likely keen to expose students to competing perspectives on and visions of the good society. Emancipatory educators who draw from Habermas are likely to reject outright the continued primacy of instrumental rationality and replace it with an interpretive approach that allows, or perhaps even presumes, that equality and justice, rather than efficient production and the expansion of capital, are of primary concern. To the extent that equality and justice are presumed ends, available visions of the good society that are offered to students are thereby delimited to visions that presuppose equality and justice as objective or universal ends. Pluralist and emancipatory educators thus agree that addressing economic inequality involves providing students with an opportunity to examine, or at a minimum consider, the rational or ideological foundation of the market system.

Does the education system generally promote the critical analysis discussed above embraced by pluralist and emancipatory educators? According to Louis Althusser (1971/2001), the answer is no; in fact, the education system functions as an ideological state apparatus that supports the interests of the existing power structure. The French-Algerian Althusser explained that, following the French Revolution, the bourgeois government wrested control of education from the Church to help ensure that French citizens adopted the values necessary for the success of the new, rationally organized, and bureaucratically managed state. According to this view, the inculcation of instrumental rationality that has since become the norm was intentional.

There are a number of actions an educator might take who believes the school is complicit in reproducing economic inequality. These include direct resistance through the counter-socialization of students,[2] and the more indirect approach of providing them with readings that both support and contest Althusser's thesis with the goal of having students consider the best arguments for each position without attempting to lead them to one conclusion or another. As developed below, the approach an educator takes to addressing economic inequality is influenced by the goals ascribed to education, especially regarding moral inculcation.

In the 1780s, Kant dared us to think for ourselves rather than accept ideas and practices based solely on tradition and authority, and promoted the application of reason to social issues in order to improve the lives of citizens. In the 1970s, Althusser argued that education systems developed in the interim compelled students to do just the opposite: to accept the dictates of authority and tradition. During intervening centuries, faith in the ability of institutionalized education to improve the lot of everyday people diminished. It did not fade completely, however, as illustrated by the chapters in this volume. In the following sections of this chapter, connections between rationality, social change, and education are explored through the scholarship of authors directly concerned with citizenship and social studies education. Drawing from a study (Johnson, 2014) of how democracy and citizenship have been understood since the 1970s, the similarities and differences between emancipatory and pluralist approaches to addressing economic inequality in social studies classrooms are further clarified.

Emancipatory Approaches to Democratic Education

In 1982, Cleo Cherryholmes, an early editor of *Theory and Research in Social Education*, saw a new perspective developing in social studies education literature. He linked this new perspective to the Frankfurt School, and particularly to Habermas's attempt to promote reflective and communicative discourse. From this new perspective developed an emancipatory approach that combined the views of Habermas with neo-Marxist elements and sought to uncover the education system's complicity in systematic forms of oppression. As understood here, however, the emancipatory project has been defined by a call to social transformation based on the belief that the existing social order is unjust.

Reflecting Althusser's thoughts on the ideological function of schools, scholars such as Jean Anyon (1978) theorized how the seemingly benign and neutral practices of social studies teachers legitimated and supported the existing, unequal system. Anyon pointed to the nature of knowledge (re)production itself, rather than the intentions of teachers, to argue that the standard practices of merely describing and explaining our existing institutions presented a logic and coherence for the system that led students to accept the status quo as natural. She argued that, because fact-based, *neutral* citizenship education that neither explicitly extols nor criticizes the existing state of affairs indirectly supports the status quo, such teaching should be understood as conservative rather than neutral. If a teacher wishes to address issues such as economic inequality, a first step, then, might be to expose students to views that directly call into question the desirability of existing economic practices and structures.

Pluralists and emancipatory social studies educators alike support Anyon's contention that students need to be exposed to sources that challenge as well as support existing institutions. An example from the late 1970s of an emancipatory, action-orientation approach can be found in an article by Giroux and Penna (1979). Argued therein was the position that a neo-Marxist framework provided "the most insightful and comprehensive model for a more progressive approach for understanding the nature of schooling and developing an emancipatory program for social education" (p. 23). A hallmark of this emancipatory vision is the desire to raise awareness of inequity and spur students to take action and become involved in transforming the unequal social and economic order. The approach discussed by Giroux and Penna involved breaking down traditional hierarchies within the classroom and exposing how the hidden curriculum represented and thus legitimated the larger, unequal structures of society.

During the 1980s, the scholarship on democratic education shifted somewhat from a concern with resisting conservative socialization to increasing political participation. These changing interests coincided with the conservative political resurgence of the same decade that, as Giroux (1989) noted, successfully laid claim to critical thinking and to a universal sense of morality. Two significant shifts made by emancipatory scholars to counter this trend during the 1980s were: (1) to more strongly emphasize the role of critical thinking in the emancipatory perspective; and (2) to further develop an emancipatory ethical vision.

Pluralists and emancipatory educators have generally supported critical examinations of existing institutions and practices, while conservatives have been more supportive of the status quo. Social studies scholarship in the 1970s, however, often pitted critical thinking against social action so that critical thinking was understood as academic, conservative, and *not enough*, while action-oriented teaching was presented as progressive and preferable. The binary allowed critics to paint emancipatory thinkers as anti-intellectual ideologues. In response, scholars such as Cherryholmes (1980, 1982), Giroux (1982, 1989), and Guyton (1988) sought to reemphasize the role of critical thinking in emancipatory social critique by revisiting the rather sophisticated intellectual arguments offered by members of the Frankfurt School.

Cherryholmes's 1982 article explained that Habermas's vision of truth and discourse can inform educators interested in equality by suggesting that, if the school is to develop in students the skills needed for a democratic society that is more equal, classroom discourse itself must become more open and less dominated by the view of the teacher or of the status quo. Students, he suggested, should be allowed to initiate discussion on topics of interest to them, to challenge the assertions of teachers and classmates, and not only to question the means to social ends but to deliberate upon desirable social ends themselves. Giroux's (1982) article from the same year likewise stressed that nurturing critical thinking was central to the goals of emancipation and social change. He proposed that critical thinking and social action might be merged through a pedagogical vision informed by critical theory:

> According to the Frankfurt School all thought and theory are tied to a specific interest in the development of a society without injustice. Theory, in this case, becomes a transformative activity that views itself as explicitly political and commits itself to the projection of a future that is as yet unfulfilled. Thus, critical theory contains a transcendent element in which critical thought becomes the precondition for human freedom.
>
> *(p. 30)*

Through the influence of critical theory, critical thinking was more comfortably reabsorbed into the emancipatory perspective. In this regard, the pluralist and emancipatory perspectives moved closer together. Another development of the 1980s, however, reiterated a difference between the two perspectives.

During the conservative revival of the 1980s, conservatives somewhat successfully connected liberalism with the political left, and both of them with relativism. In order to challenge the notion that conservatives held the moral high ground, emancipatory scholars such as Kickbusch (1987) and Giroux (1989) sought to reinvigorate the moral grounding of the emancipatory vision. Unlike liberal pluralists' inclination toward relativism, (neo-)Marxism, via Hegel, has a genealogical connection to the Judeo-Christian ethical system and is perhaps at its core a moral philosophy that understands the world as fallen and in need of redemption. The reemphasizing of the ethical element of the emancipatory perspective, characterized by equality, justice, and transformation, reiterated the prescriptive nature of the emancipatory system. This in turn allowed left-leaning emancipatory scholars to distance their views from the rational relativism of liberal pluralism. The differences between the liberal pluralists and emancipatory educators were highlighted in exchanges between Chamberlin (1990) and Ochoa (1990) and between Cornbleth (1980) and Giroux and Penna (1980).[3] Speaking of Engle and Ochoa's (1988) book *Education for Democratic Citizenship*, Chamberlin (1990), for example, claimed that the authors failed to "adequately strive for the moral principle of equality ... and [did] too little to end the role of the school in reproducing a society in which a rich, well-educated elite dominate a passive working class" (p. 179).

The decade and a half from the mid-1980s through the 1990s was a time of strong economic growth in the US. For this and other reasons, social rather than economic inequality was foregrounded in the period's democratic education literature, and with it an increased interest in multicultural education. This was informed by Habermas's goal of open dialogue, and an interest in increasing participation in the political system and in the amelioration of social inequality (see Banks, 1988; Banks and Banks, 2003; Ladson-Billings, 1995). In this literature emancipatory approaches to education that sought to promote social justice flourished (e.g., Boyle-Baise, 1995).

Following the events of September 11, 2001, discussions of multicultural education were often merged with those of global education (e.g., Evans, 2003; Mathews and Dilworth, 2008; Myers, 2006; Pang and Valle, 2004; Parker and Camicia, 2009). There was also an increase in prescriptive, action-oriented pedagogy and the desire to reassure readers that attempts to transform society and restructure students' beliefs should not be understood as dogmatic ideological indoctrination. Emancipatory educators sought to make the world a better place without crossing the line from teacher to ideologue. Mathews and Dilworth (2008), for example, wrote of the "challenges that teacher education programs face in promoting multicultural citizenship in predominately white schools of education" (p. 382), and sought to find ways for teacher educators "to confront and transform [alternative] dispositions" (p. 382). Similarly, Silva and Langhout (2011) argued for prescriptive, transformative teaching that encouraged elementary students to "be empowered to work against the matrix that oppresses them," and maintained that teachers should "instill a commitment to collective struggle rather than toward individualistic goals" (pp. 62–63). The article, an ethnographic report of teaching with these goals in mind, explained how the teacher "utilized her classroom to develop student critical consciousness that moved [the first grade students] from an individualistic to a collectivistic view of their environment, connecting individual acts of power to larger social systems that maintain unequal hierarchical power relations" (p. 85).

Over the last decade there has been an apparent increase in the confidence of educators seeking to transform their students' beliefs. Some consider using a relationship of unequal power between the student and teacher to persuade students to adopt the teacher's own social perspective, an odious form of proselytization that runs counter to the goal of helping students learn to think for themselves. From the emancipatory perspective, however, failing to challenge an unjust social and economic system is morally unacceptable. In recent years there have been attempts to articulate an emancipatory vision that respects the value of students thinking independently. One notable attempt was provided by Westheimer and Kahne (2004). There the authors suggest that there are three general approaches to citizenship education: seeking to teach students to be personally responsible; seeking to encourage students to participate in social and political affairs; and seeking to encourage students to enact systemic change. The third reflects the social justice perspective. The authors are careful to contend that this approach incorporates critical thinking and that it does not promote a particular social vision:

> The focus on social change and social justice does not imply an emphasis on particular political perspectives, conclusions, or priorities. . . . Indeed, those working to prepare justice-oriented citizens for a democracy do not aim to impart a fixed set of truths or critiques regarding the structure of the society. Rather, they work to engage students in informed analysis and discussion regarding social, political, and economic structures. They want students to consider collective strategies for change that challenge injustice and, when possible, address root causes of problems.
>
> *(pp. 242–243)*

The authors hold that conceptions of the greater good differ and that open discussion is paramount. Creating justice-oriented students without explicitly promoting a particular social vision is, however, difficult at best, and moreover relies upon the contentious notion that a social justice vision does not entail a particular social vision and set of values. Thus the Westheimer and Kahne article illustrates nicely the difficulty of encouraging social change while also encouraging students to question worldviews, ends, and presuppositions prescribed by those in authority, such as professors and teachers. It is far easier to posit a set of values or ends and have the students consider how to transform the existing structure so it more closely resembles the prescribed vision. That seems to be the current status of the emancipatory approach. Emancipatory educators can claim that economic inequality is an ethical issue via universal or natural rights. They can also value openness and critical thinking. To the extent that these two goals conflict, however, emancipatory educators defer to the belief that it is the moral duty of teachers to attempt to encourage students to adopt a justice orientation so as to make the world a better place.

To recap, since the 1970s, emancipatory scholars of democracy and citizenship education have sought to use the classroom to foster justice and equality. As suggested by Anyon (1978), an initial task for justice-oriented teachers is to take what seems natural (e.g., economic inequality) and present it as a problem that needs to be solved. Emancipatory educators might then expose students to different interpretations of the causes of inequality and to different proposed solutions. Because emancipatory educators hold that the ultimate goal is to compel students to enact social change, emancipatory educators are more likely to lead students to understand how the existing structure is unjust rather than to ask them whether or not the existing order is unjust. The emancipatory task is not over once a student acknowledges economic inequality. Equally important is creating change agents. This can be done in a number of ways. Teachers can create classroom experiences that model and enact the desired values. Students can be encouraged or compelled through service learning or other community projects to take small but material actions in the community to alleviate the symptoms of inequality. Didactic teaching combined with forcing students to experience the consequences of inequality in a more tangible way stirs the emotions in ways that academic discussion does not. Finally, emancipatory educators provide students with an interpretive framework and the corresponding language to explain inequality in reference to structural causes.

Pluralist Approaches to Democratic Education

Pluralists, as understood here, attempt to provide students with the tools to think for themselves. This section provides examples of how pluralist scholars, following in the line of Kant and the Enlightenment tradition, have approached citizenship and democratic education and how this translates to teaching about economic inequality. For the sake of unity and cohesion, the pluralist perspective is explained in comparison and contrast to that of emancipatory scholars from the same period.

Like those noted above, Cleo Cherryholmes (1977) was interested in developing rational agency and in promoting transformative social change. To illustrate, in 1976, Arthur Foshay presented a curricular model with the goal of developing politically active students who "would not stop with book knowledge [but] would be drawn by degrees into full participation in the world" (p. 5). To achieve this end, claimed Foshay, social studies needed a unified curriculum that emphasized the active pursuit of justice. Because the goal was to move beyond *mere thinking* and encourage social activism, the adoption of a standardized, narrow curriculum that would lead students quickly to social action was suggested. Cherryholmes's (1977) response was representative of pluralist concerns with transformative teaching. He contended that attempts to seek consensus on the purpose of citizenship education or to implement a single, official curriculum were misguided and that, rather than closing the perspectives made available to students on social topics, students and teachers should be given access to a varied curriculum that provided a range of accounts of the good society. According to this view, teaching issues such as income inequality is best done by exposing students to different accounts of the good society and the good citizen, and allowing students to explore those competing ideas and come to their own conclusions. Each of these steps is understood to help develop students' critical thinking skills.

As noted above, the pluralist and emancipatory approaches are in opposition to conservative approaches to education that directly seek to preserve the status quo. It is argued here that the key difference between the pluralist and emancipatory approaches, however, is that, while emancipatory educators generally advocate for a worldview aligned with equality, pluralist educators primarily seek to develop rational agency. An exchange between Cornbleth (1980) and Giroux (Giroux and Penna, 1979, 1980) further illustrates the historical differences. In their 1979 article Giroux and Penna explained that methods derived from a neo-Marxist perspective could combat the conservatism of the hidden and official curriculum. Cornbleth responded to the article by noting that she was wary of attempts to inculcate students with an egalitarian vision because doing so merely reproduces authoritarianism in a different form. Giroux and Penna (1980) rejoined, plainly enough, that "Cornbleth's position [was] relativistic" (p. 63). The emancipatory position holds that issues like economic inequality are moral issues and that students should be led to act in reference to a moral imperative. A pluralist approach to addressing economic inequality is to teach students the skills of rational analysis and to reflect on the decision about whether and how they should act on them.

Perhaps the most influential pluralist-inspired model for teaching democracy and social studies more generally was offered by Barr, Barth, and Shermis (1977, 1978, 1979). The three wrote a series of books and articles explaining what they thought to be the three main approaches to social studies education. The template provided by the three traditions model, as it was called, had an enormous impact on the field of social studies.[4] In short, Barr et al. (1978) argued that most social studies teachers sought to transmit knowledge, but that a better approach, reflective inquiry, allowed students to examine social issues of importance to them, provided the students with access to information on a topic, and taught them how to critique arguments so that students would learn how to come to their own reasoned decisions, using evidence and logic. When applied to economic inequality, this model would allow students to decide whether inequality was an issue that warranted further study. If so, the student would be directed to competing arguments and would be asked to identify theses, claims, and evidence before articulating a personal interpretation that would perhaps be offered as the starting point for a class discussion.

The final example of pluralist thinking comes from William Stanley. He began his career as an emancipatory (reconstructionist) scholar, but his view shifted toward pluralism in the early 1990s.[5] Stanley recognized the problem relativism posed for both conservative and emancipatory educators, claiming that, although relativism was a concern for many, dogmatism was unnecessary because a transformative agenda could be furthered without adopting a singular view of the good society. By incorporating postmodern insights regarding truth and subjectivity into their educational practices, teachers could open the door for social change without undermining the democratic project. His revised position was as follows:

> I now argue that the aim of social studies education should not impose or persuade students to embrace a preferred social order or set of values.... Instead, the primary purpose of social education is to enable students to become competent citizens. Put another way, we need to help students acquire the ability to make critical judgments regarding the nature of their society and how they might act, if necessary, to make it better. The task to determine what our students should become belongs to the students.
>
> *(Stanley, 1993, p. 295)*

Stanley's (1993) converted view reflected Cherryholmes (1977, 1978) and Engle and Ochoa (1988) in arguing that "there is an important difference between seeking to impose a particular social order and identifying a set of social conditions required for humans to develop the critical competence necessary to determine and act to realize their interests" (p. 296).

Stanley (1993) cautioned teachers against making the categorical mistake of subsuming the intellectual under the political and suggested that respecting and encouraging rational agency is more likely to foster social progress than prescribing our own currently held moral and political beliefs:

> No matter how strongly we as social educators have come to feel about particular social values, it is our professional obligation to help enable the next generation to claim its own set of values, even if we hope the values reflect those we presently hold. If education does not enable our students to embrace values via critical reflection, it is little more than a form of dogmatic cultural transmission. However noble the intent, this approach to instruction will serve to undermine the very basis for the democratic culture it seeks to impose.
>
> *(pp. 298–299)*

As Stanley and the other examples indicate, pluralist approaches to teaching share an affinity with Kant's desire to provide students with the tools and the courage to think for themselves. Like Hegel, however, pluralist scholars generally agree that what counts as reasonable varies in place and time and that understanding the history of political and social issues helps us make informed and rational decisions. With Weber, Horkheimer, Adorno, and Habermas, they generally hold that instrumental reason is insufficient for the development of fulfilled persons and desire to provide students with opportunities to think about ends as well as means. By having students consider what sort of society they would like to live in and why, pluralist educators provide opportunities for the next generation to decide whether they want to preserve the existing social relationships, reform them, or transform them.

The pluralist approach has two important limits regarding its applicability to teaching about income inequality. Of primary concern in this collection is that ending income inequality is not the primary goal for pluralist educators. It is at best a secondary goal behind developing the rational agency of one's students. For those whose primary educational goal is addressing income inequality, the pluralist approach will likely seem too passive. In addition, the pluralist approach is less likely to stir the emotions of students in a way that compels them to engage in transformative social action.

Closing Thoughts

I regularly tell my students that good teachers take the complex and make it simple: that we temporarily simplify events, concepts, and processes by focusing on one or a few small variables. Once an intellectual space is thereby established, we return to the simplified explanation and trouble it by introducing more variables and perspectives. This process is continued, but it is never completed, certainly not in the limited time we share with students. The task is not to transform students so they adopt the correct disposition (i.e., the teacher's own) but to provide students with the tools to compose their own interpretations of and solutions for complex and historied issues such as economic inequality. To this point my chapter has taken the form of an invitation to further study. I close, however, by explaining how these ideas influence my own practice.

The median household income in the county in which I live is about \$32,000, and the agricultural college where I teach was only a couple of decades ago an open-access community college (U.S. Census Bureau, 2015). Many of my education students already know poverty in a very personal way. Those who don't see it early in their classroom observation cycle, as there are no wealthy suburban schools in this rural area. Most of the surrounding counties have a single public high school attended by members of all socioeconomic groups present within the extended community. This reality affords certain opportunities. Introducing the topic of income inequality so that the students understand it in a personal, meaningful way, for example, requires little effort. It is as easy as asking the students to discuss some of the challenges faced by the K12 teachers in the schools they observe. Likewise, moving into discussion and the open exchange of ideas is pretty easy.

Because most of my students come from working- or middle-class backgrounds and have friends and family who have experienced sustained, intergenerational poverty, many of them have personal accounts of why the poor are poor and others are not. Of course, I do not agree with them all, nor do I expect 20-year-old education students to have exceedingly sophisticated interpretations of economic inequality. Despite the likelihood of having far more exposure to the subject, I do not disregard or discount as naïve and provincial the students' experiences and interpretations of income inequality. I do attempt to challenge and complicate their interpretations: not to lead them to any particular interpretation, but to engage them in reflective analysis. This is done in the traditionally academic way of introducing through reading and discussion the historical and intellectual context surrounding the different schools of economic thought (Marxist, Keynesian, and Austrian, in particular). It is developed by having the students apply the different interpretations, usually in small-group, jigsaw activities, to their own accounts of how economic inequality affects our local schools.

I do not seek consensus in interpretation or solution. If I intentionally move students in any direction, I do so to provoke the consideration of a multiplicity of potential analyses. This approach clearly identifies me as a pluralist. I am very deliberate in my goal to assure the students that their reasoned positions will be attended to with respect and criticism regardless of their popularity or alignment with my own position. Our goal is to discover the best argument, understanding that there is no clear-cut and universal adjudicator for these sorts of ideas.

Nonetheless, there are at times temptations to lead students to *understand* that when, in 2008, Congress decided to bail out their irresponsible corporate masters (who subsequently paid themselves enormous bonuses with the money fleeced from the present and future middle class) any reasonable semblance of market-based economics died. At times I would like to transform student beliefs so that they recognize that the Federal Reserve's continued, trickle-down practice of pumping money directly into banks and the stock market has played a role in the recent dramatic increase of income inequality, and to emancipate them from the narrative created by the military–industrial complex and parroted by the media.

It is equally tempting to discuss the absolutely revolutionary measures I think will be required to move us away from faux-democracy and toward economic equality. Although I am happy to share these opinions with peers and the general public, I refrain from doing so in class because I believe that leading students to conclusions (even my enlightened conclusions) undermines the far more pressing task of helping them learn to question authority and to think critically. So, instead of imploring students to join me in righteous struggles of political and social resistance, I expose students to different interpretations of inequality, model a willingness to listen to and engage with the reasoned positions of all students, allow students to practice critical analysis, and provide preservice teachers with pedagogical processes that allow them to teach others to do the same. In this way I encourage (working-class) students to see beyond the blue and red façade of contemporary political thinking and address economic inequality, if they choose to, in their own way.

Notes

1 See Marx (1888/1978).
2 This is discussed later in the chapter.
3 This encounter is discussed in "Pluralist Approaches to Democratic Education" below.
4 See Johnson (2014).
5 For examples of his emancipatory work, see Stanley (1981a, 1981b) and Stanley and Nelson (1986). For examples of his pluralist work see Stanley (1992, 1993, 1997).

References

Althusser, L. (2001). Ideology and ideological state apparatuses: Notes toward an investigation (trans. B. Brewster). In *Lenin and philosophy and other essays* (pp. 85–126). New York: Monthly Review Press. (Original work published 1971.)

Anyon, J. (1978). Elementary social studies textbooks and legitimating knowledge. *Theory and Research in Social Education, 6*(3), 40–55.

Banks, J. (1988). *Multiethnic education: Theory and practice* (2nd ed.). Boston: Allyn & Bacon.

Banks, J., and Banks, C. (Eds.). (2003). *Handbook of research on multicultural education*. New York: Macmillan.

Barr, R., Barth, J., and Shermis, S. (1977). *Defining the social studies*. Washington, DC: National Council for the Social Studies.

Barr, R., Barth, J., and Shermis, S. (1978). *The nature of the social studies*. Palm Springs, CA: ETC.

Barr, R., Barth, J., and Shermis, S. (1979). Defining social problems. *Theory and Research in Social Education, 7*(1), 1–19.

Boyle-Baise, M. (1995). The role of a European American scholar in multicultural education. *Theory and Research in Social Education, 23*(4), 332–341.

Chamberlin, C. (1990). Education for democratic citizenship. *Theory and Research in Social Education, 18*(2), 174–180.

Cherryholmes, C. (1977). Response to "citizenship as the aim of social studies." *Theory and Research in Social Education, 5*(1), 1–6.

Cherryholmes, C. (1978). Curriculum design as a political act: Problems and choices in teaching social justice. *Theory and Research in Social Education, 6*(4), 60–82.

Cherryholmes, C. (1980). Social knowledge and citizenship education: Two views of truth and criticism. *Curriculum Theory, 10*(2), 115–151.

Cherryholmes, C. (1982). Discourse and criticism in the social studies classroom. *Theory and Research in Social Education, 9*(4), 57–73.

Cornbleth, C. (1980). A reaction to social education in the classroom: The dynamics of the hidden curriculum. *Theory and Research in Social Education, 8*(2), 57–60.

Engle, S., and Ochoa, A. (1988). *Education for democratic citizenship: Decision making in the social studies.* New York: Teachers College Press.

Evans, R. (2003). The social studies wars revisited. *Theory and Research in Social Education, 31*(4), 523–539.

Foshay, A. W. (1976). Citizenship as the aim of the social studies. *Theory and Research in Social Education, 4*(4), 1–22.

Giroux, H. (1982). Culture and rationality in Frankfurt School thought: Ideological foundations for a theory of social education. *Theory and Research in Social Education, 9*(4), 17–51.

Giroux, H. (1989). *Schooling for democracy: Critical pedagogy in the modern age.* London: Routledge.

Giroux, H., and Penna, A. (1979). Social education in the classroom: Dynamics of the hidden curriculum. *Theory and Research in Social Education, 7*(1), 21–42.

Giroux, H., and Penna, A. (1980). Response to Cornbleth. *Theory and Research in Social Education, 8*(2), 61–64.

Guyton, E. (1988). Critical thinking and political participation: Development and assessment of a causal model. *Theory and Research in Social Education, 16*(1), 23–49.

Habermas, J. (1984). *The theory of communicative action: Reason and the rationalization of society* (trans. T. McCarthy, vol. 1). Boston, MA: Beacon Press.

Hegel, G. (1977). *Phenomenology of spirit.* Oxford: Oxford University Press. (Original work published 1807.)

Hegel, G. (1952). The philosophy of history. In *Hegel* (ed. R. Hutchins, pp. 153–369). Chicago, IL: William Benton. (Original work published 1837.)

Horkheimer, M., and Adorno, T. (1997). *Dialectic of enlightenment.* New York: Continuum. (Original work published 1944.)

Johnson, M. (2014). Reproducing and reconstructing the social order: A conceptual history of democracy and citizenship education in the journal *Theory and Research in Social Education*, 1973–2012. [Unpublished doctoral dissertation]. University of Georgia, Athens.

Kant, I. (1970). An answer to the question: "What is enlightenment?" In *Kant's political writings* (ed. H. Reiss, pp. 54–60). Cambridge: Cambridge University Press. (Original work published 1784.)

Kant, I. (1996). *Critique of pure reason.* Indianapolis, IN: Hackett. (Original work published 1781.)

Kickbusch, K. (1987). Civic education and preservice educators: Extending the boundaries of discourse. *Theory and Research in Social Education, 15*(3), 173–188.

Ladson-Billings, G. (1995). But that's just good teaching! The case for culturally relevant pedagogy. *Theory into Practice, 34*(3), 159–165.

Marx, K. (1978). Theses on Feuerbach. In K. Marx and F. Engels, *The Marx–Engels reader* (ed. R. Tucker, 2nd ed., pp. 143–145). New York: W. W. Norton. (Original work published 1888.)

Marx, K. (1990). *Capital.* New York: Penguin. (Original work published 1867.)

Marx, K., and Engels, F. (1978). *The Marx–Engels reader* (ed. R. Tucker, 2nd ed.). New York: W. W. Norton.

Mathews, S., and Dilworth, P. (2008). Case studies of preservice teachers' ideas about the role of multicultural citizenship education in social studies. *Theory and Research in Social Education, 36*(4), 356–390.

Myers, J. (2006). Rethinking the social studies curriculum in the context of globalization: Education for global citizenship in the US. *Theory and Research in Social Education*, *34*(3), 370–394.

Ochoa, A. (1990). Response to Mr. Chamberlin's review of education for democratic citizenship. *Theory and Research in Social Education*, *18*(2), 183–185.

Pang, V., and Valle, R. (2004). A change in paradigm: Applying contributions of genetic research to teaching about race and racism in social studies education. *Theory and Research in Social Education*, *32*(4), 503–522.

Parker, W., and Camicia, S. (2009). Cognitive praxis in today's "international education" movement: A case study of intents and affinities. *Theory and Research in Social Education*, *37*(1), 42–74.

Silva, J., and Langhout, R. (2011). Cultivating agents of change in children. *Theory and Research in Social Education*, *39*(1), 61–91.

Stanley, W. (1981a). The radical reconstructionist rationale for social education. *Theory and Research in Social Education*, *8*(4), 55–79.

Stanley, W. (1981b). Toward a reconstruction of social education. *Theory and Research in Social Education*, *9*(1), 67–89.

Stanley, W. (1992). *Curriculum for utopia: Social reconstructionism and critical pedagogy in the postmodern era*. Albany, NY: SUNY Press.

Stanley, W. (1993). Curricular visions and social education: A response to Ronald Evans' review of curriculum for utopia. *Theory and Research in Social Education*, *21*(3), 294–303.

Stanley, W. (1997). Reframing the question: Social education and the nature of social knowledge. *Theory and Research in Social Education*, *25*(3), 363–368.

Stanley, W., and Nelson, J. (1986). Social education for social transformation. *Social Education*, *50*(7), 528–530, 532–535.

U.S. Census Bureau. (2015). State and county QuickFacts. Retrieved from http://quickfacts.census.gov/qfd/states/13/13019.html.

Weber, M. (2002). The Protestant ethic and the "spirit" of capitalism. In *The Protestant ethic and the "spirit" of capitalism and other writings* (ed. P. Baehr and G. C. Wells). New York: Penguin. (Original work published 1905.)

Westheimer, J., and Kahne, J. (2004). What kind of citizen? The politics of educating for democracy. *American Educational Research Journal*, *41*(2), 237–269.

SECTION II
Confronting Economic Disparity

4

TEACHING ABOUT ECONOMIC INEQUALITY

Lessons from California

John Rogers and Joel Westheimer

Nina Baudin is a high school social studies teacher who sees her role as preparing young people to deliberate about complex social problems.[1] She teaches in a mid-size California city notable for its socio-economic diversity. Spacious homes in the city's south-side cost well over a million dollars, while many north-side residents live in small rent-controlled apartments. Roughly a third of Ms. Baudin's students come from low-income families, a third from middle-income families, and a third from affluent families.[2]

Ms. Baudin began to incorporate lessons about economic inequality into her 12th grade U.S. Government class because she considered it an important issue and wanted her students to be "aware of others" and to become "informed voters." She reasoned that it is not her role to "instill in my students" a particular viewpoint on economic inequality. Rather, she noted: "I want them to be aware that it exists so then they can make their own decision. . . . I just want them to think about, OK, in the world, what's my job?" Her lessons focused attention on the distribution of income, the measures that government agencies use to define poverty, and factors associated with lower and higher levels of income (like race and educational attainment). In teaching about economic disparity, Ms. Baudin reminded her students that "we're allowed to agree to disagree." Even though arguments get heated, she encouraged her class to "come back to facts, even if the facts disagree with what someone's thinking emotionally."

Ms. Baudin worried about two seemingly contradictory challenges: at times economic inequality proves either too visible or too hidden for students to interrogate. She is concerned that discussions about economic inequality can tap into students' sensitivities about their own place in the economic hierarchy—particularly when their sense of self-worth is bound up with consumer culture. "In this class . . . there are students . . . wearing the fake knock-off . . . who can't compete with the students wearing Uggs. . . . They experience income inequality; I don't want them to feel it [in my class]." At the same time, Ms. Baudin found that economic inequality is a topic often pushed to the margins of classroom discussion or avoided altogether. For example, she noted that it is "much harder" to "get them to discuss" income inequality than race. My "students can visualize racial inequality more than they can visualize income inequality," she reported.

It is not surprising that Nina Baudin, like many U.S. high school teachers today, is grappling with issues of economic inequality in her classroom. In the wake of the Occupy movement, the gap between the "haves" and the "have-nots" has become a major topic of discussion for the broader public. Questions about inequality have figured prominently in recent local, state, and national elections. High-brow publications such as the *New York Times* and *Science* have run series or created special themed issues examining inequality. Even as the din of popular media turns the public gaze elsewhere, the topic of growing economic inequality has made its way into the mainstream through documentaries, viral videos, comedic television, and popular music.

Although economic inequality increasingly is a topic of public conversation, little is known about how often these conversations are taking place in U.S. high school classrooms. A recent analysis of state social studies content standards found that, even though all 50 states in the U.S. include economics (Council for Economic Education, 2012), most states do not include issues of economic inequality, and those that do often merely acknowledge economic inequality without addressing causes or possible remedies (Rogers and Westheimer, 2015). Although illuminating, this analysis of the content standards only refers to the official social studies standards and does not necessarily address what teachers actually talk about in their classrooms.

In this chapter we aim to make an empirical contribution to the literature by reporting on California public high school teachers' responses to survey and interview questions regarding teaching about economic inequality. The study discussed in this chapter is part of a larger multinational research project (theinequalityproject.com) that seeks to understand the ways economic inequality is taught in the United States, Canada, Mexico, and elsewhere. For the California research, we considered three questions: Do public high school teachers address issues of economic inequality in their classrooms, and how and why do they do so? Does this differ by subject matter? Does this differ by the socio-economic context of the school?

The chapter proceeds as follows. First, there is a literature review about educating the public on issues of economic inequality. The chapter continues by offering an overview of our survey and interview methods. It then presents findings from the survey, with particular attention to how a teacher's subject and the school's socio-economic status are related to teacher responses. The chapter goes on to draw on teacher interviews to illuminate why teachers address economic inequality or why they do not address it, and what they do when they engage with this topic. The chapter then sets out the implications for practice and future research, before concluding. Before turning to this work, a caveat is in order. Our analysis is illuminating but necessarily partial. We report on a limited set of survey items (2) and a small number of interviews (15), and all of this data is collected in one state. Nonetheless, our findings provide a set of suggestive insights that we will explore further in future research.[3]

Literature Review

By an array of objective measures, economic inequality in the United States has risen dramatically over recent decades (Saez, 2013). While disputes remain over why economic inequality has grown, or how to reverse this trend, it is clear that the public has an interest in better understanding it. Economic inequality has emerged as an increasingly important topic within American social, political, and economic life (Duncan and Murnane, 2011; Schlozman et al., 2012; Stiglitz, 2012, 2015). General theories of democracy and democratic education suggest that democratic citizens should be able to assess evidence about contentious issues so that they can participate in consequential decisions about economic and political life (Gutmann, 1995).

Social science evidence indicates that the general public has a limited under-standing of basic facts of economic inequality, let alone of the broader debates in the field (Cruces et al., 2013; Koçer and van de Werfhorst, 2012; Morin, 2012; Osberg and Smeeding, 2006; Savani and Rattan, 2012). Norton and Ariely (2011) found that a representative group of U.S. citizens "dramatically underestimated" the proportion of wealth owned by the richest Americans. Norton (2014) also has demonstrated that the earnings ratio of CEOs to aver-age workers is ten times greater than Americans believe it to be and 50 times greater than they want it to be (see also Kiatpongsan and Norton, 2014). These findings are consistent with data from the International Social Survey Program's Social Inequality Survey, in which North American respondents were less likely than respondents from more economically egalitarian nations to have a clear understanding of income inequality and its consequences for democratic life (Hadler, 2005). Even those citizens who have information about the rise of income inequality may not understand its significance for public policy or democracy, or even have the capacities or inclinations to explore possibilities for reducing inequality. In their study of public opinion polls, McCall and Kenworthy (2009, p. 459), for example, found that, generally speaking, people "may be unsure or uninformed about how to address rising inequality" (see also Zilinsky, 2013).

Public schools are arguably the institution best situated to foster a public more informed about debates on economic inequality. Our research team's analysis of social studies content standards in the United States and Canada demonstrates wide variability across states and provinces in whether and how the standards address poverty and wealth, social mobility, or income distribution—topics that arguably form the basis of informed analysis, debate, and action. And Schug et al.'s (2009) survey of high school economics teachers suggests that the focus of most economics classes is on personal finance and consumer education.

Recent scholarly and popular literature on economic inequality highlights a set of vital questions that are of keen interest to the broader public. Drawing from this literature, we conjecture that young adults should be familiar with scholarly debates about whether economic inequality: (1) should be defined by income, assets after taxes and government transfers, or wealth (McCall and Percheski, 2010; Saez, 2013); (2) has grown because of technological change, realignment of political power, or some combination of the two (Glyn, 2007; Stiglitz, 2012; Williams, 2004); (3) produces suboptimal social behavior, such as the acceleration of credit-enabled consumption of leisure goods (Frank, 2007); (4) impacts valued social outcomes across a number of public policy domains, such as mental and physical health (Wilkinson and Pickett, 2009); (5) is related to growing political inequality and, if so, whether one is causing the other (Bartels, 2008; Stiglitz, 2012); and (6) can be ameliorated through public policy intervention (Jencks, 2002; Smeeding, 2005). These initial considerations serve as a conceptual framework for understanding the types of subject matter that might be introduced into the high school classroom.

Methods

This section discusses survey and interview data collected from California public high school teachers during the 2013–14 school year. The statewide online survey was conducted in the fall of 2013 on the broad theme of learning time. It included a question asking teachers to report on how often they talked with their students about a number of different topics in a typical class during the first couple of months of school.[4] Topics included financial literacy, racial and social inequality, economic inequality, and other issues. For each of these topics, teachers could respond: (a) "Never"; (b) "I have not done this yet"; (c) "About Once per Month"; (d) "Once per Week"; (e) "A Few Times per Week"; or (f) "Daily." Teachers who responded affirmatively regarding talking about economic inequality (responses c, d, e, or f) were then asked to indicate whether they had engaged in three specific practices related to it: reading fiction or nonfiction, watching a documentary film, and examining data. They also were asked about topics that they discussed with their students: current events, students' personal experiences, causes, and/or possible solutions.

The survey targeted groups of three to five teachers nested within 193 high schools. The sample of schools is representative of California high schools generally in terms of student socio-economic status, student language proficiency, school size, geographic region, and charter status. We used data from the California

Longitudinal Pupil Achievement Data System (CALPADS) from the 2012–13 school year to identify these representative schools. In all, 783 California high school teachers completed the 30- to 40-minute online survey.[5]

Our analysis in this chapter focuses on the 643 social studies, English, math, and science teachers who reported on regular education classes in the survey.[6] Of these teachers, 362 reported on a humanities class (social studies or English) and 281 reported on a STEM class (math or science).[7] These 643 teachers work in a diverse array of high schools, some of which enroll very few students from low-income families, and others that serve predominantly low-income communities. Table 4.1 shows the number of teachers in our sample from schools enrolling different proportions of students eligible for a free or reduced price lunch, from the most affluent quartile (Q1) to the highest-poverty quartile (Q4).

To complement the survey data, we conducted 15 interviews with teachers at seven California public schools who had participated in a separate survey we administered on civic education. Two of the schools were from the relatively affluent Quartile 2, one from Quartile 3, and four from the high-poverty Quartile 4. The interview sample was created to reflect subject matter diversity and to include teachers who rarely or frequently talked about social and political issues with their students. All of the teachers who participated had expressed a willingness to be interviewed when they took the survey.

Interviews were conducted in person and lasted approximately 30 minutes. The interview protocol explored how teachers conceive of the relationship between their classroom practice and civic education. We asked teachers if they teach about economic inequality, and we prompted them to justify why or why not. Teachers who reported teaching about economic inequality were encouraged to describe their practice. We also asked all teachers to define economic inequality, though not all teachers responded to this question directly. The audio-recorded interviews were transcribed and coded.

Survey Findings

A strong majority (60 percent) of California public high school teachers reported that they had talked with their students about economic inequality in the first few months of the 2013–14 school year. By way of contrast, 76 percent of high school teachers reported talking about social and racial inequality during this period. Whether and how frequently teachers talked about economic

TABLE 4.1 Teachers in Survey Sample from Schools by Percentage of Students Receiving Free or Reduced Price Lunch

Q1. 0–24.9%	Q2. 25–49.9%	Q3. 50–74.9%	Q4. 75–100%
132	146	194	171

inequality or social and racial inequality differed markedly by subject matter. Tables 4.2 and 4.3 show that humanities teachers were far more likely than their STEM colleagues to teach about both forms of inequality. Indeed, humanities teachers were three times as likely (44.2 percent to 14.6 percent) as STEM teachers to report that they teach about economic inequality at least once a week.

There are some differences as well in the frequency with which teachers in low- and high-poverty schools report talking about issues of economic inequality. Teachers in schools serving the highest proportion of students from low-income families were less likely to report "Never" talking about economic inequality and more likely to report talking frequently about it. These differences across school socio-economic context were more pronounced for teaching about economic inequality than teaching about racial and social inequality (see Tables 4.4 and 4.5).

Teachers who reported talking about economic inequality were asked about whether they engaged in specific instructional practices and discussed particular topics. Of the humanities teachers who taught about economic inequality, more than two-thirds used fiction or non-fiction texts and more than two-fifths used documentaries to illuminate the topic. Very few STEM teachers reported using either of these resources. Almost half of STEM teachers who talked about economic inequality asked their students to examine data on the topic—a slightly smaller proportion than humanities teachers (see Table 4.6).

Most teachers who reported talking about economic inequality noted that they discussed the topic in relationship to current events and students' personal experiences. A strong majority indicated that they discussed its causes, and a slight majority noted discussing what could be done to address it. Humanities teachers were somewhat more likely than STEM teachers to report discussing

TABLE 4.2 Frequency of Talking about Economic Inequality by Subject Area

Frequency of talking about economic inequality	Never[1]	Monthly	Weekly (or more)
Humanities teachers	22.9%	32.9%	44.2%
STEM teachers	60.9%	24.6%	14.6%

Note:[1] For the purpose of our analysis in this chapter, we treat answers of "Never" or "I have not done this yet" as "Never."

TABLE 4.3 Frequency of Talking about Social or Racial Inequality by Subject Area

Frequency of talking about social or racial inequality	Never	Monthly	Weekly (or more)
Humanities teachers	9.7%	34.8%%	55.5%
STEM teachers	41.6%	39.1%	19.2%

TABLE 4.4 Frequency of Talking about Economic Inequality by Percentage of Free or Reduced Price Lunch (FRL)

Frequency of talking about economic inequality	Never	Monthly	Weekly (or more)
0–24.9% FRL	44.7%	30.3%	25.0%
25–74.9% FRL	41.2%	28.4%	29.4%
75–100% FRL	31.6%	26.9%	41.5%

TABLE 4.5 Frequency of Talking about Social or Racial Inequality by Percentage of Free or Reduced Price Lunch (FRL)

Frequency of talking about social or racial inequality	Never	Monthly	Weekly (or more)
0–24.9% FRL	26.5%	37.9%	35.6%
25–74.9% FRL	22.7%	38.3%	39.0%
75–100% FRL	24.0%	31.6%	44.4%

TABLE 4.6 Economic Inequality Instructional Practices by Subject Area

How students learn about economic inequality	Read fiction or non-fiction	Watch documentary	Examine data
Humanities teachers	68.8%	43.0%	53.0%
STEM teachers	8.2%	12.7%	42.7%

these topics (see Table 4.7). Generally, there were not substantial differences in the responses of teachers from low- and high-poverty schools to questions about instructional strategies or topics discussed. The one exception was that teachers in the highest-poverty schools were far more likely (76.1 percent to 54.8 percent) to report that they discussed economic inequality in relationship to their students' personal experiences.

The survey findings inform our understanding of whether and how frequently different groups of California high school teachers talk with their students about economic inequality and, when they do, what instructional strategies they use

TABLE 4.7 Discussion Topics on Economic Inequality by Subject Area

	Current events	Students' personal experiences	Causes of inequality	Strategies to address inequality
Humanities teachers	90.3%	67.0%	73.0%	57.0%
STEM teachers	79.1%	59.1%	53.6%	44.5%

and which topics they address. Yet the survey data can only be suggestive of what teachers mean when they say they talk about economic inequality, and the data offer no insight into why teachers choose to remain silent or talk about this subject. We turn now to teacher interviews to illuminate these questions.

Interviews

In this section, we draw on analysis of 15 interviews with California high school teachers to elaborate on the survey findings. We begin by reporting on the rationales of teachers who do not talk with their students about economic inequality. We then highlight the different ways that teachers define it and show that these definitions are related to three distinctive approaches to teaching about it.

Teachers Who Do Not Talk about Economic Inequality

Five of the 15 teachers we interviewed do not talk with their students about economic inequality. A sixth teacher tries to avoid such discussions. These teachers work in low- and high-poverty schools and address an array of subject areas, though they are most likely to be in the STEM field (see Table 4.8).

These teachers offered several explanations for why they do not talk about economic inequality. Three of the teachers reasoned that it does not fit with the content they have been charged to teach. For Ana Lee, a science teacher at a high-poverty school, discussions about economic inequality fall outside the material she is supposed to cover. She worried that, if she pursued students' questions on such topics, her lesson might go "on a tangent" and students would not learn the mandated curriculum. Lee added that she experiences "pressure with teaching [the California science] content standards." Cathy Calabrese similarly chose to focus on her English curriculum rather than entertain discussions about economic inequality, because she feels that attending to the prescribed literature is the best way to advance students' analytic and writing skills. Whereas Lee felt pressures from the school's accountability structure, Calabrese acknowledged that these are "pressures I impose."

TABLE 4.8 Teachers Who Do Not Talk about Economic Inequality

Teacher	School	Subject	Address economic inequality?
Doyle	25–49% FRL	English	Tries to avoid
Lee	25–49% FRL	Science	No
Calabrese	50–74.9% FRL	English	No
Yates	50–74.9% FRL	Science	No
Reed	75–100% FRL	Math	No
Raneri	75–100% FRL	English	No

Note: FRL: Free or Reduced Price Lunch.

Two other teachers explained that they do not teach about economic inequality because they do not feel prepared to address it. Issues of inequality, social class, and race represent minefields for these teachers, who are not accustomed to talking with their students about topics outside of the subject matter. For example, Liz Raneri, an English teacher at a high-poverty school, chooses not to speak about inequality or poverty "because you don't want to insult anyone's parents and then kids [get] their hackles up." She added that, even if a teacher makes an accurate point, the highly charged topic of inequality may mean that "the message gets lost because of the emotion." Math teacher Alice Reed also worried about saying the wrong thing and/or having students misunderstand the underlying intent of her comments: "If you [raise questions about inequality], automatically somebody will say, 'Oh . . . She's racist . . . She said this' or 'She said that.'"

Jack Doyle, an English teacher in a socio-economically diverse school, reported that he avoids talking about economic inequality because the subject creates a "nasty filter or affective level of discomfort" that shuts down learning. "Discussing social [and] economic inequality or just economic inequality raises the level of tension amongst my students pretty dramatically. So it's not something that I'm uncomfortable discussing but I think it's something that they feel uncomfortable discussing." Doyle recounted a particular lesson that put this issue in stark relief:

> One of my other students from a relatively affluent background made [an] inappropriate comment about people's monetary status. And the student who was coming from the non-affluent background said: "You don't even know what you're talking about." And then he posed to the student: "Have you ever had to live out of your car before?" or a question something like that. And I was excited [because] he was discussing something that previously had been difficult for him to talk about even though he did it in a confrontational manner. . . . I said: "That's a great question; can anybody respond to that?" [but] it just shut the conversation down. . . . I threw out a couple more prompting questions to try to [ease] the level of combativeness and just make it a general discussion. I couldn't [make] any headway.

Much like Nina Baudin, whom we described earlier, Jack Doyle struggled with the ways that conversations about inequality in socio-economically diverse settings lead students into the trap of associating how much money someone's family has with that student's value as a person. "I think the reason the [more affluent] students are uncomfortable discussing it is because they feel like having money and talking about that with students who don't have money is sort of like passing judgment on them."

Teachers Who Teach about Economic Inequality Differ in Their Conceptions

The teachers who reported talking with their students about economic inequality differ from one another both in how they conceptualize it and in how they teach students about it. Teachers draw on their own conceptions and understandings, which can range from simply acknowledging economic inequality (it exists) to deeper forms of analysis that explore power relations and issues of fairness and justice (see Table 4.9).

Four of the teachers we interviewed defined economic inequality descriptively, highlighting the basic facts of uneven distribution of income, wealth, or resources. For example, Tia Leonard, a science teacher at a high-poverty school, defined economic inequality as "certain people having unequal access to economic, to monetary resources or financial resources, jobs, insurance, housing." Similarly, Sam West, a social studies teacher at a high-poverty school, noted that "not everyone makes the same amount of money. Not everybody lives in the same quality of home or city.... We're all at different levels." Teachers like Leonard and West depicted stratification as a natural phenomenon within social life. They define economic inequality without passing moral judgment or commenting on how or why it arises. In contrast, the definitions from five other teachers included explanations for why inequality arises. Steve Peters, a social studies teacher at a high-poverty school, offered a conditional explanation. He reasoned that all societies must make distributional decisions and these *may* produce inequality:

> At its basic form, economics is just how do we deal with resources? We have unlimited wants and limited resources.... And that's what econ is,

TABLE 4.9 Teachers Who Talk about Economic Inequality

Teacher	School	Subject	Definition	Practice
Baudin	25–49% FRL	Social studies	Descriptive	Describe
Garofalo	25–49% FRL	English	Explanatory–power	Grapple with power
Watanabee	25–49% FRL	English	Explanatory–power	Grapple with power
Leonard	75–100% FRL	Science	Description	Describe
Molina	75–100% FRL	Social studies	Description	Describe
Peters	75–100% FRL	Social studies	Explanatory–open	Open discussion
West	75–100% FRL	Social studies	Description	Open discussion
Bates	75–100% FRL	Social studies	Explanatory–power	Grapple with power
Winters	75–100% FRL	Social studies	Explanatory–power	Unclear

Note: FRL: Free or Reduced Price Lunch.

how to figure out what to do with that situation. . . . What are we going to produce? For whom are we going to produce? How much are we going to produce? . . . And all those decisions are made differently in different societies. . . . When the method by which you decide who gets what . . . is unfair, then that is inherent inequality that societies create.

All of the other teachers who provided explanations saw economic inequality as related to unequal power and a system that advantages some at the expense of others (see Table 4.9). Nick Watanabee, an English teacher at a socio-economically diverse school, associated inequality with "the 1 percent, and the rigid class structures, and the voicelessness of servants." Another English teacher, Sara Garofalo, saw economic inequality as both cause and effect of social hierarchy:

> I think we would talk about wealth and privilege, and I think those two things come with economic inequalities. One has one, and the other doesn't. And so I think, for me, it wouldn't be more of a financial number, it would be more of: what privileges do this group of people have over this group? How was this [group] empowered and this one isn't?

Similarly, Tom Bates, a social studies teacher at a high-poverty school, asserts that the relationship between unequal wealth and unequal power has become formalized within our political system. We have economic inequality, he suggests, "because of the fact that money has far more influence over the political process than it should."

Teachers Who Teach about Economic Inequality Differ in Their Goals and Approaches

Teachers' conceptualizations of economic inequality map onto three distinctive approaches for teaching about the topic: descriptive; inquiry-based; and transformative. In the first approach, teachers describe inequality, seeking to provide students with "objective" knowledge including facts concerning how people or groups are arrayed. These teachers might also encourage students to reflect on the stratification of income and resources across different social groups and its impacts. For example, science teacher Tia Leonard discussed:

> What kinds of jobs or what kind of, I don't know, resources would they have access to? And then we would compare it to someone who lives, perhaps, on the other side of the freeway. What kinds of things would they have access to? And then from there we would kind of start engaging, developing that collective understanding about the differences in those economic resources.[8]

Similarly, social studies teacher Dolores Mendez tries to "help students" at her high-poverty school "have more nuanced understanding" of the salaries associated with different jobs and the sort of consumption that these salaries afford. Mendez shared her salary and bills with students, who then compared her financial status to wealthier Americans, and to that of their parents, who earn less and often had to support several extended family members. This lesson aimed to create a basic level of financial awareness to help ensure that her students were not "walking around blind" to the economic realities in their community.

A second approach invites students to consider alternative hypotheses about economic inequality: Is economic stratification a problem? What causes it? How do different social and political arrangements exacerbate or ameliorate such stratification? These teachers articulate a commitment to open inquiry that helps students clarify their thinking. They raise questions and encourage considerations of competing perspectives on issues related to economic inequality, thereby placing students in a community of discursive inquiry. For example, social studies teacher Sam West shares information about "poverty rates, wealth distribution, unemployment," and then encourages students to develop questions. The subject matter for discussions is "whatever they come up with" to explain these inequalities. These discussions turn on both empirical and normative questions—"Does everyone have the [same] opportunities? Does everyone have the same potential?" "[Should] everyone get [paid] the same amount of money?"

Social studies teacher Steve Peters similarly invites his students to explore the causes and possible remedies for economic inequality—but he does so in the context of studying particular historical periods (the Great Depression) or particular concepts in political economy (Keynesian economics). For example, he recounts a U.S. history lesson in which he lectured on a shift from Hoover's "pull yourself up from your bootstraps" approach to Roosevelt's New Deal. After laying out Roosevelt's rationale for social welfare and jobs programs, Peters invited his students to consider the implications of these approaches for today. He asked: "Who thinks we should rely on government? Who thinks we need to do it ourselves?" "And we just talked about it." Like West, Peters believes that his role is to stimulate debate rather than advocate for a particular way of thinking about why inequality exists and how it can be addressed. "For every assignment I have that covers it, we do one side first and then the other, and . . . hopefully, if I do it well, they can't tell which side I'm role-playing and which one is mine." Teachers pursuing an inquiry-based approach pose general questions about the causes of economic inequality rather than associating it with unequal power or problems of social, political, or economic injustice (see also the related *pluralist* and *emancipatory* models described by Johnson, Chapter 3).

A third approach to teaching about economic inequality calls on students to grapple with issues of class, power, and injustice and to consider strategies for effecting social change. All of the teachers who followed this third approach defined economic inequality in relationship to unequal power and unjust social relationships. Sara Garofalo addressed these topics in a unit on Steinbeck's *East of Eden* in her 12th grade English class at a socio-economically diverse school.

Text-based discussions centered on how economic advantages and disadvantages shape the experiences of the novel's characters. Students wrote about: "What defines wealth and how does it privilege the Trasks versus the Hamiltons and how that might have been an influence on the deaths and the hardships." Garofalo then prompted her students to think about how class hierarchy in *East of Eden* relates to experiences in their school. She asked: "What can be done about this and how could you cross this boundary?" Garofalo reported that this was an "uncomfortable" discussion, because talking about class privilege was new to her students and "so they don't know what is safe and what isn't safe." But she pursued the conversation and students wrestled productively with the ways that academic tracking at their school reproduces class privileges.

Nick Watanabee also draws attention to issues of class and power in the ethnic studies classes he teaches in a socio-economically diverse school. He talks with students about which racial or ethnic groups live in different neighborhoods and how these patterns were shaped by historical practices of red-lining whereby the federal government colluded with the banking and insurance industries to create race-based restrictions on home loans and home ownership. In addition to highlighting injustice, Watanabee teaches lessons about how working-class people have changed society through grassroots organizing and labor activism. He wants his students to think about drawing on the example of "people in previous generations ... [who] work[ed] towards creating positive change within society." In contrast to Steve Peters, Watanabee believes it is important for students to understand his particular perspective on issues of class and poverty:

> When I talked about being poor, I talk about myself [when I had] 13 cents in my bank account, and when I had a college degree [and] I was scrubbing toilets, and fighting homeless ladies who would poop on my floor of the coffee shop I worked at. Or about my own grandfather who was a migrant farm worker.

Watanabee's goal is not to inculcate a particular set of beliefs. He wants students to develop a deeper sense of how differently situated people experience class and inequality:

> I try to . . . model as an adult what it means to have these conversations. . . . Here's my own personal experience which shapes the way I see the world. And this is why I think the way that I do. How about you now? What do you think? Tell me your story. Tell me your experience. . . . As long as you're speaking for yourself rather than all people, then we can build up some sort of understanding for each other.

Although Watanabee wants students to be able to dialogue across differences in perspective and opinion, he recognizes and reinforces the potential of teaching and learning about economic inequality to develop in students the inclination and capacity to imagine and help create a more just society.

Tamara L. Sober (Chapter 5) describes a similarly transformative approach to teaching about economic inequality that emphasizes close attention to power, influence, politics, and the possibilities for change. Employing a lesson on the influence of money in politics and society, she wants her students to "recognize that economic policies . . . are made by people, and can be made to disproportionately benefit one group at the expense of another."

A transformative approach to teaching about economic inequality incorporates aspects of the descriptive and inquiry-based approaches but highlights issues of power and fairness or unfairness in an effort to open up possibilities for social, political, and economic transformation. These three approaches are summarized in Table 4.10.

Summary and Implications

This chapter asked the following questions:

- Do public high school teachers address issues of economic inequality in their classrooms and, if so, how and why?
- Do their goals and practices differ by subject matter disciplines?
- Do their goals and practices differ by the socio-economic context of the school?

Our study included a survey of 643 social studies, English, math, and science teachers in 193 California public schools, as well as 15 in-depth teacher interviews. Although this study was exploratory, the results offer some valuable insights and directions for further inquiry. First, for those who see economic inequality as a problem in our society to be addressed, and who believe students should learn about it, there is both good and bad news. The good news is that approximately two-thirds of teachers are talking about economic inequality in their classes to some degree and with some level of consistency. This finding highlights the potential for wide engagement with the issue of inequality in American classrooms.

The bad news is that, to the extent teachers are talking about economic inequality, many seek to convey the facts about social and economic stratification—an important goal considering widespread ignorance about these issues in a broad swath of the American adult population—but do not always tie that knowledge to questions about the causes and consequences of inequality or to competing discourses on its importance or ways to diminish it. Teachers often draw on their own understandings and experiences of economic inequality in framing their teaching in this area. Some teachers explore power relations, issues of fairness and justice, and structural explanations of inequality; others refrain from broader concerns, choosing to focus on descriptive lessons mostly limited to conveying the existence of inequality rather than engaging in deeper analysis of causes, consequences, or possibilities for change. Like Ms. Baudin, whom we wrote about at the beginning of the chapter, many teachers want to take up economic inequality as a topic of study and discussion in their classes. Yet many teachers also worry that discussions about inequality could make variations in students' own socio-economic positions *too visible*.

It is also worth noting that more than 40 percent of teachers in high-poverty schools reported discussing economic inequality weekly, while only 25 percent of teachers in low-poverty schools reported doing so as often. It is likely that some teachers in high-poverty schools do more to draw out students' own experiences with economic inequality than their colleagues in low-poverty schools. Although this is a "thin" finding, we hope to investigate this further in our larger, ongoing bi-national study.

The variety of goals and approaches teachers express for teaching about economic inequality can be grouped in three categories: descriptive, inquiry-based, and transformative (see Table 4.10). Teachers who teach descriptively want students to know the facts about inequality. Those who focus on inquiry want students to know how to talk about economic inequality with people who agree and disagree with them; they hope students will be able to bridge an increasingly polarized political discourse and talk with others "across difference." Finally, some teachers expressed their hopes that students can use knowledge about economic inequality to help improve society. These teachers adopted a transformative approach to teaching and learning about economic inequality.

Initial findings from this California sample of teachers indicate that a significant number do not feel fully comfortable facilitating discussions about economic inequality in their classes. Policymakers and teacher educators might consider what kinds of knowledge and experiences would help teachers in this regard. Broader questions about the comfort level of students and teachers, as well as about what political environments are inhibitory or conducive to teaching and learning about economic inequality, are also worthy of further inquiry.

TABLE 4.10 Teachers' Approaches to and Reasons for Teaching about Economic Inequality

Pedagogical approach	Goals
Descriptive	It is important for students to know the facts.
Inquiry-based	It is important for students to know how to talk about economic inequality with people who agree and disagree with them, to "talk across difference."
Transformative	It is important for students to know about economic inequality and ways they might seek to ameliorate or eliminate inequality and/or its effects.

Conclusion

In 1848, in his capacity as the first Secretary of Education for the State of Massachusetts, Horace Mann noted that education, "beyond all other devices of human origin, is a great equalizer of conditions of men—the balance wheel of the social machinery." (para. 21). Today, Massachusetts has among the highest levels of economic inequality of all states (Noss, 2014). Certainly Massachusetts' income inequality cannot narrowly be explained as the result of educational failure. Many factors (including policies on manufacturing and trade, organized labor, the minimum wage, and taxation) have contributed to growing inequality in Massachusetts and elsewhere, and any substantial response to economic inequality will need to address economic and political conditions outside of schools (Stiglitz, 2015).

Yet public schools today cannot ignore issues of economic inequality. If we take seriously the promise of education to develop an informed citizenry capable of deliberating and responding to the problems of our day, then schools should provide students with an opportunity to study the causes, consequences, and potential remedies to economic inequality. In so doing, schools can play an important—though by no means exclusive—role in enhancing democracy and equalizing our shared social, political, and economic lives.

Notes

1 The teachers quoted in this chapter participated in a California-wide study that included surveys and interviews of high school teachers in social studies, English, math and science during the 2013–14 school year. The study is described in some detail in the "Methods" section of this chapter. All names are pseudonyms.
2 For the purpose of this chapter, "low-income" is defined by eligibility for the Free and Reduced Price Lunch Program. "Affluent" refers to families whose annual income is more than twice the national median household income.
3 A far more developed set of findings will emerge in the near future.
4 Teachers were asked a set of questions about their practices in a "typical class" to ground their responses in a particular class period.
5 See the methodological appendix at http://idea.gseis.ucla.edu/projects/its-about-time/Its%20About%20Time.pdf.
6 We exclude teachers from other subject areas and those reporting on small special education classes.
7 We use the term STEM teachers as shorthand for high school science and math instructors.
8 Although Leonard does teach about economic inequality, she feels some of the same accountability stress as science teacher Ana Lee. Leonard related: "As a pure science teacher, it's very difficult to make that a headlining, main part of the topic. . . . I will find ways to, but I feel like the pressure that I'm veering from the norm. I feel the pressure that I'm off, you know, my standards."

References

Bartels, L. (2008). *Unequal democracy: The political economy of the new gilded age*. New York: Russell Sage.

Council for Economic Education. (2012). *Survey of the states: Economics and personal finance education in our nation's schools.* Retrieved from http://www.councilforeconed.org/wp/wp-content/uploads/2014/02/2014-Survey-of-the-States.pdf.

Cruces, G., Perez-Truglia, R., and Tetaz, M. (2013). Biased perceptions of income distribution and preferences for redistribution: Evidence from a survey experiment. *Journal of Public Economics, 98,* 100–112.

Duncan, G. J., and Murnane, R. J. (Eds.). (2011). *Whither opportunity? Rising inequality, schools, and children's life chances.* New York: Russell Sage Foundation and Spencer Foundation.

Frank, R. (2007). *Falling behind: How rising inequality harms the middle class.* Los Angeles: University of California Press.

Glyn, A. (2007). *Capitalism unleashed: Finance globalization and welfare.* Oxford: Oxford University Press.

Gutmann, A. (1995). Civic education and social diversity. *Ethics, 105,* 557–579.

Hadler, M. (2005). Why do people accept different income ratios? A multi-level comparison of thirty countries. *Acta Sociologica, 48*(2), 131–154.

Jencks, C. (2002). Does inequality matter? *Daedulus, 131*(1), 49–65.

Kiatpongsan, S., and Norton, M. I. (2014). How much (more) should CEOs make? A universal desire for more equal pay. *Perspectives on Psychological Science, 9*(6), 587–593.

Koçer, R., and Werfhorst, H. van de. (2012). Does education affect opinions on economic inequality? A joint mean and dispersion analysis. *Acta Sociologica, 55*(3), 251–272.

Mann, H. (1848). Twelfth annual report of Horace Mann as Secretary of Massachusetts State Board of Education. Retrieved from http://usa.usembassy.de/etexts/democrac/16.htm.

McCall, L., and Kenworthy, L. (2009). Americans' social policy preferences in the era of rising inequality. *Perspectives on Politics, 7*(3), 459–484.

McCall, L., and Percheski, C. (2010). Income inequality: New trends and research directions. *Annual Review of Sociology, 36,* 329–347.

Morin, R. (2012). Rising share of Americans see conflict between rich and poor. *Pew Research Center.* Retrieved from http://www.pewsocialtrends.org/2012/01/11/rising-share-of-americans-see-conflict-between-rich-and-poor.

Norton, M. I. (2014). Unequality: Who gets what and why it matters. *Policy Insights from the Behavioral and Brain Sciences, 1*(1), 151–155.

Norton, M., and Ariely, D. (2011). Building a better America—one wealth quintile at a time. *Perspectives on Psychological Science, 6*(1), 9–12.

Noss, A. (2014). Household income: 2013. *American Community Survey Briefs* (United States Census Bureau, U.S. Department of Commerce), *13*(2), 1–6.

Osberg, L., and Smeeding, T. (2006). "Fair" inequality? Attitudes toward pay differentials: The United States in comparative perspective. *American Sociological Review, 71*(3), 450–473.

Rogers, J., and Westheimer, J. (2015). Learning inequality? A conceptual framework for examining how inequality is addressed in curricular frameworks. Presented at the meeting of the American Educational Research Association, Chicago, IL.

Saez, E. (2013). *Striking it richer: The evolution of top incomes in the United States (updated with 2012 preliminary estimates).* Retrieved from http://eml.berkeley.edu/~saez/saez-UStopincomes-2012.pdf.

Savani, K., and Rattan, A. (2012). A choice mind-set increases the acceptance and maintenance of wealth inequality. *Psychological Science, 23*(7), 796–804.

Schlozman, K., Verba, S., and Brady, H. (2012). *The unheavenly chorus: Unequal political voice and the broken promise of American democracy.* Princeton, NJ: Princeton University Press.

Schug, M., Dieterle, D., and Clark, R. (2009). Are high school economics teachers the same as other social studies teachers? The results of a national survey. *Social Education*, *73*(2), 71–75.

Smeeding, T. (2005). Public policy, economic inequality, and poverty: The United States in comparative perspective. *Social Science Quarterly*, *86*(s1), 954–983.

Stiglitz, J. (2012). *The price of inequality: How today's divided society endangers our future*. New York: W. W. Norton.

Stiglitz, J. E. (2015). *The great divide: Unequal societies and what we can do about them*. New York: W. W. Norton.

Wilkinson, R., and Pickett, K. (2009). *The spirit level: Why greater equality makes societies stronger*. New York: Bloomsbury Press.

Williams, L. (2004). The issue of our time: Economic inequality and political power in America. *Perspectives on Politics*, *2*(4), 683–689.

Zilinsky, J. (2013). Does information about income inequality shape demand for redistribution? Evidence from an on-line experiment. University of Chicago Booth School of Business. Retrieved from http://www.hanyang.ac.kr/code_html/H3HW/esSummer 2013/images/paper102.pdf.

5

TEACHING ABOUT ECONOMICS AND MONEYED INTERESTS IN TWENTY-FIRST-CENTURY DEMOCRACY

Tamara L. Sober

As a high school social studies teacher, I often found that students entering my 11th and 12th grade Government and Economics courses were unable to differentiate between democracy and capitalism. They were not naïve when it came to understanding the power of money in politics. What they lacked was: (1) exposure to *how* moneyed interests operate behind the scenes of a democracy; (2) content knowledge that demystifies economic policies; (3) real-world examples of how the power of organized people has rivaled and can continue to rival organized money; and (4) a forum to explore their own beliefs about these topics. The textbooks and curricula I was provided were silent on these topics. My goal was for students to recognize that economic policies—contrary to the neoclassical economic model's promotion of the *invisible hand of the market*—are made by people, and can be made to disproportionately benefit one group at the expense of another. These acts can lead to economic inequality that can threaten our social mobility, efforts toward equality, and ultimately our democracy.

This chapter applies an educator's approach situated within a critique of the official economics curriculum. I draw upon lesson plans and experiences integrating *Teaching Economics as if People Mattered* (Sober Giecek, 2007) into a civics course in a public high school and provide practical suggestions for teaching students to consider the human implications of various economic policies. Such suggestions necessarily create the dialogue essential to our future as a self-governing, democratic society. I use examples from lessons that examine the American Dream, institutional asset builders and blockers, and the difference between income and wealth. By providing structure, experiences, and material with which students can engage and create meaning, the lessons provide a foundation for students to understand how monetary influence is a human construction that can be reconstructed by humans.

Teaching about Economics and Moneyed Interests in Twenty-First-Century Democracy

I started the first day of a new economics unit in my 11th and 12th grade U.S. Government and Economics course by asking students to close their eyes and think about the families they've met in their life. Then I asked them to identify which of these families seemed to have the least amount of money coming in, and who seemed to have the most. I gave students a minute and instructed them to open their eyes and to discuss, in pairs, why they guessed that someone had a very low or high income. I asked them to consider what information they drew upon to make their judgment. What did they know about the way the family lived that led them to identify them as high- or low-income? I made it clear that students should not provide identifying information about any of the families. When I asked the pairs to share, and conducted a full class discussion, their answers usually focused on material items such as the types of cars, homes, or clothes the family sported. I explained that the focus of the lesson would be to examine what various occupations in the United States pay and possible explanations for those variations.

I wrote the following on the board: "What is income?" and recorded students' responses: salaries, child support, savings account interest, social security checks, rent collected from owning real estate, and profit made when something sells for more than one paid for it. I explained we were going to talk about what leads to a successful income in the U.S., and I referenced the assigned homework in which students articulated their dreams and the jobs they dreamed of doing after high school or college. Students were told not to worry about being realistic but to dream and then write about their ideal career. After several students shared, I posed these questions: "What is the American Dream?" "Some people say that anyone, including you, can one day become President or can be as rich as Bill Gates, if you work smart and hard enough. What do you think?"

Students began a discussion about the idea of the American Dream, describing it as equal opportunity for all. As the discussion evolved I encouraged them to question their assumptions, such as whether it's true that everyone in America has an equal chance to get ahead through hard work and academic achievement. "Is the American Dream true today? Do we have equal opportunity in the U.S.? Is hard work always rewarded with monetary gain? How is hard work defined?" I noted that many physically taxing jobs are not well paid. This was the starting point for introducing the idea of *meritocracy*, loosely defined as a system that rewards people for a combination of their hard work, innate abilities, the right attitude, and high moral character (McNamee, 2009).

The ideology of the American Dream presents America as a land of limitless opportunity, where individuals can go as far as their own merit takes them. Most Americans have believed, and continue to believe, that the system should and does work this way (Huber and Form, 1973; Kluegel and Smith, 1986; Ladd,

1994; McNamee, 2009). I asked my students to consider whether or not meritocracy currently exists in America. I began my economics unit with this approach because the *official curriculum* fell short of what I believed students needed to make informed economic decisions.

Limitations of the Official Economics Curriculum

A Technical, Neoclassical, and Positivist Approach

Whether stand-alone or infused in the social studies curriculum, today's official curriculum—embodied in the *Voluntary National Content Standards in Economics*, hereinafter the *Standards* (Siegfried et al., 2010), and the economics curricula, both readily promoted and available to teachers—provides a simplistic, technical, and neoclassical approach to economics (Maier and Nelson, 2007). Yet there has been little discussion or debate from prominent scholars and associations in the economic academic community about K–12 economic education's narrowed approach (Maier and Nelson, 2007).[1] The authors of the *Standards* justified their singular approach as: an effort to preclude confusing and frustrating teachers with minority viewpoints for which they claim students and teachers possess an insufficient foundation for understanding; a decision to use the predominant paradigm; and a tradeoff between parsimony and accuracy (Siegfried et al., 2010).

Chang (2014) summarized that Adam Smith's metaphor of the *invisible hand of the market* plays out in neoclassical economics in the belief that people are rational actors, driven by self-interest, and competitive markets help ensure that their actions collectively produce good outcomes for society when the market is left alone. This economic model is based on the belief that the free market replaces the functions of government and labor on behalf of citizens. In reality the market only looks free because its underlying restrictions are so readily accepted that we fail to see them. For example, child labor laws are so conventional that no one sees them as a government intervention or an infringement on the market (Chang, 2010).

Chang (2014) asserted that there are numerous schools of economic thought with distinctive ways of conceptualizing and explaining the economy, and that none of these can claim a hold on universal truth. No theory, including those of the natural sciences, can address all aspects and complexities of the real world. Chang (2014) and Nelson (2011) argued that different economic theories possess particular strengths and weaknesses, depending upon what they highlight and ignore and how they conceptualize and analyze relationships. Nelson (2011) advocated a pluralist and inclusive approach to economic education, drawing on a variety of perspectives to help students apply critical thinking to real-world problems. Although the academic field of economics is open to ontological and epistemological questioning (Davis, 2006) it would appear that K–12 economics is not. My review of the K–12 economics education literature and standards found pluralist or inclusive approaches to be rare, if not absent.

A Focus on Financial Literacy

Much of what is taught in K–12 economic education as a whole can be traced to the influence of the Council for Economic Education (CEE). The CEE was founded over 65 years ago by business and education leaders. Its website states its current goal of creating an "informed citizenry capable of making better decisions as savers, investors, borrowers, voters, and participants in the global economy" (Council for Economic Education, 2015). The Council's policy and advocacy portion of its website focuses on the need for additional financial literacy testing, while touting growth in personal finance course graduation requirements, with the current total of 17 states (Council for Economic Education, 2014).

The 2008 recession in the United States is often used as a rationale, both domestically and internationally, to incorporate more personal finance into the school curriculum, and this rationale is almost entirely cast in terms of the personal responsibility of the consumer (Davies, 2015). Davies (2015) wrote: "definitions of financial literacy make no reference to citizens' understanding of the roles of banks or governments in the conduct of financial systems" (p. 301). In 2013 the CEE introduced the *National Standards for Financial Literacy* (*NSFL*), supported by the corporate finance sector (Buckles et al., 2013). The *NSFL* focus on individual choices—while omitting macroeconomic and structural solutions—and are poised to shape the economics and personal finance content of the Common Core Standards Initiative (Maier et al., 2014). Maier et al. offered a detailed critique of the underlying assumptions in the standards, with recommendations for teaching about the wider context within which financial decisions are made, including a discussion of the role of government, labor, non-profits, income distribution, and corporate power. Scholars such as Grimes (2012) and Miller and VanFossen (2008) warn of the predominance of personal financial education, arguing that "financial lessons crowd out more traditional and broader-based economics lessons" (Grimes, 2012, p. 261), and that, "in spite of the historical distinction between personal finance (or consumer) education and economic education, it appears possible (even likely) that financial literacy will become an increasingly important part of economic literacy and thus economic education" (Miller and VanFossen, 2008, p. 300).

The *NSFL* approach aligns with the neoclassical economic belief that the market replaces the functions of government and labor on behalf of citizens. Davies (2006, 2015) and Arthur (2012) cautioned, however, that if economics education is reduced to teaching students how to be good consumers we will fail to educate citizens about the democratic choices that need to be made about the economy, and specifically about the role of citizen oversight of financial regulatory structures. The shift towards microeconomics—specifically personal finance—is problematic in light of the long-standing calls by leading economic educators for more research into students' macroeconomic reasoning (Miller and VanFossen, 2008; Schug and Walstad, 1991).

A Normative Economics Approach

A key component of teaching for democracy in an age of increasing economic disparity is to provide a distinction between political and economic systems and to have students develop critical analysis skills for understanding how the two interact (Domhoff, 2006). I reasoned that exclusively teaching *positive economics*—the branch of economics that focuses on cause and effect behavior and uses empirical evidence to test economic theories (Samuelson and Nordhaus, 2010)—fails to equip students for twenty-first-century democracy. It may even foster apathy and cynicism, especially in light of my students' expressed awareness of the monetary influence on our political system. I supplemented the curriculum with *normative economics*—economics that expresses values or judgments about economic fairness or what the outcome of economic policies should be (Samuelson and Nordhaus, 2010). My purpose was to provide a foundation for students to understand how monetary influence has been humanly constructed and therefore can be humanly reconstructed. This was relatively new territory for most of my students, many of whom viewed democracy and capitalism as one and the same.

Looking beyond economics curricula toward literature on citizenship education for insights into the role of economic thinking in the civics classroom, Davies (2006) noted: "the place of economic understanding in educating citizens is neither widely recognized nor substantially articulated in the literature" (p. 15). He summarized evidence that a primarily individual responsibility approach to economic literacy has resulted in students' lack of understanding of the economic relationships between benefits and opportunity costs between individuals and society (Davies, 2006). He also argued that "teaching students how to evaluate alternative modes of economic engagement (through the market, government, social organizations, etc.) is the most appropriate basis for the economic elements in citizenship education" (p. 17). I used this alternative mode of economic engagement with my students. My goal was to foster realistic hope by providing students with examples of how the democratic political process has been used to create economic policies that perpetuate moneyed interests at democracy's expense, and to limit moneyed interests and protect democracy.

As I share excerpts and summaries in this chapter of what transpired in my high school Government and Economics classroom over several years I make no formal research claims about generalizability, but scholars have established that results from case study research helps to shed light on situations that expand the discourse of the phenomena in question (Flyvbjerg, 2001, 2006; Yin, 2014). A reasonable argument can be made that conveying my experiences of implementing normative economics in my classroom falls within what Flyvbjerg (2006) wrote about the importance of context-dependent knowledge: "in the study of human affairs, there appears to exist only context-dependent knowledge" (p. 221). In this vein, I will use the following examples to illuminate how economics education could be incorporated into the civics classroom.

I taught in a large, affluent suburban county. Approximately 85 percent of each graduating class enrolled in college, and the majority of the students would be considered "privileged" (Swalwell, 2013). There were more than 30 students in each of my five classes, and each year we began this unit in the late spring when class norms, relationships, and a safe classroom environment were well established. Although a fifth of the state course standards addressed economic concepts, no textbooks or official economics materials were provided. The assigned textbook on American government gave little attention to the role of economic thinking in the context of citizenship education, and teachers were left to find their own resources to address the economic standards. My search for supplementary materials revealed a dearth of resources that went beyond teaching the theory of competitive markets, with materials such as the popular *Stock Market Game* (Sifma Foundation, 2015) or the entrepreneurship-focused Junior Achievement (n.d.).

Teaching Economics as if People Mattered

Seeing the need for materials that helped students take a critical and constructive view of economic policies within a democratic system spurred my collaboration with United for a Fair Economy[2] on *Teaching Economics as if People Mattered* (Sober Giecek, 2007). The curriculum was designed to supplement traditional economics curricula and could easily be integrated into a civics course. The lessons provide structure, experiences, and material with which students can engage and create meaning about the human influences on economic policy-making in a democratic society. The lessons employ critical pedagogy (McLaren, 2015) and constructivist pedagogy (Merriam et al., 2012) using techniques such as inquiry- or problem-based learning (Loyens and Rikers, 2011), peer interactions (Wentzel and Watkins, 2011), and discussion (Hess, 2009; Hess and Posselt, 2002; Murphy et al., 2011). Students: evaluate their prior knowledge, experiences, and values; explore economic data, trends, and issues; and dialogue about problems to construct democratic economic policy solutions.

In my experience students are not naïve when it comes to understanding the power of money in politics. What they often lack is: (1) exposure to *how* moneyed interests operate behind the scenes of a democracy; (2) content knowledge that demystifies economic policies; (3) real-world examples of how the power of organized people has rivaled, and can continue to rival, organized money; and (4) a forum to explore their own beliefs about these topics. From this standpoint this curriculum provides concrete examples of the outcomes of economic policies, to reveal—contrary to the *invisible hand* dogma discussed above—that economic policies are made by people and can be made to disproportionately benefit one group at the expense of another.

The American Dream versus the American Reality

Teaching for democracy in the twenty-first century means exposing students to a realistic perspective of what it takes to bring about change. Successful community organizers have long recognized the need to begin any change effort by recognizing the world as it is as opposed to the world as it should be (Gecan, 2004). Grounding a civics class economics unit in a world-as-it-is perspective means asking students to examine to what extent meritocracy exists in America.

In a society where it is considered impolite to discuss income, and where few economic textbooks address the distribution of income and wealth (Maier and Nelson, 2007), students have little exposure to what various occupations pay. This lesson provides average annual salaries for a sample of occupations and a frame of reference for students to view these salaries in relation to the cost of living and the poverty line. After introducing the meritocracy concept, I write "The American Dream vs. the American Reality" on the board and solicit students' understandings of the differences between these concepts, and their opinions about the idea that hard work and a good education lead to a higher income. I ask whether differences in income are always due to education and effort, and inquire about other factors that may affect people's income. Students usually offer parents' income level, the city where people live, and the availability of well-paying jobs. If they don't mention race, gender, and the quality of schools I add them to the conversation. I fill in the following words on the board: "The American Dream: Work hard and get ahead"; "The American Reality: Many people who work hard are still poor and often there are unfair reasons for pay differences."

We move into an activity where student volunteers create a human bar graph depicting the variation between incomes and the cost of living and poverty lines. Students begin by standing on the cost of living line,[3] explained as the minimal amount it takes to buy housing, child care, food, transportation, health care, and other necessities, and pay taxes for a family of three. Each of the seven students is given an 8½ × 11-inch card to display, with the occupation title visible, and asked to line up shoulder to shoulder. One by one each student flips his or her card to reveal the average income level for that occupation. For each $5,000 above or below the cost of living line the student moves one step forward or back, moving further from or closer to the poverty line, a helpful instructional strategy, especially for visual and kinesthetic learners.[4]

As the salaries are revealed we discuss the required background for different jobs and how often during their daily lives students interact with people making these various levels of income. My students were often surprised that some traditional blue-collar careers, such as plumbing, paid more than traditional white-collar careers. We discuss what types of workers likely earn the minimum wage, such as fast-food workers, agricultural workers, and teachers' and hospital aides. Students seem surprised to realize how close to the poverty line most people they come into daily contact with are, or how many occupations barely pay enough for people to make ends meet. Some students find it difficult to understand how someone can work full time and still remain below the poverty line. This activity helps to expose the limits of the individual responsibility framework for economic literacy, and asks students to consider institutional and structural influences, such as the variation in school quality, employee rights, union activity, discrimination, and the existence or absence of employee protection policies (Maier et al., 2014). The class chooses one of these institutional influences for further discussion. For example, a discussion of school quality reveals how inequities such as the opportunity gap (Darling-Hammond, 2010; Ladson-Billings, 2006, 2013) impact long-term economic mobility and stability. I prompt students to consider the role of citizen action in creating or supporting policies that encourage economic opportunity. This lesson usually culminates in discussions about fairness. Seeing these salary figures and connecting them to people in students' lives helps students put human faces on what might otherwise be a sterile and abstract conversation about meritocracy. As a result, students are faced with the confounding notion that the ideological myth of meritocracy thwarts democratic efforts to create economic policies to lift more people out of poverty. This sets the tone for future lessons where students learn about wealth and explore institutional asset builders and blockers.

Visualizing the Power of Concentrated Wealth

This lesson begins by distinguishing wealth from income, clarifying that wealth is what you own minus what you owe, providing examples of wealth from different income groups, and illustrating changes in wealth since 1976. Students then pair off and brainstorm examples of the types of wealth different income groups might possess, such as: cash, television sets, and used cars for lower-income earners; checking accounts and equity in a house for middle-income earners; luxury cars, a vacation home, and stocks for upper-income earners; and several houses, real estate, large stock holdings, and businesses for the top 1 percent of income earners. I take the time to discuss "negative wealth" (owing more than is owned), known as debt, and the percentage of the population in debt. I also bring to students' attention the growing number of college graduates exiting college with huge debt, and ask them to consider which of the discussed assets gain or lose value over time.

To provide students with a visualization of U.S. wealth distribution and the change in that distribution over time, I line up ten armless chairs across the front of the room facing the students and ask for ten volunteers. I identify one person who represents the wealthiest 10 percent of the U.S. population and give that student a card with that title to hold. While the volunteers stand shoulder to shoulder, one behind each of the chairs, I explain that each chair represents 10 percent of all the private wealth in the U.S. and that each volunteer represents 10 percent of the population, with the student holding the sign representing the wealthiest 10 percent of the population (Sober Giecek, 2007). I explain that this is what wealth would look like if it were evenly distributed and encourage students to guess the net worth of every household if wealth were evenly distributed, which in 2012 was $343,000 (Saez and Zucman, 2014).

Students are then asked to guess what percentage of the total wealth they think the wealthiest 10 percent of the population owned in 2012. I ask the students to move to sit on the chairs according to the real distribution of wealth. In 2012 the top 10 percent owned approximately 77 percent of the nation's wealth (Saez and Zucman, 2014), and therefore the student bearing the top 10 percent title lies across seven and a half of the chairs, while the other nine students squeeze onto the remaining two and a half chairs. I purposely don't allow students to stand behind the chairs, because the discomfort provides an opportunity to discuss how anger over economic injustice manifests itself in scapegoating among the bottom 90 percent. I ask the person farthest from the "top 10 percent" if she can even see the person at the top. Students often respond that the person they are bothered by the most is the one pushing them off the chair and onto the floor. This provides an opportunity to discuss possible real-life scapegoats, such as undocumented immigrants, beneficiaries of affirmative action policies, or welfare recipients. I point out that wealth is even more concentrated when we examine ownership by the top 1 percent. As of 2014, the top 1 percent owned almost 40 percent of all household wealth (Saez and Zucman, 2014), up from 22 percent in 1976 (Sober Giecek, 2007).

Additions to this lesson include looking at wealth through race and gender lenses. Household median net worth by race reveals African-American households with less than $5,000, Latino households with approximately $7,500, Asian households with $69,000, and Whites with a little over $110,000. I ask students for possible explanations of the racial wealth gap, pointing towards the next lesson that tackles how wealth is built. To give an additional layer of complexity, it is useful to add gender to question why—as Engebretson and Hollett point out in Chapter 7—the confluence of race and gender tends to exacerbate the economic disparities that exist in the United States.

I provide students with graphs mirroring the wealth distributions they physically depicted. Of equal importance to the memorable visual is time for students to discuss and make meaning about the potential threats from the power of concentrated wealth, which have been well documented by Piketty (2014), Stiglitz (2015), and others. I ask students to brainstorm the unfair power that people with huge amounts of wealth may have over others. Further, I encourage them to provide specific examples such as individual campaign contributions that buy access to politicians, resulting in tax breaks for wealthy individuals, and corporate welfare for specific industries.[5]

Another example of the power of concentrated wealth is the ability of owners of large companies to shut down their businesses, lay off hundreds of employees, and move their companies to developing countries as retribution for tax breaks denied to them. Huge amounts of concentrated wealth create the power to buy up competitors' companies and shut them down to gather more customers, creating monopolies and driving up prices for consumers. It is also important to include advantages that wealth affords some and denies others that may seem less significant on the surface but are nevertheless affordances that may contribute to growing inequality. These advantages include—among others—the time to visit and lobby legislators, hiring lobbyists on one's own behalf, and attending public hearings during the day while others are at their jobs. Painting a clear picture of how laws have been and can be made to benefit the wealthy helps students understand the potential for extreme wealth to interfere with the democratic process. In contrast, for the average family their finances provide an economic safety net rather than a source of social power and political advantage.

Understanding the Wealth Building Train

In a follow-up lesson I ask students to break into small groups to discuss and record their answers to the following questions: Considering as much as you know about your family's history, going back two to three generations, what were significant events or milestones in terms of homeownership or other ways of building assets? For example, do your parents or grandparents own a home or a business? Did they get any assistance from family members or the government to buy their car or home?

Asking students to consider key barriers to wealth accumulation, such as how job loss due to corporate downsizing may place a family in financial hardship, provides specific examples that demonstrate the fragility of our meritocracy. To get students started on this activity I provide examples from my own family history, such as how my parents purchased a home with a down payment on loan from family members. We discuss the biggest factor in wealth accumulation—the family of origin's wealth—and how wealth accumulation is generational. The timing of when a person's family first boarded the wealth building train greatly influences subsequent generations in terms of their opportunity to board and remain on the train (Conley, 1999). This lesson should only be conducted after relationships and trust have been built and classroom norms about discussing sensitive topics have been well established.

Examining individual asset builders and blockers provides a segue into a discussion of how institutional barriers such as Jim Crow laws, or more proximal factors such as the practice of *redlining* (Hodgson, 2009; Reich, Stemhagen, and

Siegel-Hawley, 2014; Sugrue, 2014), placed significant barriers in the way of people of color, which has long-lasting consequences in contemporary America made manifest in the racial wealth gap. It also provides a platform to review how organized people, for instance in the civil rights movement, came together to combat these barriers and rival organized money.

Experience taught me that introducing too much new content about the realities of economic inequality without balancing that information with successful historical accounts of how it has been addressed in the past created a sense of hopelessness. I began to include more historical and present-day examples of people coming together to successfully address injustices. A favorite, concise resource that captures the behind-the-scenes work that goes into a successful organizing action is Kohl's (1994) "The Politics of Children's Literature: What's Wrong with the Rosa Parks Myth." Kohl provided the necessary details to move students beyond a simplistic interpretation of the familiar story. Parks was obviously a brave and courageous woman, but she and her fellow activists were also strategic and had been planning and training for the bus boycott for some time. I incorporated present-day stories of the living wage movement and provided specific details about students organizing and advocating for local living wage ordinances on college campuses (15 Now, n.d.; Living Wage at UVA, n.d.).

Rationale for a Normative Approach to Economics

Timeliness

The institutional forces that have defined what is considered legitimate economic knowledge have coincided with several important historical developments: the fall of Communism, the rise of globalization, the colossal growth of the financial industry, the decline of organized labor, and growing income and wealth inequality (Piketty, 2014). Tracing the narrowing of the debate reveals the power of the dominant class to protect their interests by creating, funding, advocating, and researching economics curricula that secure the consent of those least likely to benefit from such a system—which just so happens to be the majority of Americans. Although not referring specifically to economics, McLaren (2015) pointed to the dangers of curricula where the "basis of social authority and the unequal relations of power and privilege remain hidden" and where curricula function to supply the "terms of reference . . . against which all individuals are expected to live their lives" (pp. 140–141). It is our role as social studies teachers to help students uncover these hidden power relations and to provide students with a balanced approach for addressing societal issues (National Council for the Social Studies, 2008). A normative approach helps students to demystify economics, which has increasingly—yet misleadingly—positioned itself as a precise science that uses mathematics to offer predictive answers to society's challenges (Chang, 2014).

Social Sciences Excel in Analysis and Values Discussions

Economics falls under the aegis of the social sciences (Solow, 1985). Although he does not specifically address economics, Flyvbjerg (2001) argued that the social sciences differ from the natural sciences in that they excel not in providing accurate prognostic and prescriptive models for policy development, but rather in the analysis and discussion of outcomes that reflect our values and interests. Flyvbjerg (2001) contended that discussions of values and interests are the prerequisite for society's enlightened political, economic, and cultural development and herein lies the strength of the social sciences. He presented a modern interpretation of the Aristotelian concept of *phronesis*, defined as a "'true state, reasoned, and capable of action with regard to things that are good or bad for man'" (as cited in Flyvbjerg, 2001, p. 2). Moreover, "phronesis moves beyond analytical, scientific knowledge (episteme) and technical knowledge or know-how (techne) and involves judgments and decisions" (Flyvbjerg, 2001, p. 2). Flyvbjerg reasoned that attempts to reduce social science and its related theories, and by extension economics and economic theory, to either episteme or techne are misguided.

Building on this interpretation of the social sciences, I assert that K–12 economics curricula's reliance on an epistemological and technological approach to the discipline (Davis, 2006) ignores phronetic questions. Social science discussions of values and interests inherently involve ideology, and yet K–12 economics education—as shaped by the *Standards* (Siegfried et al., 2010) and the *NSFL* (Buckles et al., 2013)—ignores the selective process of the adoption of an economic ideology, and elevates positive economics to the status of natural law, beyond human control.

Values Discussions Are Critical When Economic Disparity Threatens Democracy and More

Values discussions are particularly important in a time when economic disparity is poised to threaten democracy. Piketty (2014) writes:

> When the rate of return on capital exceeds the rate of growth of output and income, as it did in the nineteenth century and seems quite likely to do again in the twenty-first, capitalism automatically generates arbitrary and unsustainable inequalities that radically undermine the meritocratic values on which democratic societies are based.
>
> *(p. 1)*

Wilkinson and Pickett (2009) documented the numerous and varied costs of economic inequality that manifest themselves in dysfunctional community and social relations, mental and physical health problems, educational inequities, violence, crime, and more. As Journell et al. discuss in Chapter 6, the U.S.

Supreme Court's *Citizens United v. Federal Election Commission* (2010) decision, effectively equating money to free speech, as well as related cases and legislation, is a testament to how these policies are generated by political institutions. These human-designed artifices necessitate that students have access to the discussions and perspectives that a normative approach to teaching economics provides.

Democracy depends upon an educated citizenry capable of making informed choices. If economics is taught as a discipline that exists outside the realm of human influence, then citizens' ability to make informed choices about whether current economic patterns serve valuable ends is limited, even co-opted by those who maintain privileged access to this knowledge. Ultimately the privileging of this knowledge places citizens at a disadvantage. Their inability to recognize their role or ability to shape economic policies in determining the kind of society in which they prefer to live handicaps our nation and promulgates a system that continues to disadvantage the majority of Americans. If we are to begin to address economic disparity, we need to begin providing our students with the tools and understandings they need to engage with this problem at both its practical and its ideological roots.

Notes

1 A review of the literature reveals that the last rich and nuanced discussion of what constitutes economic literacy by economists and economic educators from across the ideological and political spectrum was in an issue of the *Journal of Economic Education* (Goldberg, 1987). These critiques from the field's greatest minds were largely ignored (Saunders and Gilliard, 1995); the subsequently developed *Voluntary National Content Standards in Economics* promotes a model of smoothly functioning, perfectly competitive markets that contradicts the views of many professional economists (Maier and Nelson, 2007).
2 See *Teaching Economics as if People Mattered* for downloadable lessons: https://scottfen wickteachingeconomics.wikispaces.com/file/view/TEAIPM_2007.pdf.
3 The cost of living line is based on the self-sufficiency standard, defined as the amount of net income necessary to meet basic needs without public subsidies (e.g., public housing, food stamps, Medicaid, or child care) and without private/informal assistance (e.g., free babysitting by a relative or friend, food provided by churches or local food banks, or shared housing). To find the most recent self-sufficiency standards for your state go to: www.selfsufficiencystandard.org.
4 The poverty thresholds are the original version of the federal poverty measure. They are updated each year by the Census Bureau and are used mainly for statistical purposes such as preparing estimates of the number of Americans in poverty each year (U.S. Department of Health and Human Services, 2015).
5 A number of examples of corporate welfare can be found on www.goodjobsfirst.org.

References

15 Now. (n.d.). Retrieved November 24, 2015 from https://15now.org/.
Arthur, C. (2012). Consumers or critical citizens? Financial literacy education and freedom. *Critical Education*, 3(6), 1–24.

Buckles, S., Hill, A., Meszaros, B., Staten, M., Suiter, M., and Walstad, W. (2013). *National standards for financial literacy*. Retrieved from http://www.councilforeconed. org/wp/wp-content/uploads/2013/02/national-standards-for-financial literacy. pdf.

Chang, H. J. (2010). *23 things they don't tell you about capitalism*. New York: Bloomsbury Press.

Chang, H. J. (2014). *Economics: The user's guide*. New York: Bloomsbury Press.

Citizens United v. Federal Election Commission, 130 S.Ct. 876 (2010).

Conley, D. (1999). *Being Black, living in the red: Race, wealth, and social policy in America*. Berkeley: University of California Press.

Council for Economic Education (CEE). (2014). *Survey of the states: Economics and personal financial education in our nation's schools, 2014*. New York: CEE. Retrieved from http://www.councilforeconed.org/policy-and-advocacy/survey-of-the-states/.

Council for Economic Education (CEE). (2015). *About CEE*. Retrieved from http:// www.councilforeconed.org/about/.

Darling-Hammond, L. (2010). *The flat world and education: How America's commitment to equity will determine our future*. New York: Teachers College Press.

Davies, P. (2006). Educating citizens for changing economies. *Journal of Curriculum Studies, 38*(1), 15–30.

Davies, P. (2015). Towards a framework for financial literacy in the context of democracy. *Journal of Curriculum Studies, 47*(2), 300–316.

Davis, J. B. (2006). Heterodox economics, the fragmentation of the mainstream, and embedded individual analysis. In J. T. Harvey and R. F. Garnett (Eds.), *Future directions in heterodox economics* (pp. 57–72). Ann Arbor: University of Michigan Press.

Domhoff, G. W. (2006). *Who rules America? Power and politics, and social change*. New York: McGraw-Hill Humanities, Social Sciences and World Languages.

Flyvbjerg, B. (2001). *Making social science matter, why social inquiry fails and how it might succeed again*. Cambridge: Cambridge University Press.

Flyvbjerg, B. (2006). Five misunderstandings about case-study research. *Qualitative Inquiry, 12*(2), 219–245.

Gecan, M. (2004). *Going public: An organizer's guide to citizen action*. New York: Anchor Books.

Goldberg, K. (Ed.). (1987). *Journal of Economic Education, 18*(2), 97–254.

Grimes, P. W. (2012). Economic education in American elementary and secondary schools. In G. Hoyt and K. McGoldrick (Eds.), *International handbook on teaching and learning economics* (pp. 259–272). Cheltenham, UK: Edward Elgar.

Hess, D. E. (2009). *Controversy in the classroom: The democratic power of discussion*. New York: Routledge.

Hess, D., and Posselt, J. (2002). How high school students experience and learn from the discussion of controversial public issues. *Journal of Curriculum and Supervision, 17*(4), 283–314.

Hodgson, G. (2009). *More equal than others: America from Nixon to the new century*. Princeton, NJ: Princeton University Press.

Huber, J., and Form, W. H. (1973). *Income and ideology: An analysis of the American political formula*. New York: Free Press.

Junior Achievement. (n.d.). Educators. Retrieved from http:///www.juniorachievement. org.

Kluegel, J. R., and Smith, E. R. (1986). *Beliefs about inequality: Americans' views of what is and what ought to be*. Piscataway, NJ: Transaction.

Kohl, H. (1994). The politics of children's literature: What's wrong with the Rosa Parks myth. In W. Au, B. Bigelow, and S. Karp (Eds.), *Rethinking our classrooms* (vol. 1, pp. 137–140). Milwaukee WI: Rethinking Schools. Retrieved from http://www.wou.edu/~ulvelad/courses/ED632Spring11/Assets/RosaParks.pdf.

Ladd, E. C. (1994). *The American ideology: An exploration of the origins, meaning, and role of American political ideas* (Report No. 1). Ithaca, NY: Roper Center for Public Opinion Research.

Ladson-Billings, G. (2006). From the achievement gap to the education debt: Understanding achievement in US schools. *Educational Researcher, 35*(7), 3–12.

Ladson-Billings, G. (2013). Lack of achievement or loss of opportunity. In P. L. Carter and K. G. Welner (Eds.), *Closing the opportunity gap: What America must do to give every child an even chance* (pp. 11–22). New York: Oxford University Press.

Living Wage at UVA. (n.d.). Retrieved from http://www.livingwageatuva.org/.

Loyens, S. M. M., and Rikers, R. M. J. P. (2011). Instruction based on feedback. In R. E. Mayer and P. A. Alexander (Eds.), *Handbook of research on learning and instruction* (pp. 361–381). New York: Routledge.

Maier, M. H., and Nelson, J. A. (2007). *Introducing economics: A critical guide for teaching.* Armonk, NY: M. E. Sharpe.

Maier, M. H., Figart, D. M., and Nelson, J. A. (2014). Proposed national standards for financial literacy: What's in? What's out? *Social Education, 78*(2), 77–79.

McLaren, P. (2015). *Life in schools: An introduction to critical pedagogy in the foundations of education* (6th ed.). Boulder, CO: Paradigm.

McNamee, S. J. (2009). *The meritocracy myth.* Lanham, MD: Rowman & Littlefield.

Merriam, S. B., Caffarella, R. S., and Baumgartner, L. M. (2012). *Learning in adulthood: A comprehensive guide.* Hoboken, NJ: John Wiley & Sons.

Miller, S. L., and VanFossen, P. J. (2008). Recent research on the teaching and learning of pre-collegiate economics. In L. Levstik and C. Tyson (Eds.), *Handbook of research in social studies education* (pp. 284–304). New York: Routledge.

Murphy, P. K., Wilkinson, I. A., and Soter, A. O. (2011). Instruction based on examples. In R. E. Mayer and P. A. Alexander (Eds.), *Handbook of research on learning and instruction* (pp. 382–407). New York: Routledge.

National Council for the Social Studies. (2008). A vision of powerful teaching and learning in the social studies: Building social understanding and civic efficacy. Retrieved from http://www.socialstudies.org/positions/powerful.

Nelson, J. A. (2011). Broader questions and a bigger toolbox: A problem-centered and student-centered approach to teaching pluralist economics. *Economics Faculty Publication Series*, Paper 31. Retrieved from http://scholarworks.umb.edu/econ_faculty_pubs/31.

Piketty, T. (2014). *Capital in the twenty-first century.* Cambridge, MA: Belknap Press.

Reich, G. A., Stemhagen, K., and Siegel-Hawley, G. (2014). Educational research and the metropolitan mindset. *Journal of Thought, 48*(3/4), 57–72.

Saez, E., and Zucman, G. (2014). *Wealth inequality in the United States since 1913: Evidence from capitalized income tax data* (No. w20625). Cambridge, MA: National Bureau of Economic Research. Retrieved from http://goodtimesweb.org/industrial-policy/2014/SaezZucman2014.pdf.

Samuelson, P. A., and Nordhaus, W. D. (2010). *Economics* (19th ed.). New York: McGraw-Hill.

Saunders, P., and Gilliard, J. V. (1995). *A framework for teaching basic economic concepts with scope and sequence guidelines K–12.* New York: National Council on Economic Education.

Schug, M., and Walstad, W. (1991). Teaching and learning economics. In J. P. Shaver (Ed.), *Handbook of research on social studies teaching and learning* (pp. 411–419). New York: Routledge.

Siegfried, J., Krueger, A., Collins, S., Frank, R., MacDonald, R., McGoldrick, K., Taylor, J., and Vredeveld, G. (2010). *Voluntary national content standards in economics.* Retrieved from http://www.councilforeconed.org/wp/wp-content/uploads/2012/03/voluntary-national-content-standards-2010.pdf.

Sifma Foundation. (2015). *The stock market game.* [Online video game]. New York: Sifma Foundation.

Sober Giecek, T. (2007). *Teaching economics as if people mattered.* Boston, MA: United for a Fair Economy.

Solow, R. M. (1985). Economic history and economics. *American Economic Review, 75*(2), 328–331.

Stiglitz, J. (2015). *The great divide: Unequal societies and what we can do about them.* New York: W. W. Norton.

Sugrue, T. J. (2014). *The origins of the urban crisis: Race and inequality in postwar Detroit.* Princeton, NJ: Princeton University Press.

Swalwell, K. (2013). "With great power comes great responsibility": Privileged students' conceptions of justice-oriented citizenship. *Democracy and Education, 21*(1), 1–11.

U.S. Department of Health and Human Services. (2015). *Poverty thresholds for 2014 by size of family and number of related children under 18 years.* Retrieved from http://aspe.hhs.gov/poverty/15poverty.cfm#thresholds.

Wentzel, K. R., and Watkins, D. E. (2011). Instruction based on peer interactions. In R. E. Mayer and P. A. Alexander (Eds.), *Handbook of research on learning and instruction* (pp. 322–343). New York: Routledge.

Wilkinson, R., and Pickett, K. (2009). *The spirit level: Why more equal societies almost always do better.* New York: Bloomsbury Press.

Yin, R. K. (2014). *Case study research: Design and methods* (5th ed.). Thousand Oaks, CA: Sage.

6

HELPING STUDENTS ADDRESS THE ELEPHANT IN DEMOCRACY'S ROOM

An Interactive Approach to Teaching about Campaign Finance

Wayne Journell, Brett L. M. Levy, and James M. M. Hartwick

Election campaigns in the United States have been primarily financed by private contributions since the nineteenth century, but, with recent increases in election spending, questions about who can give money to campaigns and how much have become central political concerns of the early twenty-first century. In many ways, this issue runs parallel to the increasing economic disparity in the United States, which, as Sober argues in Chapter 5, is detrimentally impacting American democracy. If the gap between rich and poor continues to grow, then our elections will increasingly be financed by the former, especially in an era of unprecedented deregulation of campaign contributions. In this chapter, we summarize recent changes in campaign finance regulations, describe different perspectives on the issue, and outline ways that teachers can spark students' interest in campaign finance controversies. Then we discuss strategies for fostering students' exploration of the role of money on politics and suggest ways that teachers can help students become involved in collective advocacy efforts where their voices can be heard within the political arena.

Recent Shifts in Campaign Spending Regulations

For more than a century, Congress has been making laws to regulate and limit how federal election campaigns can be financed. In response to the increases in campaign spending during the twentieth century, several laws, such as the bipartisan McCain–Feingold Act, placed caps on what individuals and groups could contribute to campaigns and other political groups. But over the past few years most of these modest reforms have begun to unravel.

In January 2010, the Supreme Court's decision in *Citizens United v. Federal Election Commission* was the first big step to relax these regulations. This 5–4 ruling first reaffirmed an existing precedent that how one chooses to spend money can be viewed as a form of "speech" under the First Amendment.[1] Then, in the most controversial part of the decision, the Court ruled that corporations and unions have similar free speech rights to individual citizens and that many previously established attempts to limit those rights were unconstitutional. This made it legal for such groups to make unlimited contributions to political action committees (PACs and SuperPACs), which could spend money to support their favored candidates.

Shortly thereafter, two other major rulings opened the door further to greater campaign spending. In March 2010, the *Speechnow.org v. Federal Election Commission* decision in the DC Circuit Court of Appeals eliminated the cap on what individuals, corporations, and unions could contribute to PACs. Then in 2014 another 5–4 Supreme Court decision, *McCutcheon et al. v. Federal Election Commission*, struck down all combined total limits that individuals could contribute to political parties, candidates, and PACs.

These rulings and their aftermath have sparked heated political discourse. The week after the *Citizens United* ruling, President Obama publicly rebuked the decision at his State of the Union address (White House, 2010), and, with each of the subsequent aforementioned decisions, the debate over whether the ruling was a victory for free speech or a way for wealthy individuals to unduly influence the democratic process has been argued in various media outlets. Even Pope Francis recently admonished the influence of money on politics and called for the public financing of elections (Jaffe, 2015). While many conservatives favor the rulings and liberals tend to dislike them, the consequences of *Citizens United*, *Speechnow*, and *McCutcheon* transcend partisan politics and political ideology.[2]

Indeed politicians from both major parties appear quite willing to accept money from big donors (Center for Responsive Politics (CRP), 2015), and for good reason. In this era of ubiquitous technology, social media, and 24-hour cable news networks, public opinion is determined via various forms of media as much as it is through elections, and these venues cost money. Without sufficient funds, candidates and interest groups cannot adequately advertise their issues or advocate for certain policies or candidates.

Nonetheless, the majority of Americans are concerned about the current state of federal campaign finance rules. A recent survey conducted by the *New York Times* found that 84 percent of Americans believe that money has too much influence on the political process. Fifty-five percent of those surveyed also expressed concern that candidates who win public office choose to promote policies that directly help those individuals and groups who helped finance their campaigns ("Americans' views," 2015). In short, many Americans today believe that the democratic process is unduly influenced by a small number of wealthy individuals and groups.

Campaign finance data support these fears. The Center for Responsive Politics (2015), a non-partisan research group that tracks money in American politics using data from the Federal Election Commission (FEC), reports that over $1.6 billion was raised by candidates in the 2014 House and Senate elections, with Republicans raising more than Democrats.[3] Out of the hundreds of thousands of Americans who contributed money in the election, the top 100 donors gave over $305 million, about 19 percent of the total. These 100 individuals represented less than 0.05 percent of the contributors and a far smaller proportion of the general population. Thus, a small number of big money donors are contributing a sizeable percentage of the funding that candidates and political organizations receive.

Individual donations, however, only represent a portion of overall campaign donations in an election cycle. Since the *Speechnow.org* ruling, organizations and corporations have been able to give unlimited amounts of money to PACs. During the 2014 midterm elections, the top 50 organizations donated over $561 million to PACs (CRP, 2015).[4] In addition, a growing source of revenue for political campaigns is "dark money," a term for funds given to nonprofit 501(c)(4) political organizations that are not required to disclose their donors.[5] The exact amount of dark money spent in an election is difficult to track, but estimates suggest that approximately $200 million in dark money was spent in the 2014 midterms (Blumenthal, 2014a), with the vast majority of that money supporting Republican candidates (Olsen-Phillips, 2014). Altogether the 2014 elections cost nearly *$4 billion*, which were the most expensive midterm elections in history (CRP, 2015), and with the current regulations on campaign finance the amount of money spent on political campaigns is likely to increase in future elections.

Whereas some find these large expenditures counterproductive for the democratic process, others consider them essential for fostering healthy debate. Public interest groups with various perspectives on the issue have become increasingly active, and the debate over campaign finance reform seems likely to grow more intense. The growing controversy over campaign spending and the role it plays in our democracy demands that high school and middle school students should develop informed views on this issue.

Different Perspectives on Campaign Finance[6]

Campaign finance reform is an example of what Hess (2009) described as an "open" issue, meaning that there are multiple, rational perspectives that individuals can take when considering what, if anything, we should do about the current state of affairs. We believe that there are five main schools of thought regarding campaign finance reform, and if students explore each of these approaches in depth they should be well positioned to make informed decisions. Below we briefly discuss each of these schools of thought, but we also encourage those interested in more thorough explanations of each approach to visit http://www. teachingcampaignfinance.org, which provides resources to help teachers address issues related to campaign finance.

The Status Quo

Perhaps the simplest approach to campaign finance reform is to leave the current regulations in place. Those who advocate for this way of thinking agree with the majority decision in *Citizens United* that "Corporations and other associations, like individuals, contribute to the 'discussion, debate, and the dissemination of information and ideas' that the First Amendment seeks to foster" (*Citizens United v. Federal Election Commission*, 2010, para. 57). For example, the American Civil Liberties Union (2015) is outspoken in that the organization "does not support campaign finance regulation premised on the notion that the answer to money in politics is *to ban political speech*" (para. 3, emphasis in original).

Further, those who advocate maintaining the status quo argue that democracy is best served by "more speech, not less" (*Citizens United v. Federal Election Commission*, 2010, para. 102). As Christopher Horner (2015), a senior fellow for the libertarian Competitive Enterprise Institute, recently wrote, "among the bases for the First Amendment's guarantee is the reality that competition in the marketplace of ideas makes our system a healthier one" (para. 14). In other words, the money being spent on elections increases awareness about candidates and issues. More money, therefore, equates to more information being disseminated, which in turn leads to more informed voters and fairer, more competitive elections. Without this influx of money in the political process, the argument goes, incumbents would have an even more competitive advantage than they already do based on their familiarity with voters. Further, they argue, by limiting the amount of money that can be used in the political process, one is inherently advocating for fewer challenges to those in power.

Judicial Action

For those who disagree with the precedent set by *Citizens United* and advocate for stricter campaign finance regulations, there exist several possible methods to achieve that goal. The most direct avenue for change would be for the Supreme Court to reverse its decision in *Citizens United*. Although it is a rare event, the Supreme Court has overturned previous rulings before; however, in most of those cases, the composition of the Court had changed considerably since the original ruling. Although *Citizens United* was a 5–4 decision, the Court recently affirmed its position on campaign finance reform in *McCutcheon*, so it is unlikely that the current Court will reverse its stance in the near future.

Realistically, the likelihood of a judicial reversal of *Citizens United* will rest on the outcome of the 2016 presidential election and the health or retirement plans of the current members of the Court. It is probable that whoever succeeds President Obama will be able to fill one or more vacancies in the Court during his or her term. Which seats on the Court open up and how those vacancies are filled will determine whether the Court will shift ideologically enough to open the possibility of overturning *Citizens United* and other related decisions.

Legislative Action

Opportunities also exist to tighten campaign finance regulations through legislative action at both federal and state levels. Any law, of course, is subject to the review of the federal court system, but it is possible that some elements of campaign finance reform—especially those related to disclosure or political coordination between parties and donors—could be passed that would not violate the precedent set by *Citizens United* and subsequent decisions. For example, eight of the nine Supreme Court justices have indicated that they would uphold laws that require political organizations to disclose the identities of large donors, which in turn would force individuals and groups to publicly stand behind their contributions (Backer, 2012).[7] Moreover, many states have passed disclosure laws and other legislative measures designed to minimize the influence of wealthy donors on the political process (Blumenthal, 2014b).

Another way that Congress could encourage politicians to be less reliant on private fundraising is by increasing the amount of public funding options that exist and making public funding available for all federal elections. Currently, presidential candidates can accept $91 million in public monies for their campaigns if they agree not to accept private donations, but no public funding exists for Congressional candidates.[8] Of course, the question then becomes how much money would need to be offered to candidates for them to opt for public funds. If the figures presented at the beginning of this chapter are any indication, the number would have to be well above the current rate of federal support. It is worth noting that, in 2012, both President Obama and Governor Romney declined to accept public funds for their campaigns, which was the first time both major party presidential nominees had refused to participate in the public funding program.

Democratizing Corporate and Organizational Governance

A third way to reduce corporate influence on the political process is from within. Shareholders, employees, and consumers often have a vested interest in how organizations spend their money. Certain organizational structures, such as shareholder and employee voting procedures, can provide shareholders and employees with more input on how such large organizations do or do not contribute to political causes. The proposed Shareholder Protection Act (S. 824, 2013) attempts to give shareholders more input on these decisions, but it has not yet been passed.

In addition, consumers can vote with their dollars and voices to influence corporate or union political spending. A perfect example can be found in the controversy surrounding Chick-fil-A after it was reported that the fast food franchise had donated over $3 million between 2010 and 2011 to several political organizations that opposed same-sex marriage (Israel, 2014; O'Connor, 2012). The story became a nightly staple on mainstream and cable news outlets, and organized boycotts of Chick-fil-A restaurants occurred throughout the nation. In little over a month, the company had issued a statement indicating that it would remove itself from the political arena with respect to same-sex marriage, and according to the franchise's 2012 tax filings Chick-fil-A had ceased all funding to the vast majority of the controversial political organizations it had donated to in the past (Comer, 2014; Israel, 2014).[9]

Although Chick-fil-A survived the incident, the negative press created enough concern for it to change its donation practices. When organizations enter the political arena, they must recognize that their actions may not be reflective of the values of their constituents or customers. If legislation requires corporations and other collective entities to disclose their political spending to their shareholders—and mass media outlets help to publicize such contributions—then in the spirit of maximizing profits it may be less likely that corporations will use their money to support potentially controversial political issues.

Constitutional Amendment

Perhaps the only surefire way to address the influx of money into the political process is to pass a Constitutional amendment that allows limits on the amount of money individuals and groups can give to candidates, parties, and/or political organizations. A Constitutional amendment would "force" the courts to consider campaign finance reform measures constitutional, which would effectively nullify the rulings in *Citizens United* and subsequent Supreme Court cases on campaign finance. Of course, there is a reason why the Constitution has only been amended 17 times since 1791—it is extremely difficult to do! The most common way to amend the Constitution (26 of the 27 amendments have been added this way) is for two-thirds of the House and Senate to approve a proposed amendment and then for three-fourths of the state legislatures to do so.

In recent years, Congress has proposed numerous resolutions calling for such an amendment. The most recent attempt, which had modest bipartisan support and the backing of 16 states, was unanimously rejected by Senate Republicans (Everett, 2014; Udall and Simpson, 2014). Although passing a Constitutional amendment on campaign finance in this era of divisive political discourse may seem impossible, activity at the state level suggests that the potential for a grassroots movement exists. A growing number of state legislatures have passed resolutions for a Constitutional amendment, and, in Colorado and Montana, voters approved ballot initiatives in support of an amendment. Currently, these efforts indicate significant voter concern regarding the influence of money on elections, and if the matter is not resolved in another way it is possible that the passage of such resolutions could grow into a groundswell of support for a Constitutional amendment.

Helping Students Understand the Issue

Although these different schools of thought are useful to help students contextualize the various options available for campaign finance reform efforts, additional scaffolding is needed for students to be able to develop their own opinions about it. An open-ended framing question for lessons or units about this issue could be: "What, if anything, can and should be done about the influence of money on U.S. elections?" This section will discuss possible steps that teachers can take to help their students deliberate on that question and encourage them to become active participants in the public discourse surrounding it.[10]

Piquing Student Interest

We suggest that the first step to helping students understand its importance is to "show them the money." There are several organizations, such as the Center for Responsive Politics and the Sunlight Foundation, that provide a comprehensive analysis of the amount of money spent in the political arena. Students could use these websites to acquire data that can then be used as the basis for further analysis.[11]

For example, in a recent study of teachers during the 2012 presidential election, Journell et al. (2015) observed a teacher who made a concerted effort to have his students track campaign donations and expenditures as a way to have them better understand the role of money in the election. The teacher had his students use openly available campaign finance data to compare differences in the types of funding that Obama and Romney had received, and how the source of funding correlated with each candidate's support for particular policies. For example, on October 9th, his students used a *New York Times* website to find that Obama's contributions were primarily "hard" money that was subject to federal regulation, whereas Romney's money was from a variety of unregulated—or "soft"—sources. The teacher then had students respond to the following questions: "What does this information tell you about each candidate, the campaign, and the likelihood of winning the election? Do you think it is fair for one candidate to have such a monetary advantage? What could be some alternatives to the current system?" As one might expect, students had conflicting opinions on the use of unregulated money, ranging from believing that soft money was a "good loophole" for candidates, to describing this type of fundraising as "a little sketchy."

Teachers could also engage students by using examples of popular culture that frame the campaign finance reform debate in approachable or humorous ways. For example, in 2011, television host and political satirist Stephen

Colbert created a PAC that was designed to fund his farcical campaign for the 2012 South Carolina Republican primary election. For the better part of a year, Colbert's PAC was a reoccurring theme on his show, and many aspects of how PACs work—from filing paperwork with the FEC to the rules regulating how PACs can coordinate with political candidates—were humorously lampooned. Colbert won a Peabody Award for his efforts (Subramanian, 2012), and a study by researchers at the Annenberg Public Policy Center at the University of Pennsylvania found that individuals who viewed the PAC storyline on *The Colbert Report* were better informed about PACs and other 501(c)(4) groups than individuals who received their political information from other media sources (Hardy et al., 2014). Archives of these episodes can be found online through both the Comedy Central website and YouTube.[12]

Once students' interest is piqued, teachers can transition into a more detailed analysis of campaign finance reform. An obvious place to start would be to have students analyze the *Citizens United* decision, specifically comparing Justice Kennedy's majority opinion and Justice Stevens's dissenting opinion. Then students could read articles and/or watch videos that outline both sides of the issue.

Creating Spaces for Discussion

There is considerable educational value to having students engage in discussions of controversial public issues (Hess, 2009). Students gain practice in defending their beliefs while also learning to be understanding and tolerant of opposing viewpoints. In this sense, discussion acts not only as a pedagogical tool, but also as an instructional goal unto itself (Parker and Hess, 2001). Given the educational benefits associated with engaging in discussions of controversial public issues and the vigorous public debate on campaign finance reform, students should be invited to engage in authentic discussion and deliberation on this topic of public import.

It is possible that students may not see tolerant discourse at home, and they are likely not seeing it on cable news networks or on social media (Sobieraj and Berry, 2011). Research suggests that, if students are allowed to freely discuss issues without any training or expectations of civility, then verbal exchanges can quickly turn hostile, leaving those holding minority opinions feeling marginalized or ostracized (e.g., Hess and Ganzler, 2007; Journell, 2012; Levy, 2014). Teachers, therefore, need to explain and model their expectations for tolerant discourse before jumping into discussions of a controversial nature.

One format that seems particularly useful for discussing campaign finance reform is structured academic controversy (SAC) (Johnson and Johnson, 1979, 1993). The SAC process involves examining two sides of an issue that can be framed dichotomously, such as "Should the United States amend the Constitution to eliminate corporate personhood and allow Congress to limit corporate and union political contributions?"[13] Students are then placed in even-numbered groups (four is an ideal number), and half of the group is asked to create an argument for the "pro" side and the other half of the group is asked to do the same for the "con" side. Teachers should provide each side with relevant and accurate resources. Having students research the issue of campaign finance on their own may also be an option for teachers; however, if teachers choose this approach, it is essential that they evaluate the accuracy of students' sources before engaging in an SAC. There exists quite a bit of misinformation about campaign finance on the Internet, and, in order for a SAC to be successful, students need to be privy to accurate information on both sides of the issue being discussed.

After reviewing the arguments for their assigned side, each pair or group presents its arguments to the other side. As the arguing side in each group conveys its argument, the other students listen and take notes without interrupting, other than to ask questions for clarification. Teachers may also choose to have students flip roles so that all students have the opportunity to defend each side. After both sides have been presented, the groups can then have a general discussion of the issue or the teacher can choose to lead a whole-class discussion (see Avery et al., 2013; Hartwick and Levy, 2012).

Regardless of what format the discussion takes, it should serve two main purposes. First, the discussion should take the form of a seminar, which Parker and Hess (2001) define as a discussion where the "purpose is deepened and widened understanding" (p. 282). Then, once students have developed a position, the discussion can change into more of a deliberation, which Parker and Hess (2001) describe as an "action plan that will resolve a problem" (p. 282). At this point, it would be useful for students to revisit the five schools of thought discussed previously. Students who favor campaign finance reform, for example, could deliberate which of the proposed paths is most viable.

Taking Action

Too often the civic education students receive in schools does not make the leap from awareness to action, which prompts political scientists to criticize that schools "often teach *about* citizenship and government without teaching students the skills that are necessary to become active citizens themselves" (Macedo et al., 2005, p. 33, emphasis in original). If schools are to become the "laboratories for democracy" as Dewey (1938) hoped they would, then teachers have a responsibility to channel students' passions into real-world opportunities for civic engagement.

Another goal of civic education is to increase students' political efficacy, which can be defined as "the feeling that individual political action does have, or can have, an impact on the political process. . . . It is the feeling that political and social change is possible, and that the individual citizen can play a part in bringing about this change" (Campbell et al., 1954, p. 187). Research suggests that, when individuals identify strongly with an issue, group, or political party, and actively work on behalf of it, their political efficacy increases (e.g., Koch, 1993; Louis et al., 2004; Steinberger, 1981). Further, research within K–12 education suggests that students' political efficacy increases when they are allowed to engage with civic action projects that focus on issues of personal and collective (societal or community) importance (e.g., Levy, 2011; Serriere, 2014; Serriere et al., 2011).

Thus, to support students' political efficacy, we believe that, in addition to teaching students about campaign finance, teachers should guide students to take basic political action. For example, teachers could require students to write letters to their elected representatives or volunteer for political campaigns with local candidates whose stances on campaign finance reform align with the students' viewpoints. More ambitious students could even attempt to write op-eds to the local newspaper or give presentations at town meetings or local community organizations, such as the local chapter of the Veterans of Foreign Wars, as a way to educate voters about their positions on campaign finance. Another small-scale project could involve contacting a local university and offering to assist faculty with research on issues related to campaign finance.

Other options for local political involvement could be for students to attend meetings, lectures, demonstrations, or other events that would allow them to interact with others who share their beliefs regarding campaign finance. Students could even choose to volunteer for a reform group or an organization that holds campaign finance as an area of interest, such as the League of Women Voters.

The Internet and social media also provide unprecedented opportunities for students to become engaged with groups and issues in ways that allow them to connect to national or global audiences (e.g., Journell et al., 2013; Krutka, 2014). As Krutka and Carpenter point out in Chapter 14, the political landscape is shifting in response to changing technological contexts, which necessitates that civic education evolves too. Teachers could easily make students aware of various organizations at the local, state, and national levels that have taken a stand for or against campaign finance reform, and structure assignments that facilitate students' support of such groups.[14] Table 6.1 offers examples of such groups.

After researching organizations that correspond to their beliefs on campaign finance reform, students could choose one to join, which might allow them to interact with others through that organization's website, blog, social media accounts, or mailing lists. Simply becoming affiliated with an established organization could immerse students in an authentic political conversation that extends well beyond school walls.

A civic action project should not be a "one size fits all" type of assignment. Forcing dispassionate or shy students to speak at an interest group meeting could be counterproductive by having the opposite effect and discourage them from becoming politically engaged in the future. For some students, having them follow and reflect upon, or analyze, a political organization's entries on Twitter or weekly blogs might be the spark that slowly leads them closer to the

TABLE 6.1 Advocacy Organizations on Campaign Finance

Status quo	Judicial action	Corporate governance	Amend the Constitution	Legislation
Citizens United	Move On	Corporate Reform Coalition	Common Cause	Mayday PAC
citizensunited. org	moveon. org	corporatereform coalition.org	commoncause. org	mayday.us
Center for Competitive Politics	Alliance for Justice	SomeOfUs	Move to Amend	Brennan Center for Justice
campaignfreedom. org	afj.org	sumofus.org	movetoamend. org	brennancenter. org

political sphere. As long as the students' choice in activity moves beyond knowledge acquisition about campaign finance reform and toward active political engagement, the activity can give students valuable experience in the political arena that could be a foundation for future involvement.

Reflection

The final step in this process should be individual and/or collective reflection about the experience as a whole. This reflection should move beyond simply reflecting about the issue of campaign finance reform; it should also focus on the process of moving from political knowledge to political action. Students should consider the following questions, which are designed to help students better understand the experiential learning process they have just completed (Boyd and Fales, 1983; Kolb, 2015): (1) What did I learn from becoming involved within the public discussion on campaign finance reform? (2) How was I able to use my political voice to support the cause I believed in? (3) What were the pros and cons of working with the organizations that I chose? (4) What did I learn about the value of collective versus individual action? (5) If I had the opportunity, what would I do differently? (6) What will be my next steps in exploring or advocating on this issue?

Although campaign finance reform is an essential issue that needs to be addressed, it is far from the only pressing issue that holds implications for our democratic society. If students can learn to become more politically active through an activity on campaign finance reform, they may be more likely to take stands on other issues about which they feel passionate.

Conclusion

In a seminal article, discussed here by Johnson (Chapter 3), Westheimer and Kahne (2004) outlined three types of citizens that schools produce. Although they suggest that learning about issues is important, they argue that it is insufficient for preparing students to respond to them. The approach outlined in this chapter encourages students to become both participatory and justice-oriented citizens. After students develop an understanding of, and perspective on, campaign finance reform, teachers can encourage their students to become politically involved with others. Although we should always applaud individuals for taking stands on their own, students need to know that political reform often requires collective organization, mobilization, and action.

Again, we believe that the process described in this chapter is more universally important than the issue of campaign finance reform. It is essential for all students to develop their political voices and better understand how they can use them to advocate for policies and positions that reflect their beliefs. Campaign finance reform is a timely and important issue, and an important pillar upon which a more economically equitable society rests. This topic can serve fruitfully as a vehicle for teaching students the types of justice-oriented citizenship skills they need in an age of social connectivity, especially since individuals have more opportunities for collective political mobilization than ever before.

Notes

1 This precedent was set by two earlier Supreme Court decisions, *Buckley v. Valeo* in 1976 and *First National Bank of Boston v. Bellotti* in 1978.

2 Two prominent examples of exceptions are John McCain, senator from Arizona and the 2008 Republican presidential nominee, who called the *Citizens United* ruling the "worst decision ever" (Wing, 2012), and the American Civil Liberties Union, which has openly championed the Court's decision as a protection of free speech (American Civil Liberties Union, 2015).

3 Over $198 million was donated to candidates by liberal-leaning PACs and over $252 million was donated by conservative-leaning PACs in the 2014 election cycle. Individual donations constituted over $479 million for Democrats and over $514 million for Republicans (CRP, 2015).

4 A list of those top 50 organizations and the amount of money they gave can be found at https://www.opensecrets.org/overview/toporgs.php.

5 The term "501(c) organization" comes from the section of the tax code that gives such organizations tax-exempt status.

6 This section draws heavily from articles published in *Social Education* (Hartwick and Levy, 2012) and *The Social Studies* (Levy et al., 2014).

7 In 2012, a Disclose Act was proposed in the Senate, but Republican senators filibustered the bill so no vote was ever taken on it.

8 A proposed law entitled the Fair Elections Now Act was proposed during the 2013–14 legislative session that sought to provide options for public funding for Congressional elections. The bill is currently sitting in committee in both the House of Representatives and the Senate.

9 According to its tax information, Chick-Fil-A stopped giving money to all of the organizations that were believed to actively oppose same-sex marriage with the exception of the Fellowship of Christian Athletes. The franchise gave a little more than $25,000 to that organization.

10 A variety of useful resources for helping students understand the issue of campaign finance reform can be found in Hartwick and Levy (2012) and at http://www.teaching campaignfinance.org.

11 The Center for Responsive Politics website is https://www.opensecrets.org/. The Sunlight Foundation website is http://sunlightfoundation.com/.

12 An archive of all of *The Colbert Report* episodes can be found at http://thecolbertreport. cc.com/. It should be noted, however, that, although political satire shows like *The Colbert Report* and *The Daily Show* have often been found to be more informative than mainstream media outlets (e.g., Baym, 2010; Hardy et al., 2014) and, thus, pedagogically useful (Garrett and Schmeichel, 2012), these shows often contain adult themes that may not be appropriate for all classrooms.

13 Although relevant to this discussion, corporate personhood encompasses more than just election contributions. Corporate personhood, from a legal perspective, means that corporations can legally be disassociated from their human workers (e.g., owners, managers, and employees) and enjoy many of the same legal rights as American citizens. The notion of corporate personhood in the United States dates back to the nineteenth century, and the 1886 case of *Santa Clara v. Southern Pacific*. Although the case itself did not deal with this issue, the case's abstract, written by a clerk sympathetic to corporations, included a statement that the justices agreed that corporations were persons. This briefing has been used subsequently as a precedent for other decisions that have reified this position (see Hartmann, 2010). Corporate personhood is often used to justify the *Citizens United* decision and other campaign finance-related rulings.

14 We acknowledge, however, that it may be harder for students to find grassroots organizations in favor of the status quo, which is a limitation to this type of assignment.

References

American Civil Liberties Union. (2015). The ACLU and *Citizens United*. Retrieved from https://www.aclu.org/free-speech/aclu-and-citizens-united.

"Americans' views on money in politics." (2015, June 2). *New York Times*. Retrieved from http://www.nytimes.com/interactive/2015/06/02/us/politics/money-in-politics-poll.html?_r=0.

Avery, P. G., Levy, S. A., and Simmons, A. M. M. (2013). Deliberating controversial public issues as a part of civic education. *Social Studies, 104*(3), 105–114.

Backer, J. (2012). Not buying Senator McConnell's position on disclosure. Retrieved from http://www.brennancenter.org/blog/not-buying-senator-mcconnells-position-disclosure.

Baym, G. (2010). *From Cronkite to Colbert: The evolution of broadcast news*. Boulder, CO: Paradigm.

Blumenthal, P. (2014a). Dark money concentrates in a small number of pivotal 2014 races. Retrieved from http://www.huffingtonpost.com/2014/10/15/dark-money-2014_n_5991978.html.

Blumenthal, P. (2014b). Here's where campaign finance reform may move ahead as Congress dithers. Retrieved from http://www.huffingtonpost.com/2014/12/20/campaign-finance-reform-states_n_6357182.html.

Boyd, E. M., and Fales, A. W. (1983). Reflective learning: Key to learning from experience. *Journal of Humanistic Psychology, 23*, 99–117.

Campbell, A., Gurin, G., and Miller, W. (1954). *The voter decides*. Evanston, IL: Row, Peterson.

Center for Responsive Politics (CRP). (2015). 2014 election overview. Retrieved from https://www.opensecrets.org/overview/.

Citizens United v. Federal Election Commission, 558 U.S. 310 (2010).

Comer, M. (2014). New Chick-fil-A filings show decrease in anti-LGBT funding. Retrieved from http://goqnotes.com/27860/new-chick-fil-a-filings-show-decrease-in-anti-lgbt-funding/.

Dewey, J. (1938). *Experience and education.* New York: Touchstone.

Everett, B. (2014). Senate blocks campaign finance amendment. Retrieved from http://www.politico.com/story/2014/09/senate-block-campaign-finance-amendment-110864.html.

Garrett, H. J., and Schmeichel, M. (2012). Using *The Daily Show* to promote media literacy. *Social Education, 76*(4), 211–215.

Hardy, B. W., Gottfried, J. A., Winneg, K. M., and Jamieson, K. H. (2014). Stephen Colbert's civics lesson: How Colbert super PAC taught viewers about campaign finance. *Mass Communication and Society, 17*(3), 329–353.

Hartmann, T. (2010). *Unequal protection: How corporations became "people"—and how you can fight back* (2nd ed.). San Francisco, CA: Berrett-Koehler.

Hartwick, J. M. M., and Levy, B. L. M. (2012). Teaching about big money in elections: To amend or not to amend the U.S. Constitution? *Social Education, 76*(5), 236–241.

Hess, D. E. (2009). *Controversy in the classroom: The democratic power of discussion.* New York: Routledge.

Hess, D., and Ganzler, L. (2007). Patriotism and ideological diversity in the classroom. In J. Westheimer (Ed.), *Pledging allegiance: The politics of patriotism in America's schools* (pp. 131–138). New York: Teachers College Press.

Horner, C. C. (2015). In support of Citizens United, against targeting political speech. Retrieved from http://thehill.com/blogs/congress-blog/politics/232535-in-support-of-citizens-united-against-targeting-political-speech.

Israel, J. (2014). Chick-fil-A's foundations dramatically reduce anti-LGBT giving (updated). Retrieved from http://thinkprogress.org/lgbt/2014/03/03/3355701/chick-fil-2012-giving/.

Jaffe, A. (2015). The Pope gives his blessing to campaign finance reform. Retrieved from http://www.cnn.com/2015/03/12/politics/pope-francis-campaign-finance-reform/.

Johnson, D. W., and Johnson, R. T. (1979). Conflict in the classroom: Controversy and learning. *Review of Educational Research, 49*(1), 51–70.

Johnson, D.W., and Johnson, R.T. (1993). Creative and critical thinking through academic controversy. *American Behavioral Scientist, 37*(1), 40–53.

Journell, W. (2012). Ideological homogeneity, school leadership, and political intolerance in secondary education: A study of three high schools during the 2008 presidential election. *Journal of School Leadership, 22*(3), 569–599.

Journell, W., Ayers, C. A., and Beeson, M. W. (2013). Joining the conversation: Twitter as a tool for student political engagement. *Educational Forum, 77*(4), 466–480.

Journell, W., Beeson, M. W., and Ayers, C. A. (2015). Learning to think politically: Toward more complete disciplinary knowledge in civics and government courses. *Theory and Research in Social Education, 43*(1), 28–67.

Koch, J. W. (1993). Assessments of group influence, subjective political competence, and interest group membership. *Political Behavior, 15*(4), 309–325.

Kolb, D. A. (2015). *Experiential learning: Experience as the source of learning and development* (2nd ed.). Upper Saddle River, NJ: Pearson.

Krutka, D. G. (2014). Democratic twittering: Microblogging for a more participatory social studies. *Social Education, 78*(2), 86–89.

Levy, B. L. M. (2011). Fostering cautious political efficacy through civic advocacy projects: A mixed methods case study of an innovative high school class. *Theory and Research in Social Education, 39*(2), 238–277.

Levy, B. L. M. (2014). Teaching about the 2012 presidential election in a swing state: Opportunities and challenges related to fostering youth political interest. Paper presented at the annual meeting of the American Educational Research Association, Philadelphia, PA.

Levy, B. L. M., Hartwick, J. M. M., Munoz, S. P., and Gudgel, S. (2014). What's money got to do with it? Fostering productive discussions about campaign finance. *Social Studies, 105*(5), 213–221.

Louis, W. R., Taylor, D. M., and Neil, T. (2004). Cost–benefit analysis for your group and yourself: The rationality of decision-making in conflict. *International Journal of Conflict Management, 15*(2), 110–143.

Macedo, S., Alex-Assensoh, Y., Berry, J. M., Brintnall, M., Campbell, D. E., Fraga, L. R., Fung, A., Galston, W. A., Karpowitz, C. F., Levi, M., Levinson, M., Lipsitz, K., Niemi, R. G., Putnam, R. D., Rahn, W. M., Reich, R., Rodgers, R. R., Swanstrom, T., and Walsh, K. C. (2005). *Democracy at risk: How political choices undermine citizen participation, and what we can do about it.* Washington, DC: Brookings Institution.

O'Connor, C. (2012). Meet the Cathys: Your guide to the billionaires behind Chick-fil-A. Retrieved from http://www.forbes.com/sites/clareoconnor/2012/08/03/meet-the-cathys-your-guide-to-the-billionaires-behind-chick-fil-a/.

Olsen-Phillips, P. (2014). Dark money still a Republican game. Retrieved from http://sunlightfoundation.com/blog/2014/10/28/dark-money-still-a-republican-game/.

Parker, W. C., and Hess, D. (2001). Teaching with and for discussion. *Teaching and Teacher Education, 17*(3), 273–289.

Serriere, S. C. (2014). The role of the elementary teacher in fostering civic efficacy. *Social Studies, 105*(1), 45–56.

Serriere, S. C., Mitra, D., and Reed, K. (2011). Student voice in the elementary years: Fostering youth–adult partnerships in elementary service learning. *Theory and Research in Social Education, 39*(4), 541–575.

Shareholder Protection Act, S. 824, 113th Cong. (2013). Retrieved from https://www.congress.gov/bill/113th-congress/senate-bill/824.

Sobieraj, S., and Berry, J. M. (2011). From incivility to outrage: Political discourse in blogs, talk radio, and cable news. *Political Communication, 28*(1), 19–41.

Steinberger, P. J. (1981). Social context and political efficacy. *Sociology and Social Research, 65*(2), 129–141.

Subramanian, C. (2012). Stephen Colbert's super PAC satire lands him a Peabody. Retrieved from http://newsfeed.time.com/2012/04/05/stephen-colberts-super-pac-satire-lands-him-a-peabody/.

Udall, T., and Simpson, A. (2014). Bipartisan case for a Constitutional amendment on campaign finance. Retrieved from http://thehill.com/opinion/op-ed/216809-bipartisan-case-for-a-constitutional-amendment-on-campaign-finance.

Westheimer, J., and Kahne, J. (2004). What kind of citizen? The politics of educating for democracy. *American Educational Research Journal, 41*(2), 237–269.

White House. (2010). Remarks by the President in State of the Union Address. Retrieved from https://www.whitehouse.gov/the-press-office/remarks-president-state-union-address.

Wing, N. (2012). John McCain: Citizens United is "worst decision ever"..."money is money," not free speech. Retrieved from http://www.huffingtonpost.com/2012/10/12/john-mccain-citizens-united_n_1960996.html.

Building Spaces to Nurture Student Action

7

TOWARD GENDER EQUITY

Imagining New Spaces for Empowerment through Feminist Pedagogy in Democratic Classrooms

Kathryn E. Engebretson and Alexandria Hollett

When gender equity is considered, it is common for an image of women earning the right to vote or work for equal pay to arise. Of course, these are hallmarks of the move toward gender equity; however, it can be politically expedient to claim a coherent and stable classification of "women" in order to highlight national trends that speak to the persistence or eradication of gender-based inequity in society. Consider, for example, the apparent gains made by women within the realm of school. Since 2000, women have increased their college attendance and graduation rates (U.S. Census Bureau, 2011), and National Assessment of Educational Progress (NAEP) tests show nearly equal performance between boys and girls (Corbett et al., 2008). SAT and ACT scores reveal a small yet persistent gap, with boys scoring higher on math, science, and composite scores of these tests, whereas girls score higher on the English sections of both exams (Corbett et al., 2008). An increasing number of women entering academia is also encouraging, although as of 2009 only 38.8 percent of academics who have achieved the level of full professor were women (WIA Report, 2012). Still, with the more equitable representation of women and girls in these areas, as well as evidence of the slow closure of the gender gap, it is clear that progress has been made.

Notwithstanding these gains, gender inequity persists both in and outside of school, even though gender can no longer be used to limit voting rights, funding for school sports and activities, or employment opportunities. The political landscape reveals that the number of women serving in Congress is disproportionately low compared to men—only 313 women have ever served in either house, with the current percentage being 19.4 percent (Office of the Clerk, 2015), and the United States has never—as of this writing—had a female candidate endorsed by either major party for president. Economically, women still face at least an 18 percent wage gap compared to men (U.S. Bureau of Labor Statistics, 2014), women CEOs are a minuscule minority at 1.5 percent of the world's 2,000 top-performing companies (Ibarra and Hansen, 2009), and hidden discrimination is still present in hiring and firing practices. Married women, on average, work more hours than ever before, as many of the household duties continue to fall to them, regardless of whether they hold full-time employment outside the home (Bureau of Labor Statistics, 2015).

Even in typically feminized professions such as education, women are over-represented as teachers but under-represented in administrative positions, and when in those positions the work of promoting gender equity is still needed (Rusch and Marshall, 2006). It is worth mentioning that these administrative positions typically held by men not only allow those who occupy them to make key decisions regarding all aspects of school and schooling, but also pay the high-est salaries, which has repercussions for the social, political, and economic agency of women on a broader level.

Economic inequity as it relates to earnings is still more troubling when both race and gender are considered together; for example, a study on the weekly earnings of women with advanced degrees showed that in 2010 white women made, on average, $1,169, Latinas earned $1,126, and African-American women earned $1,010. Although Latina, African-American, and Native American women have historically earned the lowest wages while being at the highest risk of poverty (Browne, 2000), these statistics reveal that, even when making higher salaries, they still earn less than their white counterparts. Women of color are also at the greatest disadvantage when it comes to employment mobility, particularly when they are members of older generations. Some causes of this heightened inequality have been attributed to unequal access to education, socialization into certain types of work that do not allow for the transfer of skills across jobs, and deindustrialization—or the disappearance of the low-skilled factory work that was once a relatively stable source of income (Browne, 2000). Still others attribute both wage and employment discrepancies for women of color to racial segregation—particularly in major cities—as well as persistent achievement gaps in educational institutions which limit opportunities and the ability to access the high-skilled, tech-based jobs that are currently in demand in the United States (Massey and Denton, 1993; Tienda et al., 1992; Tomaskovic-Devey, 1993).

Differences in salary and employment protections are also disheartening when we look beyond the binary categorization of gender as "man" or "woman" and consider the rights and (in)visibility of the trans and genderqueer commu-nity. While statistics are difficult to obtain because of concerns of privacy, safety, and identity, the available information regarding the experiences of transgen-der individuals and the discrimination they face in hiring, wages, and broader society is alarming (Badgett et al., 2007). Interestingly, in examining the work-place experiences of 64 transgender individuals, Schilt and Wiswall (2008) found that earnings for female-to-male transgender workers slightly increased, while earnings for male-to-female transgender workers fell by nearly one-third after their gender transitions. The researchers theorize that this disparity is linked to persistent—if subtle—gender discrimination that continues to favor masculine performance in the workplace.

This status quo of gender disparity fails to ensure equal pay for equal work, further marginalizes women of color as well as trans individuals, supports the over-representation of men in political and economic positions of power, and most glaringly fails to achieve the vision of the United States as a place that equitably serves the needs of those living in a pluralistic and democratic society. Despite this sobering realization, it is heartening to imagine a reality in which our classrooms and schools confront gender inequity as it exists in the present. In particular, if our social studies classrooms are sites for learning about and practicing democracy, they must become spaces where issues of gender are addressed, both discretely and in relation to the economic, political, and social forms of capital granted to those who make the most money. In order to confront the aforementioned injustices, and build upon the foundation laid by Crocco (2001), Levstik (2001), and others, this chapter will show how incorporating feminism and "discomfort" pedagogies into democratic classrooms can empower our students to begin to work together to address these societal problems that have become manifest as severe economic disadvantages for those of the non-dominant gender.

Feminism Is a Dirty Word

Although there are multiple, and sometimes conflicting, interpretations of feminism, most would agree that the term evokes images of women (and, to a lesser extent, men) fighting for an end to gender-based oppression. At the beginning of the twentieth century in the U.S. and other parts of the Western world, women's movements were largely concerned with legal issues, primarily voting and property rights. In the 1960s, influenced in part by the sex education curricula of prior decades, feminism would turn its attention to reproductive justice, sexual liberation, family structures, and women in the workplace (Freeman, 2008). It is important to note, however, that these movements have largely subsumed the concerns of queer women and women of color under white, heterosexual agendas (Davis, 1981), which troubles perceptions of "women" as a coherent identity marker (Riley, 1988) as well as calls into question which women have or have not benefited from feminist agendas throughout history. It is with this knowledge in mind that we align ourselves with the post-structural frameworks of third-wave feminism and advance the definition suggested by bell hooks (1981):

> Feminism is not simply a struggle to end male chauvinism or a movement to ensure that women have equal rights with men; it is a commitment to eradicating the ideology of domination that permeates Western culture

on various levels—sex, race, class to name a few, and a commitment to reorganizing U.S. society so that the self-development of people can take precedence over imperialism, economic expansion, and material desires.

(p. 194)

Among other things, hooks ties feminism directly to economic concerns, implying that feminism stands in opposition to a capitalism that correlates success with the acquisition of commodities and bases itself on the exploitation of vulnerable populations. hooks also offers an understanding of feminism that is predicated on the ability to see various oppressions as connected under the broader umbrella of an "ideology of domination" and asserts the inherent limitations of treating gender inequity as a discrete form of injustice. We further argue that feminisms which do not provide a framework for viewing the operation of gender oppression as an "always already" racialized and classed set of interlocking systems are most in danger of replicating the privileged status of, among other things, the white and middle- to upper-class gendered identities that most closely align with existing power structures.

This particular brand of feminism therefore requires the development of a critical lens with which to view relations between simultaneous forms of oppression that wax or wane in various contexts. It is equally necessary to turn this lens on the systems that undergird society more generally. Economic parity for all genders, for example, is an issue that many feminists in the U.S. believe critical to broader conversations about gender justice. However, it is arguable that, without a corresponding critique of capitalism as an inherently unjust economic system, achieving parity without restructuring this system may actually further marginalize impoverished communities and deplete world resources. This is not to say that men, women, and trans individuals should not make the same amount of money for the completion of similar tasks, but rather that capitalist economic structures often necessitate the maintenance of profits at the expense of the environment, other humans, or both. Therefore, for economic parity to be truly just, it is necessary to not only eradicate disparate pay scales based on gender difference, but also to address the conditions of oppression upon which capitalism is built.

As a result of these considerations, it is understandable that feminism, and therefore feminist teaching, appears an overwhelming undertaking. In school settings, much research has been done to show that both current and preservice teachers either hesitate to introduce or vehemently resist curricula that discuss oppression (Levstik, 2001; Lundeberg, 1997; Sadker, 1999; Titus, 2000; Webber, 2005). In regard to issues of gender specifically, Baumgardner and Richards (2000) point out the difficulty that women in particular have in admitting that they are subject to social, economic, and political oppression. Feminism has been construed as a dirty word; we argue here that it is not the word, but the *work* of feminism, that is dirty. It is the hard intellectual, emotional, and practical labor of dismantling systems of supremacy and unjust social and economic hierarchies; it is also work that is liberating, transformative, and urgent.

Democratic Classrooms

Democracy is also a messy undertaking replete with risks. Like feminism, it is a useful stance from which to approach education. In both student and teacher education theory and research, democratic classrooms as an extension of democratic education have been written about widely (Gillaspie et al., 1996; Landau and Gathercoal, 2000; Marri, 2005, 2009). While there are differences in how democratic education is implemented, democratic classrooms frequently seek to promote the elevation of student voice, participation through discussion and joint decision-making, open-mindedness, and appropriate student autonomy in the classroom. These classrooms are characterized as being active and student-centered, and based upon the liberal democratic ideals of equality and diversity. Proponents indicate that students who are able to practice democracy in the classroom are more likely to do so in their adult lives, and that this practice can extend beyond their local communities to help them develop conceptions of global citizenship (Zong et al., 2008). Unfortunately, while these outcomes support the utility of its framework, democratic classrooms are not a panacea for making the world a better place, because they do not require social transformation as a marker of their success.

Simply including democratic practices in a classroom does not "ensure the interruption of human-created hierarchies and the conditions of alienation, domination, and exploitation that they engender" (North, 2009, p. 574). Herein lies the major limitation of democratic classrooms. Without the ideological underpinning of a justice framework, these classrooms can just as easily perpetuate injustice as they can empower students to practice civic responsibility and become agents of equity. These classrooms risk functioning as bodies without souls; they are little democracies without a democratic ethos. In order to solve this problem, we return to feminism, and in particular feminist pedagogy, as a way to complement, complicate, and ultimately elevate the democratic classroom.

Feminist Pedagogy

Democratic classrooms seek to promote the ethics of equality of all members, the sharing of classroom space, the presence of student voice in decision-making, and connections to the community. Feminist pedagogy takes these ideals a step further; this approach is predicated upon the presence and nurturance of a multi-voiced community of learners, shared ownership of the material and class, empowerment of those in the community, and the valuing of multiple discourses (Crabtree and Sapp, 2003). It necessitates the opportunities for students to engage in intentional emancipatory experiences with space to grapple with social justice issues. Both conditions are prerequisites for enabling the process through which the benefits of the democratic classroom can spill over into other classes and areas of students' lives.

Emancipatory experiences are at the heart of feminist pedagogy and require students to think critically about their own lives and agency. As the student population in the United States changes and becomes more diverse, students will continue to strive to situate themselves and others into the fabric of the greater society. It is often through the classroom that students are socialized into a world different from the one they are accustomed to, and for some it may be the first place where they recognize that their voices matter as much as the voices of those in power. Shrewsbury (1987) states that "empowerment is only possible when there is a sense of mutuality" between the people involved (p. 10). In the democratic feminist classroom, students learn to share power through the division of labor, time management, and meaningful connection-making with other students and the curriculum. Daily processes (refining the class schedule, offering a time for questions, setting the next unit plan, or even choosing the break time), when negotiated in a way that honors all members and their individual perspectives, clears the path for student authenticity. In fact, this emphasis on student voice and the de-centering of the teacher is one of the most important elements of feminist pedagogy and of teaching students how to participate actively in a democratic community. Crabtree and Sapp (2003) state that feminist pedagogy is a complex interaction of ethics, beliefs, and practices that should not allow the teacher to "substitute one authoritarian discourse for another" (p. 132). Therefore, it is in the democratic feminist classroom that students find commonality, struggle with difference, and learn to engage in processes involving community choice and consequence *together*, both with each other and with the teacher.

Aside from providing opportunities for emancipation and autonomy, a classroom based on the principles of feminist pedagogy also requires its members to interrogate issues of injustice and inequity. Given the myriad ways our identities work to promote or deny our full access to society, it is critical that the democratic feminist classroom elevate the voices of those on the margins—which Hyland-Russell and Syrnyk discuss more extensively in Chapter 13. This requires infusing the curricular space with the perspectives and ideas of antiracists, feminists of color, queer feminists, and Marxist feminists.

Consider, for example, the economic disparities related to concerns of gender, class, and race mentioned earlier in this chapter. Incorporating feminist theory into the democratic classroom might require students to study the statistics on current economic trends for women, women of color, and trans women, including but not limited to wages, employment mobility, job security, health benefits provided (or not) by employers, taxation rates, or the possibility to participate in pension plans or labor unions. Doing so will likely reveal stark disparities between individuals based on race, class, gender performance, and perhaps even sexual orientation. Students may begin to see relations between structural racism, heterosexism, and sexism, and how these "isms" affect economic opportunities for people with marginalized identities and therefore influence the economic system as a whole. The evidence of these inequities supports the arguments of Ferber and Nelson (2009) that, like gender, economic practices are social constructs, influenced by the "limitations implicit in human cognition and the social, cultural . . . and political milieu in which [they] have been created" (p. 1).

In this way, students are challenged to expand their conceptions of feminism beyond gender discrimination and begin to see its potential for empowering all identities. We live in a time of social unrest and growing conversations regarding our collective experiences at the intersections of democracy and inequity. These include, among other examples, people of color and state violence, the privatization of public spaces, the continued harassment of LGBTQ youth and adults, the vulnerability of undocumented workers to wage theft and deportation, and the perilously fragile state of economic stability facing an enormous number of American families. Fostering a generation of people who can see and address oppression and liberation at a macroscopic level (with specific emphasis on the ways in which these concepts intersect between marginalized groups), while providing them with the tools to do so efficaciously, would be a powerful force toward reimagining and creating a more equitable society.

Tensions and Solutions

There are, however, particular challenges to creating feminist-imbued democratic spaces. Becoming empowered and taking ownership in the class is risky for teachers and students alike. Fear of what others will think, how one will be perceived, who will respond, and the nature of those responses all limit the honesty that community members are willing to bring into the classroom. Potential problems arise if students resist the methods, dominate the space, or reject the material. These could be particularly difficult hurdles to overcome if students are farther along in their academic careers but have not experienced education as the practice of freedom (Freire, 1970/2005). Many students will not have had the experience of learning in democratic classrooms rooted within a feminist framework and may struggle with the new demands that will be placed on them, not least of which is self-liberation in the face of economic, social, and political inequities.

The negotiations of power between teacher–students and student–teachers (Freire, 1970/2005) could be jarring for some. For those students or teachers who may not want to, or do not think they can, handle a shift in consciousness, these practices could appear threatening to the status quo—which, of course, they are; this perceived threat may also extend to their conceptions of themselves, and to their place in society. The effect of this dysphoria could be more devastating than their potential discomfort—it could result in students' avoidance of classes that use this framework or teachers refusing to provide these classes in the first place. Trust and time are therefore necessities in opening spaces for emancipatory education. Luckily, if intersectional feminist democratic classrooms bring discomfort to the surface, they also hold the key to harnessing powerful emotions in order to advance agendas of justice and equity.

Embracing Discomfort and Emotion

Feminist theory and practices, which value personal experiences in relation to structural inequities, view discomfort, pain, and even anger as useful tools with which to help create environments in which people and their ideas can develop authentically. Often referred to as a pedagogy of discomfort, this framework seeks to reclaim the political, rational, and social roles that affect plays in the educative process (Zembylas, 2014). Boler (1999) argues that emotion, which is generally affixed to the feminine gender, is frequently used as a form of social control in order to reify existing hegemonic structures. She stated that affect has been unfairly contrasted with reason—which has a privileged position in our society. This established binary qualifies emotion, and therefore women, as holding less value than reason and notions of masculinity to which reason is attributed, particularly in academic and professional settings. As a result of this valuation, emotions, as part of the social body, are disparaged as well as policed, thus reifying the dominant values of a patriarchal and instrumentalist culture. When students and teachers cite discomfort as a way to get out of critical conversations about justice and oppression, they are adhering to structural conventions that have conveniently persuaded them to perceive feelings of discomfort as negative, perhaps even harmful (Sheppard et al., 2015). In these moments, feelings of discomfort are often alleviated by ending the conversation at the expense of ending the injustice that prompted the feeling.

Therefore, reclaiming emotion—and the discomfort it can produce—is a necessary aspect of the learning environment, one that is a critical part of the transformative promise of a justice-oriented curriculum (Brooks and Devasahayam, 2011). Practitioners interested in addressing the injustices of society can use this feeling not only to incite action but also to provoke intellectual inquiry on the part of students (Engebretson and Weiss, 2015). The rigorous demands of feminist pedagogy and the pedagogy of discomfort ask students to honor their individual experiences while also requiring them to grapple with broader societal issues of marginalization, privilege, and oppression that they may be either hesitant to explore or even completely oblivious to. Directing student learning to issues of inequity, injustice, privilege, and power through the curriculum is an area where feminist pedagogy is essential to helping ensure that the democratic classroom actualizes its full potential. In order to do this, teachers should bring in conflictual or controversial issues to study (Hess, 2008), without which the democratic community risks superficiality. If members are allowed to voice their opinions, question, and participate in conflictual pedagogy without any conflictual content, the effort is futile (Bickmore, 1993).

Because addressing issues of injustice as well as explicitly discussing personal connections to oppression—particularly gendered oppression—is not part of the state standards or mandated testing that currently drives so much of the curriculum, teachers must find creative ways to use feminist content to achieve the objectives of particular standards and testing requirements. Thankfully, this is not as daunting as it once might have been given current emphases on skills such as critical thinking and connection-making (Bellanca and Brandt, 2010; Trilling and Fadel, 2009). Furthermore, although feminist pedagogy stems from gender injustice, it welcomes multiple manifestations of oppression to become open topics in the classroom (Fisher, 2001). Starting these conversations with students is a primary goal of feminist pedagogy (Crabtree and Sapp, 2003). And, when combined with the structure of the democratic classroom, this approach provides students with the resources necessary to engage effectively in the work of community building, personal growth, societal responsibility, and eventually societal change (Crabtree et al., 2009).

Helping to ensure an environment that is safe enough for students to feel discomfort, express themselves honestly, and approach the process of learning about societal problems and ways to confront them with humility and dedication may be the most important task for any educator. As several authors in this volume have illustrated, the elements of the democratic classroom offer a toolbox from which feminist pedagogy may draw to actualize in the classroom a more responsive, reflective, and proactive approach to democratic education.

The Need to Nurture

Another key challenge with these types of classrooms is that the time necessary to create a nurturing environment, aid in the actualization of the self, build community, and grow a group of individuals into a community that can then transform or transgress the status quo may be prohibitive in some instances. For example, if a class only meets a few times a week for a semester, as is the case in some schools, the potential to see this approach come to fruition is inhibited. Nevertheless, we believe that the insufficiency of time is not a valid excuse for rejecting the combination of democratic classrooms, feminist pedagogy, and discourses of discomfort.

Part of nurturing this stance requires teachers to develop the aptitude to complicate issues with a variety of perspectives from multicultural and social justice education, and to do so without unintentionally reinforcing social and political hierarchies (Ellsworth, 1989; Kumashiro, 2000). Not only must teachers draw increased attention to positive representations of diversity within the curriculum and climate of the school as an important step toward justice and equity; they must also seek to promote intersectional activism inside and outside the school setting. Too often we emphasize helping students feel "empowered" as a means to effect change, but these ideas of empowerment often "fail to challenge any identifiable social or political position, institution, or group" (Ellsworth, 1989, p. 307). Justice frameworks are at their most transformative when they provide students not only with platforms from which to speak but also with concrete, student-identified actions that will be taken to combat oppression(s) that are manifested in their lives and communities.

Turning Affect into Action

Turning now to the intersection of economic justice and gender, students may, for example, decide to use research to investigate discrepancies between the wages of women and men, white women and women of color, or gender-conforming and genderqueer individuals as the foundation for an activist project. This project could evolve into the production of educational materials for their school and communities, which might involve the planning of actions, rallies, or protests of organizations that do not provide fair wages to women workers, the building of intentional coalitions and alliances across organizations, and even creating activist art—which Arend and Cuenca discuss at length in Chapter 12. Each of the three composite elements of democratic education, feminist pedagogy, and pedagogy of discomfort help students to develop and personalize their rationales and their mission and vision, while also providing them with the tools to enact their vision of what is possible as a result of their work towards it.

The potential for success throughout the unit requires: that students' decisions and leadership drive the project from beginning to end; that they have opportunities to interrogate disparities, as well as the hegemonic values and oppressive structures that perpetuate them; and that they have spaces provided for them that nurture their ability to undertake, and work through the discomfort of, projects that are seen as controversial or risky. This is but one example of how to bridge democratic classrooms, feminist pedagogy, and a pedagogy of discomfort on a broad scale. We recognize that teaching according to these considerations in a project is not the same as doing so on a daily basis, which often proves more difficult.

Theory into Practice

Given the concerns of the previous section, the more elusive "how" questions remain the sticking points. How does a teacher blend democratic classrooms, feminist pedagogy, and pedagogies of discomfort? How does a lesson plan look within this framework? And how does that look in a classroom when put into practice? The answer to these questions is at times both liberating and frustrating, in part because this process defies the presentation of a single model to offer to teachers; employing must necessarily be done in context, thus making each manifestation of it unique. Simply put, democratic feminist classrooms will not look the same everywhere. This approach is not a "teacher-proof" curriculum; it demands that the teacher is deeply tapped into the realities of the students, that their concerns and interests drive the curriculum, and that teachers are able to embrace a fluid, "chaordic" classroom environment (see Wright-Maley, 2015). Further, it requires teachers to be connected to the world and the community around the students, and to employ issues of justice that matter deeply in their overlapping social contexts. For those looking for a place to begin, the following entry points offer opportunities to open the space to begin this "dirty" work.

Pedagogical Entry Points

- Share authority with the students by co-constructing the syllabus or assignments.
- Hold regular class meetings where students can bring topics of conversation or concern to the whole group.
- Implement cooperative learning as a norm of the class.
- Weave self- and group reflections into the course and the content.
- Consult students on how to resolve dilemmas or conflicts that arise in the classroom or school. Trust their perspectives.
- Promote gender equality in the classroom in speaking, participation, and leadership roles.
- Position male students and teachers as allies working for the equality of all genders in the classroom community.
- Allow students to share their interests and devote regular time to discussing their concerns about the world.
- Incorporate activism into the curriculum; allow students to design and implement projects that directly and specifically challenge oppression and injustice.
- Resist the belief that student empowerment cannot happen or the fear that teaching differently will fail.

Curricular Entry Points

- Introduce feminist content into the curriculum: critique power relations, study ethnocentrism, investigate the current and past roles of gender-diverse individuals throughout literature, art, history, and contemporary life.
- Highlight gender inequality and the victories toward abolishing it.
- Study the roles and contributions of women throughout history equally to those of men.
- Engage students in discussions of why history texts and trade books are biased toward the contributions of men.
- Choose to teach about intersections of identity for both contemporary and historical people.

- When misconceptions present themselves in your classrooms, engage the students to dig deeper by asking "What do you mean?" and "How do you know?"
- Share annual reports from trusted sources about economic disparities for different genders (as well as those reflecting intersecting identities). Investigate the macro-situation with large statistics and the micro-situation with individual person studies.
- Present students with a global view of economics and the role of women in the global economy. Study microfinance and why women are the target population for it.
- Engage even young children in discussions of economics and oppression by studying the supply chain of an item they are interested in (e.g., "Teaching social issues," 2010).

The combination of feminist pedagogy, pedagogy of discomfort, and democratic classroom environments not only encourages all students' voices to be heard but creates active sites for resisting oppression and imagining conditions beyond the status quo in which all people regardless of their genders or other identities are valued equally. This framework encourages students to develop the capacity for leadership, critical thinking, and radical reflexivity necessary to succeed in their efforts to undertake and realize the justice that would make these conditions manifest in the world. It also asks students to connect various injustices to each other in order to help ensure that one group's liberation does not come at the expense of another's. Failing to attend to issues of gender disparity, particularly in terms of economic opportunities, employment mobility, job protections, and the various "isms" (sexism, racism, classism, etc.) associated with them, supports the endurance of oppression and the stagnation or even regression of gender equity. Teaching for democracy in an age of economic disparity necessitates more than just an attendance to the structures and tools of democracy; it requires a framework within which students can make sense of how and why to use them. The approach we have advanced here offers a potentially powerful way to do so.

References

Badgett, M. V. L., Lau, H., Sears, B., and Ho, D. (2007). *Bias in the workplace: Consistent evidence of sexual orientation and gender identity discrimination*. Retrieved from http://williamsinstitute.law.ucla.edu/wp-content/uploads/Badgett-Sears-Lau-Ho-Bias-in-the-Workplace-Jun-2007.pdf.

Baumgardner, J., and Richards, A. (2000). *Manifesta: Young women, feminism, and the future*. New York: Farrar, Straus and Giroux.

Bellanca, J., and Brandt, R. (Eds.). (2010). *21st century skills: Rethinking how students learn*. Bloomington, IN: Solution Tree Press.

Bickmore, K. (1993). Learning inclusion/inclusion in learning: Citizenship education for a pluralistic society. *Theory and Research in Social Studies Education, 21*(4), 341–384.

Boler, M. (1999). *Feeling power: Emotions and education.* New York: Routledge.

Brooks, A., and Devasahayam, T. (2011). *Gender, emotions, and labour markets: Asian and Western perspectives.* London: Routledge.

Browne, I. (Ed.). (2000). *Latinas and African American women at work: Race, gender, and economic inequality.* New York: Russell Sage.

Bureau of Labor Statistics, U.S. Department of Labor. (2015). How do married parents use their time? Retrieved from http://www.bls.gov/opub/ted/2012/ted_20120829.htm.

Corbett, C., Hill, C., and St. Rose, A. (2008). *Where the girls are: Facts about gender equity in education.* Retrieved from http://www.aauw.org/learn/research/upload/where GirlsAre.pdf.

Crabtree, R. D., and Sapp, D. A. (2003). Theoretical, political, and pedagogical challenges in the feminist classroom: Our struggles to walk the walk. *College Teaching, 51*(4), 131–140.

Crabtree, R. D., Sapp, D. A., and Licona, A. C. (2009). *Feminist pedagogy: Looking back to move forward.* Baltimore, MD: Johns Hopkins University Press.

Crocco, M. S. (2001). The missing discourse about gender and sexuality in the social studies. *Theory into Practice, 40*(1), 65–71.

Davis, A. (1981). *Women, race, and class.* New York: Vintage Books.

Ellsworth, E. (1989). Why doesn't this feel empowering? Working through the repressive myths of critical pedagogy. *Harvard Educational Review, 59*(3), 297–324.

Engebretson, K. E., and Weiss, A. M. (2015). A brave new curriculum: Empowering teachers and students in times of trauma. *Curriculum and Teaching Dialogue, 17*(1), 57–68.

Ferber, M., and Nelson, J. (Eds.). (2009). The social construction of economics and the social construction of gender. *Beyond economic man: Feminist theory and economics.* Chicago, IL: University of Chicago Press.

Fisher, B. M. (2001). *No angel in the classroom: Teaching through feminist discourse.* Lanham, MD: Rowman & Littlefield.

Freeman, S. (2008). *Sex goes to school: Girls and sex education before the 1960s.* Urbana: University of Illinois Press.

Freire, P. (2005). *Pedagogy of the oppressed.* New York: Continuum. (Original work published 1970.)

Gillaspie, L. C., Harrington, M., Van Tassel, F., and Watkins, R. M. (1996). Classrooms as democratic communities. Paper presented at the summer workshop of the Association of Teacher Education, Tarpon Springs, FL.

Hess, D. (2008). Controversial issues and democratic discourse. In L. S. Levstik and C. A. Tyson (Eds.), *Handbook of research in social studies education* (pp. 124–136). New York: Routledge.

hooks, b. (1981). *Ain't I a woman: Black women and feminism.* Cambridge, MA: South End Press.

Ibarra, H., and Hansen, M. T. (2009). Women CEOs: Why so few? [Blog post]. Retrieved from http://blogs.hbr.org/cs/2009/12/women_ceo_why_so_few.html.

Kumashiro, K. (2000). Toward a theory of antioppressive education. *Review of Educational Research, 70*(1), 25–53.

Landau, B. M., and Gathercoal, P. (2000). Creating peaceful classrooms. *Phi Delta Kappan, 81*(6), 450–454.

Levstik, L. S. (2001). Daily acts of ordinary courage: Gender-equitable practice in the social studies classroom. In P. O'Reilly, E. M. Penn, and K. deMarrais (Eds.), *Educating young adolescent girls.* Mahwah, NJ: Lawrence Erlbaum Associates.

Lundeberg, M. (1997). "You guys are over-reacting": Teaching prospective teachers about subtle gender bias. *Journal of Teacher Education, 48*(1), 55–61.

Marri, A. R. (2005). Building a framework for classroom-based multicultural democratic education: Learning from three skilled teachers. *Teachers College Record*, *107*(5), 1036–1059.

Marri, A. R. (2009). Creating citizens: Lessons in relationships, personal growth, and community in one secondary social studies classroom. *Multicultural Perspectives*, *11*(1), 12–18.

Massey, D. S., and Denton, N. A. (1993). *American apartheid: Segregation and the making of the underclass.* Cambridge, MA: Harvard University Press.

North, C. E. (2009). The promise and perils of developing democratic literacy for social justice. *Curriculum Inquiry*, *39*(4), 555–579.

Office of the Clerk. (2015). *Women in Congress: Historical data.* Retrieved from http://womenincongress.house.gov/historical-data/.

Riley, D. (1988). *Am I that name? Feminism and the category of women.* Minneapolis: University of Minnesota Press.

Rusch, E. R., and Marshall, C. (2006). Gender filters and leadership: Plotting a course to equity. *International Journal of Leadership in Education*, *9*(3), 229–250.

Sadker, D. (1999). Gender equity: Still knocking at the classroom door. *Educational Leadership*, *56*(7), 22–26.

Schilt, K., and Wiswall, M. (2008). Before and after: Gender transitions, human capital, and workplace experiences. *B.E. Journal of Economic Analysis and Policy*, *8*(1), 1–26.

Sheppard, M., Katz, D., and Grosland, T. (2015). Conceptualizing emotions in social studies education. *Theory and Research in Social Education*, *43*(2), 147–178.

Shrewsbury, C. M. (1987). What is feminist pedagogy? *Women's Studies Quarterly*, *15*(3/4), 6–14.

"Teaching social issues in elementary school." (2010). Retrieved from http://socialjustice teaching.tumblr.com/post/1613721338/in-this-film-paula-and-her-first-grade-students#notes.

Tienda, M., Donato, K., and Cordero-Guzmán, H. (1992). Schooling, color and the labor force activity of women. *Social Forces*, *71*(2), 365–396.

Titus, J. J. (2000). Engaging student resistance to feminism: "How is this stuff going to make us better teachers?" *Gender and Education*, *12*(1), 21–37.

Tomaskovic-Devey, D. (1993). *Gender and racial inequality at work: The sources and consequences of job segregation.* Ithaca, NY: Cornell University Press.

Trilling, B., and Fadel, C. (2009). *21st century skills: Learning for life in our times.* San Francisco, CA: Jossey-Bass.

U.S. Bureau of Labor Statistics. (2014). *Women in the labor force: A databook.* Retrieved from http://www.bls.gov/opub/reports/cps/women-in-the-labor-force-a-databook-2014.pdf.

U.S. Census Bureau. (2011). *More working women than men have college degrees, Census Bureau reports.* Retrieved from http://www.census.gov/newsroom/releases/archives/education/cb11-72.html.

Webber, M. (2005). "Don't be so feminist": Exploring student resistance to feminist approaches in a Canadian university. *Women's Studies International Forum*, *28*(2–3), 181–194.

WIA Report. (2012). *The large persisting gender gap in faculty posts in higher education.* Retrieved from http://www.wiareport.com/2012/07/the-large-persisting-gender-gap-in-faculty-posts-in-higher-education/.

Wright-Maley, C. (2015). On "stepping back and letting go": The role of control in the success or failure of social studies simulations. *Theory and Research in Social Education*, *43*(2), 206–243.

Zembylas, M. (2014). Theorizing "difficult knowledge" in the aftermath of the "affective turn": Implications for curriculum and pedagogy in handling traumatic representations. *Curriculum Inquiry*, *44*(3), 390–412.

Zong, G., Wilson, A. H., and Quashiga, A. Y. (2008). Global education. In L. S. Levstik and C. A. Tyson (Eds.), *Handbook of research in social studies education* (pp. 197–216). New York: Routledge.

8

LITERACY INSTRUCTION AS A TOOL FOR VIBRANT CIVIC VOICE

Jennifer E. Dolan and Douglas Kaufman

The numbers of socially and economically marginalized students in U.S. classrooms are increasing at an unprecedented pace. Sadker and Zittleman (2013) report that the percentage of children living in poverty in the United States increased from 16.9 percent in 2006 to nearly 22 percent in 2010, and that the percentage of children living in poverty was highest for Blacks (35 percent), American Indians/Alaska Natives (33 percent), and Latino/as (27 percent). In a country founded on a promise of life, liberty, and the pursuit of happiness, social mobility is only a dream. Sharkey (2008) noted, "More than 70% of Black children who are raised in the poorest quarter of American neighborhoods will continue to live in the poorest quarter of neighborhoods as adults" (p. 933). Horace Mann (1848) called education the "the great equalizer," yet "groups that are the most socially and economically disadvantaged have the lowest levels of civic knowledge and engagement, and therefore are also politically disadvantaged" (Wilkenfeld, 2009, p. 1; see also Nichols, Chapter 2). Still, schools can be institutions for promoting change. Berson and Berson (2011) state, "Schools are the most systematically and directly responsible [institutions] for catalyzing civic engagement by facilitating students' skills to mobilize their voices, access resources, and develop innovative solutions for public problems" (p. 6). The teachers in these schools are tasked with the enormous responsibility of engaging and motivating their students to develop strong civic voices, whether or not they yet know how to help their students reach that goal.

As teacher educators in a highly regarded five-year teacher preparation program at the University of Connecticut's Neag School of Education, one of the first questions we ask our preservice teachers is, "What is the purpose of education?" A surprising number answer: "To prepare students to participate in a democratic society." This ideal appears central to many teachers' beliefs, and they hold steadfast to it.

We define civic voice as the ability to participate in the discourses of one's community and society at large, communicating ideas and beliefs effectively in order to create positive social change. Helping children develop their civic voices is a dynamic endeavor, and it is not automatic: it must be nurtured—a position that Engebretson and Hollett take in Chapter 7, as well. Teachers must continually adapt to both the growth and development of individual children and changes in society. Furthermore, teachers must recognize that external factors can specifically inhibit the development of civic voice for socially and economically disadvantaged children. These factors include power differentials within and among the social strata, language differences, lack of education opportunities, and other forms of sociopolitical oppression. We must help our students, especially those who are limited by our social and political system, to oppose and mitigate these barriers to their success. To do so, as teachers, we must first model civic participation by using our own civic voices and then remove obstacles that stand in our students' ways. We must create democratic classroom communities to encourage and develop—even demand—all our students' civic voices through opportunities to participate: voting in class elections, choosing curricular topics, self-evaluating, actively protesting unfair school practices or presenting a case for new ones, and engaging in the larger community outside of the school walls.

As teacher educators who teach a variety of introductory and elementary literacy methods courses, we try to live by these ideals, and we help our elementary preservice teachers recognize the necessity of developing strong literacy skills for communicating effectively as citizens in a democratic society. However, these ideals often differ from reality. In today's public schools, teachers face obstacles that dissuade or prevent them from helping their students to develop strong civic voices (Hursh, 2007; Picower, 2011). Rudimentary demands become their priority, while more complex issues of social justice languish.

In this chapter, we draw on relevant literature and our own experiences as teacher educators to: (1) explore the obstacles preventing new and practicing teachers from promoting students' civic voices; (2) examine how teachers learn about their students; (3) discuss building optimal classroom environments for fostering students' civic voices; and (4) suggest strategies and models of literacy practices that promote students' civic voices.

Obstacles to Students' Civic Voices

A Culture of Standardization

With the advent of the No Child Left Behind Act of 2001 (NCLB) (Library of Congress, 2001) and the subsequent implementation of the Common Core State Standards (CCSS) (National Governors Association Center for Best Practices and Council of Chief State School Officers, 2010) and its corresponding tests—the Smarter Balanced Assessment Consortium (SBAC) and the Partnership for Assessment of Readiness for College and Careers (PARCC, 2015) tests and the competitive grant program entitled Race to the Top (U.S. Department of Education, 2009)—school curricula in almost all states have changed significantly. To meet proficiency standards, many districts have narrowed their curricula, in some cases teaching only test-specific content. Even in districts where a range of subjects is taught, teachers may lack freedom to develop curricula based on their students' needs or interests. Schools in socioeconomically disadvantaged areas, especially, utilize scripted curricula through which teachers act as functionaries, presenting material in the exact same way to every student. As Milner (2014) stated, "teachers are to act as robots rather than professionals" (p. 747). In addition, the rigid program structures serve to alienate, and even deprive, culturally, linguistically, and socioeconomically diverse students. Test preparation pedagogy prevails, creating situations in which students complete test packets or perform practice exercises for hours.

The consequences are enormous. Sacks (1999) stated, "in all its various incarnations, teaching to big-stakes tests has made our children dumber than they would have otherwise been" (p. 125). For example, time for disciplines such as science, social studies, music, art, and physical education—typically not included in standardized testing regimens—has been shortened or cut completely. But it is in these discarded disciplines that marginalized students often reveal their abilities and where their voices are heard most clearly (Au, W., and Temple, 2012; Lomax et al., 1995; Ricci, 2004). Misco (2005) compared the marginalization of social studies through narrowed curricula and increased test preparation—especially in low-performing schools—to the actions of totalitarian states, which "aim for student acceptance of specific attitudes and habits, as well as an awareness of a body of facts that are carefully selected for consumption" (p. 3). It is here that economic disparity plays an oppressive role in schools. As Joseph R. Nichols, Jr. points out in Chapter 2, the focus on standardized testing promulgates economic notions of citizenship while undermining civic-oriented citizenship. In these communities, parent groups often lack the civic efficacy to push back against these forces. This sharply contrasts to the democratic belief that "the *process* of education is exceedingly significant as students must develop the knowledge, skills, and dispositions in ways that perpetuate free, active, and harmonious social life with no definite end, for ends change as a result of new experiences" (Misco, 2005, p. 3, emphasis in original).

A focus on discrete knowledge or skills promotes the assimilation of students to a national standard at the expense of the pluralistic identities and perspectives that constitute essential attributes of a healthy democracy. This is not a new phenomenon. John Dewey (1937) recognized how schools oversimplified our notion of democracy and the apathy this engendered in education:

The trouble . . . is that we have taken democracy for granted; we have thought and acted as if our forefathers had founded it once and for all. We have forgotten that it has to be enacted anew in every generation, in every year and day, in the living relations of person to person in all social forms and institutions. Forgetting this . . . we have been negligent even in creating a school that should be the constant nurse of democracy.

(p. 238)

As we move through the twenty-first century, we must explore democracy with children, recognizing that it is an inherently complex process to promote and nurture democracy in a diverse nation.

Acceptance of a Pedagogy of Poverty

Haberman (1991) asserted that the dumbing down of curricula was not simply a consequence of testing, but a culturally accepted model of pedagogy. Authoritarian norms still exist in many schools serving students of color and students living in poverty. Rather than providing environments where students participate in developing classroom agreements, conduct independent investigations, or get involved in community issues, these schools systematically demand that students must passively receive directions, seatwork, tests, and lectures. Haberman (1991) uses the term "pedagogy of poverty" to describe this system. School curricula that function only to improve marginalized students' test scores, rather than to prepare them to participate fully in society, fail to provide students with the tools to participate in democratic society, and yet schools place the blame on students for this deficiency (pp. 290–291). As Kohn sarcastically charges, "It's how you are *supposed* to teach kids of color" (2013, p. 218). In schools that promote a pedagogy of poverty, teachers take charge while students maintain "appropriate" behavior. Success is measured through student assimilation, passive acquiescence to hegemony, and their silenced civic voices (Haberman, 1991, p. 291).

The pedagogy of poverty is compounded when teachers with good intentions nevertheless fail to see the problem. As classrooms in the United States house increasingly diverse sets of students, the teachers who inhabit them remain over 80 percent White, middle-class, and female (U.S. Department of Education, 2014; Feistritzer, 2011). Preservice teachers look little different and can often revert to deficit theories when engaging with and assessing students with different socioeconomic, linguistic, or cultural backgrounds: "It is imperative that preservice teachers learn how to avoid the tendency to measure a student's world view, thinking, communication, and mode of behavior by their own yardstick that is often based on the values and expectations of the dominant U.S. culture" (Taylor and Sobel, 2001, p. 501). Given this tendency, teacher educators must systematically address issues of culture, race, power, and privilege that complicate and enhance teacher–student relationships. Unfortunately, many teacher education programs may serve to further, rather than ameliorate, the problem, owing to the lack of required multicultural coursework. Commensurately, teacher education faculty may view multicultural education as political rather than educational (Garcia and Pugh, 1992; Sleeter, 2001).

Teacher Education Programs That Promote the Status Quo

In many teacher preparation programs, little, if any, coursework in multiculturalism, human rights, or social democracy occurs before students participate in practicum experiences (Menchaca, 1996; Neumann, 2010). As a consequence, teacher education can reify preservice teachers' preexisting, and often stereotypical, perspectives of people from different backgrounds. In addition, when culturally, linguistically, and economically diverse students engage in many strong literate practices not traditionally affiliated with school, their teachers may not honor these as "academic" practices (Boyd et al., 2006). These literate practices may include movies (Morrell, 2002); new literacies such as IMs, blogs, vlogs, texts, memes, and so on (Coiro et al., 2008); and rap or hip hop (Christianakis, 2011). Preservice coursework must explore the dynamics of cultural identity, and teacher educators must design courses that empower preservice teachers to understand, evaluate, and challenge current educational systems.

As literacy teacher educators, we strive to help preservice teachers grow in multiple ways: to evolve personal philosophies of language arts learning and teaching; to understand, develop, and practice effective instruction; to understand theories of language learning; to understand and practice effective evaluation of literacy growth; to learn to create environments for effective learning; to understand language conventions and mechanics; and to become acquainted with children's literature, to name a few. Noting all of these requirements, there appears to be little room to explore and negotiate positions of power and how to develop voices capable of changing societal structures.

Our preservice teachers want to provide equitable literacy classrooms for their marginalized students, but they rarely know how to begin. Therefore, as literacy teacher educators, we are compelled to incorporate ideals of inclusive learning environments effectively into our courses. As Canestrari and Marlowe (2013) state,

> "New teachers need models of critical reflection (and even dissent) in order to help them develop their own critical questions, their own voice, by being given the opportunity to engage in serious conversations about learning and teaching in the context of increasing pressures for accountability and uniformity of instruction."
>
> *(p. 204)*

Simply providing preservice teachers with multiple methods courses or multiple teaching experiences that "appear to deny the very need for critical thinking" is not acceptable (Giroux, 2013, p. 191). They need opportunities to ask and answer challenging questions, deeply investigate whether "research based practices" are equitable, moral, and inclusive for all of their students, and then know how to advocate for their students, to be "transformative intellectuals" (p. 193). The following sections describe specific steps that we have taken toward this end.

Learning Deeply about Your Students: Transforming from Teacher to Learner

In the classic teacher–student relationship, an inherent power differential can weaken opportunities for students to develop strong civic voices. To foster an environment where students can share their ideas and beliefs and are willing to take action, they must feel safe, valued, and heard. They must also be given many opportunities to develop and practice using their civic voices. Therefore, we must re-envision our own identities, learning how to speak less and listen more.

When teachers recognize their students' diversity as strengths, they begin to incorporate *difference* into the fabric of classroom life. To begin, teachers must learn who their students are—their interests, cultural practices, and social and emotional strengths and needs. There are numerous ways to do this in a literacy classroom, but we find the following to be effective in promoting teacher learning and offering students platforms for developing strong, unique civic voices.

Daily Class Discussions

Freire (2005a) wrote, "If we dream about democracy, let us fight day and night for a school in which we talk to and with the learners so that, hearing them, we could be heard by them as well" (p. 121). However, once teachers enter daily practice, this democratic vision does not often occur in practice. As Peterson (2012) noted, "A lack of reflective dialogue is all too common in American schools. Less than 1% of instructional time in high school is devoted to discussion that requires reasoning, or an opinion from students" (p. 50).

Teachers must create spaces where students can express their perspectives, listen to others, learn how to agree and disagree, and discover what is happening in their communities and the world. We suggest using a problem-posing approach (Freire, 1970/2005b). For example, Lind (2008) advocates for daily "dilemma discussions" (p. 330)—formally scheduled daily discussion times in which students bring in questions or concerns regarding conflicts that arise among them during lunch, at recess, or on the bus; for reflections on current events and community issues; or for discussions of issues such as respect, honesty, inclusion, and bias. Let students struggle with the moral challenge of the dilemma while you offer only necessary support. Allow time for students to develop plans for taking action. These discussions can quickly turn into sophisticated debates about morals, values, and social responsibility.

Mary Cowhey (2006), a well-known social justice educator, tells the story about an invasion of black ants in her kindergarten classroom that was "met by vigorous stomping and a cry of protest [that] engaged every member of the class, within seconds" (p. 12). One student, a Buddhist, believed that no living thing must be hurt. Her students, from many different ethnicities, faiths, and backgrounds, investigated this everyday event, and she led five-year-olds to ponder issues of religion, war, and the power of protest. These discussions may serve as the foundation of a literacy curriculum that promotes civic voice. However, as do Engebretson and Hollett in Chapter 7, we hold that the responsibility for creating environments in which rich discussions arise begins with the teacher.

Surveys and Interviews

Surveys and interviews uncover background information about students, helping teachers to adapt the curriculum to their particular needs, interests, and cultural values, which may ultimately lead to opportunities for students to share authority and take social action (Schultz and Oyler, 2006). Teachers can create many different types of surveys and interviews for their students throughout the year. In our experience, surveys and inventories are living documents that should be accessed, reflected upon, and updated consistently. A few suggestions include developing online surveys for easier access and aggregating data, involving students in survey creation, specifically creating surveys for students' families, and translating surveys into the languages spoken in your classroom. Survey questions may include:

- What kinds of books do you like to read or what kinds of stories do you like to write?
- What else do you like to do outside of school? Hobbies? Collections?
- What is something I should know about you as a learner?
- Tell me about an important tradition you share with your family.
- What do you care about that we could bring into our classroom?
- What is going on in your neighborhood (or the world) that you are passionate about?

Journals

Often called "writer's notebooks" (Fletcher and Portalupi, 2001), "daybooks" (Murray, 1998), or "writers' logs" (Rief, 2014), students' personal journals should be an integral part of a literacy classroom. As students document their observations, experiences, and writing ideas, they again reveal to teachers aspects of their lives. As Penny Kittle (2008) stated, "the notebook is where we mine the world for story. The notebook is where we find our voices" (pp. 25–26).

Students' Free Choice of Reading Books, Writing Topics, and Writing Genres

As a democratically determined array of routines and organization, a literacy workshop approach promotes an environment where students have a greater ability to choose the books they read, the topics they write about, and the genres in which they write (Atwell, 2015; Graves, 1994; Kaufman, 2000). In terms of learning about students, these practices are profoundly revealing. Students' choices directly reflect their interests, experiences, and knowledge. By creating systems in which we document and reflect upon their choices over time, we develop a database that allows us to learn much more about their multifaceted identities. More importantly, when we give individuals the power to choose what they read and write, they engage with literacy deeply and feel legitimized when they share their perspectives with others; and ultimately they develop their voices (Atwell, 2015; Graves, 1983; Rief, 2014).

Reading and Writing Conferences

Another component of a workshop is the conference, an event that occurs while the class engages in daily independent reading and writing. The teacher interacts with individual students to help them solve identified problems and take advantage of reading and writing strengths. "As teachers in a workshop, we want children to find their voices. . . . When teachers are conferring with students and giving them feedback about their writing it is important that they listen for student voice and hear what the writer has to say" (Mulcahy, 2010, p. 41). Listening carefully and taking extensive notes, we learn even more about children through the ways that they express themselves, the particular problems that they pose, their topics of conversation, the knowledge that they display, and the social and cultural values that they share.

Building an Optimal Learning Community

The Importance of Community in Nurturing Civic Voices

We have offered a number of ways that literacy teachers can begin to learn deeply about their students. In order to help students take advantage of the resources that they bring with them to school, teachers must then create communities that leverage them. In this section we address how the physical environment and the curriculum, among other conditions, either support or limit students' sense of safety, levels of engagement, and, ultimately, their development of civic voices.

A primary reason that teachers must learn about their students is that it is the first step in creating a community that fosters children's civic voices. A community is sometimes defined by the *similarities* of its members. However, we look at a classroom community as driven by the unity found in celebrating and taking advantage of the *differences* in children's interests, abilities, cultural backgrounds, languages, identities, and experiences. For children to develop independent civic voices, each needs to feel personal ownership of the classroom. Ownership may be expressed through participation in democratic practices such as co-creating classroom constitutions, sharing responsibilities for determining curricular content, or making independent decisions over activities.

Create an Environment That Supports Communication and Represents Students

What is on your classroom's walls and on your bookshelves? How does it support students' ability to communicate? Often, what teachers display can unintentionally stifle students' voices. Classrooms adorned with commercial messages touting how hard work alone leads to achievement can send the opposite message. Kohn (2010) argues: "Rather than being invited to consider the existence of structural barriers and pronounced disparities in resources and opportunities, we're fed the line that there are no limits to what each of us can accomplish on our own if we just buckle down" (p. 4). Instead of displaying materials created by corporations with no situational knowledge, classrooms should reflect the cultural, emotional, and intellectual perspectives of the students who occupy them.

Represent Children's Lives on the Walls

Classroom walls are wide spaces full of potential. Gay (2002) calls displays that fill these spaces the "symbolic curriculum," which includes images, symbols, icons, mottos, and awards (p. 108). Children should decorate the walls with artifacts that reflect and celebrate their multicultural, multifaceted identities. The walls become a public gallery where students notice both surprising connections among themselves and brand new points of view. As the year moves forward and children gain new understandings and develop stronger voices through writing, reading, and discussion, teachers and students can add to the gallery or regularly rotate through new exhibitions.

Create Seating Arrangements That Promote Communication

To develop civic voices, students must have the opportunity to speak. Therefore, the classroom design should be flexible enough to create various configurations for communication and collaboration for students in pairs, in small groups, in large groups, and as a whole class. Au (2007) wrote: "The goal of using a variety of groupings is to create a classroom in which every student can comfortably participate at least part of the time" (p. 14). This is a necessary step to nurturing the "practices [that] are rarely seen in classrooms with students of diverse backgrounds" (p. 15), but that developed the civic voices of those who are socially and economically disadvantaged. Students should have space to stand together to work on projects that require physical activity, and spaces where they can sit together to listen to stories, be read to, or share and discuss their work. Seating arrangements may not seem particularly relevant to promoting students' civic voices, yet easy access to rich communication is crucial, especially for children learning English and children with disabilities (Lucas et al., 2008; Morocco and Hindin, 2002). Collective discourse demands that students negotiate, support, listen, consider, and compromise.

Create Classroom Libraries That Speak to Children

Classroom libraries should reflect the students' multifaceted identities. When teachers know their students' identities, they can then directly acknowledge them by adding new texts. Classroom libraries should represent a wide variety of countries, cultures, and languages, as well as many political, social, family diversity, and life challenge topics. Texts should not only mirror children's experiences and identities, but also provide windows to new perspectives. As classrooms change, they present opportunities to partner with students in a critical and reciprocal selection process (see Meller and Hatch, 2008 for suggestions how to choose critical literacy texts).

Models of Literacy Practices That Promote Students' Civic Voices

Literacy Curricula That Include Students' Lives

Owing to the increased emphasis on standardized testing, civics education and social studies curricula have been increasingly either relegated to part-time status or absorbed into the literacy curriculum (Bolick et al., 2010; Boyle-Baise et al., 2008; Fitchett and Heafner, 2010; Levine et al., 2008). In response, teachers must develop a rich literacy curriculum drawn from students' own lives, as well as from local and global communities. By being responsive to students' interests, identities, and experiences, we enable their voices to drive the curriculum, rather than using the curriculum to dictate what standardized content receives their attention. Banks's (2006) multicultural education framework demands that a curriculum address both *knowledge construction* and *equity pedagogy*. *Knowledge construction* is defined as how teachers help students understand, investigate, and determine the implicit cultural assumptions, frames of reference, and perspectives of the discipline taught. For instance, one of the authors, Jennifer E. Dolan, launched a Literacy through Photography initiative (see https://literacythroughphotography.wordpress.com/wendy-ewald/), supplying fifth graders with cameras to photograph the people, places, and things meaningful to their lives;

they then used the images to create personal narratives. In the process, social studies, science, and literacy were interwoven, providing students with a forum for speaking about their out-of-school lives, questioning their view through their lenses, and expressing their vision to a wide audience.

Equity pedagogy arises from the teaching strategies and classroom environments that help students from diverse cultural backgrounds attain the knowledge, skills, and attitudes necessary to participate and thrive within a just and humane democratic society (Banks, 2006, p. 34). In response to this challenge, Jennifer E. Dolan launched a school-wide celebration of the International Day of Peace (see http://internationaldayofpeace.org), through which her students connected with fifth graders in Bogotá, Colombia. Partnering on literacy and art projects to share their ideas for peace, students expanded their conceptions of the world and their roles within it, and gave voice to their beliefs.

A good curriculum is responsive, continually adapted "in order to contextualize issues within race, class, ethnicity, and gender, and include multiple kinds of knowledge and perspectives" (Gay, 2002, p. 108). Teachers must examine content, searching to find points of both connection and disconnection with their students' lives. Ask: "How will students who are different than me receive this material?" "Does this leverage or ignore their particular cultural histories?" "What content arising from students' lives can be incorporated?" "How can I adapt my current curriculum to meet students' needs?"

Begin with students' home literacy practices. Encourage students to: read and write in their first languages; speak in their home vernaculars, such as African American Vernacular English (AAVE); and integrate new literacies such as texting, memes, blogs, vlogs, and fanfiction. When teachers engage in these practices, they lay the foundation for curricula that draw from many disciplines. For example, in Morrell's (2002) study of popular culture texts, students watched the movie *A Time to Kill* and "discussed justice in the context of the lives of Wright's Bigger Thomas and Schumaker's Carl Lee Hailey." They "examined their own school for examples of injustice" and "creat[ed] a magazine that depicted the injustices they experienced as students at an underresourced urban school" (p. 75). An integrated instructional approach promotes the inclusion of multiple subject areas, helps students make important connections across different disciplines, and offers students opportunities to use their civic voices.

Time to Communicate and Make Meaning

Students must have more time to read, write, and speak, which the literacy workshop approach provides. The independent reading and writing choices that children make turn instruction on its head as students become co-responsible for course content. A workshop eschews long sessions of teacher content delivery in favor of time for students' independent exploration. A classic workshop session begins with a targeted mini-lesson (Calkins, 1994) lasting from only 5 to 15 minutes. This reduces the teacher–student power differential and allows more time for authentic practice, as students work independently. Students also have more time to process and voice their views during conferences with one another and the teacher. Consistent attention to these conversational skills gives students the impetus to use their voices beyond that space. However, we believe that simply giving students the power to turn and talk does not automatically result in the development of civic voices. The literacy environment must encourage and teach children to advocate for themselves and others, and engage with their peers about important issues that impact their daily lives, their community, and the world.

Support Students in Confronting Difficult Social Justice and Equity Issues

Literacy work that involves engaging in social responsibility can deeply trouble teachers with limited coursework in critical pedagogy or personal experience in multicultural communities. Teachers may question the power, right, or responsibility they have to introduce issues of social and cultural importance, particularly when it upsets the status quo. In Chapter 7, Engebretson and Hollett describe the importance of engaging students in a pedagogy of discomfort. Teachers, therefore, need to see this approach in practice during their training. Preservice teachers today who have grown up in the standardized school era may find using their own voices to be difficult, or they may push back against the introduction of relevant social issues into the curriculum. For instance, when teaching critical literacy through picture books in one of our literacy courses, we shared titles such as *The Giving Tree* (Silverstein, 1964), *And Tango Makes Three* (Richardson et al., 2005), and *Wings* (Myers, 2000). Although many of our students were open to viewing texts through alternate lenses, others had difficulty seeing their childhood favorites in negative lights (e.g., *The Giving Tree* could be about an imbalance of power in relationships), or they abdicated their power to act as transformative intellectuals (Giroux, 2013), expressing fears about parent refusals or district bans to the texts they wished to use. Phillips and Larson (2011) similarly found that their preservice teachers ceded their decision-making power to these other groups when introduced to *And Tango Makes Three*.

When teachers silence their own voices by avoiding topics or issues deemed taboo by privileged majorities, they directly silence their students' voices, in particular those from historically marginalized groups (Evans et al., 1999). Therefore, we attempt to empower the teachers with whom we work by having them critically analyze their own beliefs, perspectives, and definitions of literacy. They must explore counter-narratives that challenge the master narratives that are "directed by advantaging dominant groups and disadvantaging members of marginalized groups such as women and people of color" (Berry et al., 2011, p. 11).

Counter-narratives question the traditional, hegemonic structure of schools, classroom hierarchies, and discourses. Teachers must find counter-narratives (Chang, 2013; Milner, 2008) through the types of texts that they offer, how they create and implement the curriculum, and how they share democratic roles with students. In our courses, we problematize discourse by publicly scrutinizing our curricular materials, just as we ask our preservice teachers to scrutinize the materials in their classrooms. For instance, we have deconstructed reading anthologies and content area textbooks, discovering how often they portray diverse students in stereotyped ways—or neglect to include their voices at all. For example, our preservice teachers uncovered a fifth grade social studies text that directly stated the falsehood "Connecticut did not have many slaves" (Ifkovik, 2002, p. 71)—one of the only sentences in the entire chapter referencing the African American experience (Dolan and Colwell, 2014). Recently, a Texas high school student and his mother became social media sensations when they discovered the same troubling issues within a high school textbook, which called African Americans kidnapped and brought to the US between 1500 and 1800 "'workers' rather than slaves" (Fernandez and Houser, 2015).

As educators, we will only be able to nurture others when more of us engage with civic issues and seek out knowledge about democratic processes, cultural foundations, and issues of social justice and equity. To quote Huse (2008), "We must infect students with enthusiasm for knowledge and civic responsibility; which calls upon us to become more inspired ourselves, particularly on the occasions when we wish to turn students' attention to areas in our democracy's evolution where critical evaluation and change is necessary" (p. 344).

Helping students gain powerful civic voices can be a process for teachers who have rarely used their own. Winfield (2013) gives a number of suggestions for teachers who wish to learn how to do so in order to challenge the status quo and be transformative in their teaching:

- Read often and deeply.
- Expose yourselves to art, music, theatre, politics, and literature.
- Seek out a variety of sources for news.
- When you are unsure about what to do, put your students' needs first.
- Interact, examine, explore, compare, and critique with your colleagues as much as possible.
- Never lose sight of the big picture; context is necessary—ask difficult questions.

(pp. 246–247)

The Ultimate Goal: Sharing rather than Seeking Power

When children develop civic voices, they gain power, and there is an inherent tension in this relationship. It can arise in those who have power and are afraid to lose it, and in those without power who are unsure what to do once they gain it. Tensions arise in teachers who equate shared power in a classroom with loss of control. Studies have shown that a primary concern of preservice and new teachers is behavior management (Jackson et al., 2013; Kaufman and Moss, 2010; Veenman, 1984). We believe that student protests—often disguised as unproductive behaviors—actually arise from power*less* students in their classroom communities. Irwin (1996) describes two classroom power scenarios: (a) "*power over*"; and (b) "*power to/power with*" (p. 344). *Power over* relationships occur when the teacher is the keeper of knowledge, imparting wisdom and control. In *power to/power with* relationships, teachers and students share classroom responsibility. In a *power over* model, students fight to gain brief moments of control, often manifested in refusals to do work or breaking "rules." We contend that negative behavior is symptomatic of underlying issues; it is a call from students attempting to use their civic voices, albeit in misdirected or misunderstood ways. Instead of rushing to punish students, teachers must instead seek to uncover students' motivations. Consistently ask: "Do students feel safe and valued? Is the curriculum engaging and tied to their particular backgrounds and interests? Are organizational systems and routines in place to allow all students to work independently and effectively? How well do I know my students? How can I help my students develop and use their voices to contribute to society, fight injustices, and improve the quality of their lives and the lives of others?" Martin Luther King, Jr. articulated, "faith is taking the first step even when you don't see the whole staircase" (King Center, 2013). When we ask and act upon questions that promote power to/power with relationships and help our students develop effective civic voices, we take the first step together toward engaging as stewards of democracy and equity.

References

Atwell, N. (2015). *In the middle: A lifetime of learning about writing, reading, and adolescents.* Portsmouth, NH: Heinemann.

Au, K. H. (2007). Culturally responsive instruction: Application to multiethnic classrooms. *Pedagogies: An International Journal, 2*(1), 1–18.

Au, W., and Tempel, M. (2012). *Pencils down: Rethinking high-stakes testing and accountability in public schools.* Milwaukee, WI: Rethinking Schools.

Banks, J. A. (2006). *Cultural diversity and education: Foundations, curriculum, and teaching* (5th ed.). Boston, MA: Allyn & Bacon.

Berry, R., Thunder, K., and McClain, O. (2011). Counter narratives: Examining the mathematics and racial identities of Black boys who are successful with mathematics. *Journal of African-American Males in Education, 2*(1), 10–23.

Berson, I., and Berson, M. (2011). *Civic education as a poverty reduction strategy: A conceptual overview.* National Social Studies Supervisors Association. Retrieved from http://loufreyinstitute.org/uploads/2011/12/NSSSA-Leader-2011-Berson-Berson.pdf.

Bolick, C. M., Adams, R., and Willox, L. (2010). The marginalization of elementary social studies in teacher education. *Social Studies Research and Practice, 5*(1), 1–22. Retrieved from http://www.socstrp.org/issues/PDF/5.2.3.pdf.

Boyd, F., Ariail, M., Williams, R., Jocson, K., Sachs, G., and McNeal, K., with Fecho, B., Fisher, M., Healy, M., Meyer, T., and Morrell, E. (2006). Real teaching for real diversity: Preparing English language arts teachers for 21st-century classrooms. *English Education, 38*(4), 329–350.

Boyle-Baise, M., Hsu, M., Johnnson, S., Serriere, S. C., and Stewart, D. (2008). Putting reading first: Teaching social studies in elementary classrooms. *Theory and Research in Social Education, 36*(3), 233–255.

Calkins, L. M. (1994). *The art of teaching writing* (2nd ed.). Portsmouth, NH: Heinemann.

Canestrari, A., and Marlowe, B. (Eds.). (2013). *Educational foundations: An anthology of critical readings.* Thousand Oaks, CA: Sage.

Chang, B. (2013). Voice of the voiceless? Multiethnic student voices in critical approaches to race, pedagogy, literacy and agency. *Linguistics and Education, 24*(3), 348–360.

Christianakis, M. (2011). Hybrid texts: Fifth graders, rap music and writing. *Urban Education, 46*(5), 1131–1168.

Coiro, J., Knobel, M., Lankshear, C., and Leu, D. J. (Eds.). (2008). *Handbook of research in new literacies.* Mahwah, NJ: Lawrence Erlbaum Associates.

Cowhey, M. (2006). *Black ants and Buddhists: Thinking critically and teaching differently in the primary grades.* Portland, ME: Stenhouse.

Dewey, J. (1937). Education and social change. *Teachers College Record, 3*(26), 235–238.

Dolan, J., and Colwell, R. (2013). Zooming in: Close reading through critical questioning. Presented at the Connecticut Reading Association conference, Cromwell, CT.

Evans, R. W., Avery, P. G., and Pederson, P. V. (1999). Taboo topics: Cultural restraint on teaching social issues. *Social Studies, 90*(5), 218–224.

Feistritzer, C. (2011). *Profile of teachers in the U.S. 2011.* Washington, DC: National Center for Education Information. Retrieved from http://www.edweek.org/media/pot2011final-blog.pdf.

Fernandez, M., and Houser, C. (2015, October 5). Texas mother teaches textbook company a lesson on accuracy. *New York Times.* Retrieved from http://www.nytimes.com/2015/10/06/us/publisher-promises-revisions-after-textbook-refers-to-african-slaves-as-workers.html?_r=0.

Fitchett, P. G., and Heafner, T. L. (2010). A national perspective on the effects of high-stakes testing and standardization on elementary social studies marginalization. *Theory and Research in Social Education, 38*(1), 114–130.

Fletcher, R., and Portalupi, J. (2001). *Writing workshop: The essential guide.* Portsmouth, NH: Heinemann.

Freire, P. (2005a). *Teachers as cultural workers: Letters to those who dare teach.* Boulder, CO: Westview Press.

Freire, P. (2005b). *Pedagogy of the oppressed.* New York: Continuum. (Original work published 1970.)

Garcia, J., and Pugh, S. (1992). Multicultural education in teacher preparation programs: A political or an educational concept? *Phi Delta Kappan, 74*(3), 214–219.

Gay, G. (2002). Preparing for culturally responsive teaching. *Journal of Teacher Education, 53*(2), 106–116.

Giroux, H. A. (2013). Teachers as transformative intellectuals. In A. Canestrari and B. Marlowe (Eds.), *Educational foundations: An anthology of critical readings* (pp. 189–198). Thousand Oaks, CA: Sage.

Graves, D. H. (1983). *Writing: Teachers and children at work.* Portsmouth, NH: Heinemann.

Graves, D. H. (1994). *A fresh look at writing.* Portsmouth, NH: Heinemann.

Haberman, M. (1991). The pedagogy of poverty vs. good teaching. *Phi Delta Kappan*, *73*(4), 290–294.

Hursh, D. (2007). Assessing No Child Left Behind and the rise of neoliberal education policies. *American Educational Research Journal*, *44*(3), 493–518.

Huse, H. (2008). Don't teach me what I don't know: Fostering democratic literacy. In D. Lund and P. Carr (Eds.), *Doing democracy: Striving for political literacy and social justice* (pp. 337–350). New York: Peter Lang.

Ifkovik, J. W. (2002). *The Connecticut adventure*. Salt Lake City, UT: Gibbs-Smith.

Irwin, J. (1996). *Empowering ourselves and transforming schools: Educators making a difference.* Albany, NY: SUNY Press.

Jackson, C., Simoncini, K., and Davidson, M. (2013). Classroom profiling training: Preservice teachers' confidence and knowledge of classroom management skills. *Australian Journal of Teacher Education*, *38*(8), 30–46.

Kaufman, D. (2000). *Conferences and conversations: Listening to the literate classroom.* Portsmouth, NH: Heinemann.

Kaufman, D., and Moss, D. M. (2010). A new look at preservice teachers' conceptions of classroom management and organization: Uncovering complexity and dissonance. *Teacher Educator*, *45*(2), 118–136.

King Center. (2013). MLK quote of the week. Retrieved from http://www.theking center.org/blog/mlk-quote-week-faith-taking-first-step.

Kittle, P. (2008). *Write beside them: Risk, voice and clarity in high school writing*. Portsmouth, NH: Heinemann.

Kohn, A. (2010). Bad signs. *Kappa Delta Pi Record*, *47*(1), 4–9.

Kohn, A. (2013). Poor teaching for poor children . . . in the name of reform. In A. Canestrari and B. Marlowe (Eds.), *Educational foundations: An anthology of critical readings* (pp. 217–221). Thousand Oaks, CA: Sage.

Levine, P., Lopez, M. H., and Marcelo, K. B. (2008). *Getting narrower at the base: The American curriculum after NCLB*. Medford, MA: Center for Information and Research on Civic Learning and Engagement.

Library of Congress. (2001). H.R.1: No Child Left Behind Act of 2001. 107th Congress 2001–2002. Retrieved from https://www.congress.gov/bill/107th-congress/house-bill/1.

Lind, G. (2008). Teaching students to speak up and listen to others: Fostering moral democratic competencies. In D. Lund and P. Carr (Eds.), *Doing democracy: Striving for political literacy and social justice* (pp. 319–335). New York: Peter Lang.

Lomax, R., West, M., Harmon, M., Viator, K., and Madaus, G. (1995). The impact of mandated standardized testing on minority students. *Journal of Negro Education*, *64*(2), 171–185.

Lucas, T., Villegas, A. M., and Freedson-Gonzalez, M. (2008). Linguistically responsive teacher education: Preparing classroom teachers to teach English language learners. *Journal of Teacher Education*, *59*(4), 361–373.

Mann, H. (1848). Twelfth annual report of Horace Mann as secretary of Massachusetts State Board of Education. Retrieved from http://usa.usembassy.de/etexts/democrac/16.htm.

Meller, W., and Hatch, J. A. (2008). Introductory critical literacy practices for urban preservice teachers. *New Educator*, *4*(4), 330–348.

Menchaca, V. (1996). Multicultural education: The missing link in teacher education programs. *Journal of Educational Issues of Language Minority Students*, *17*, 1–8.

Milner, H. (2008). Disrupting deficit notions of difference: Counter narratives of teachers and community in teacher education. *Teaching and Teacher Education, 24*(6), 1573–1588.

Milner, H. (2014). Scripted and narrowed curriculum reform in urban schools. *Urban Education, 49*(7), 743–749.

Misco, T. (2005). In response to NCLB: A case for retaining the social studies. Retrieved from http://www.usca.edu/essays/vol152005/misco.pdf.

Morocco, C. C., and Hindin, A. (2002). The role of conversation in a thematic understanding of literature. *Learning Disabilities Research and Practice, 17*(3), 144–159.

Morrell, E. (2002). Toward a critical pedagogy of popular culture: Literacy development among urban youth. *Journal of Adolescent and Adult Literacy, 46*(1), 72–77.

Mulcahy, C. (2010). *Marginalized literacies: Critical literacy in the language arts classroom.* Charlotte, NC: Information Age.

Murray, D. (1998). *Write to learn.* Philadelphia, PA: Harcourt Brace College.

Myers, C. (2000). *Wings.* New York: Scholastic Press.

National Governors Association Center for Best Practices and Council of Chief State School Officers. (2010). *Common Core State Standards.* Washington, DC: National Governors Association Center for Best Practices and Council of Chief State School Officers.

Neumann, R. (2010). Social foundations and multicultural education course requirements in teacher preparation programs in the United States. *Educational Foundations, 24*(3–4), 3–17.

Partnership for Assessment of Readiness for College and Careers (PARCC). (2015). Retrieved from http://www.parcconline.org/.

Peterson, B. (2012). Teaching for social justice: One teacher's journey. In L. Christensen, M. Hansen, B. Peterson, E. Schlessman, and D. Watson (Eds.), *Rethinking elementary education* (pp. 49–56). Milwaukee, WI: Rethinking Schools.

Phillips, D., and Larson, M. (2011). Preservice teachers respond to *And Tango makes three*: Deconstructing disciplinary power and the heteronormative in teacher education. *Gender and Education, 24*(2), 159–175.

Picower, B. (2011). Resisting compliance: Learning to teach for social justice in a neoliberal context. *Teachers College Record, 113*(5), 1105–1134.

Ricci, C. (2004). The case against standardized testing and the call for a revitalization of democracy. *Review of Education, Pedagogy, and Cultural Studies, 26*(4), 339–361.

Richardson, J., Parnell, P., and Cole, H. (2005). *And Tango makes three.* New York: Simon & Schuster.

Rief, L. (2014). *Read write teach: Choice and challenge in the reading writing workshop.* Portsmouth, NH: Heinemann.

Sacks, P. (1999). *Standardized minds: The high price of America's testing culture and what we can do to change it.* New York: Da Capo Press.

Sadker, D., and Zittleman, K. (2013). *Teachers, schools and society.* New York: McGraw-Hill.

Schultz, B. D., and Oyler, C. (2006). We make this road as we walk together: Sharing teacher authority in a social action curriculum project. *Curriculum Inquiry, 36*(4), 423–451.

Sharkey, P. (2008). The intergenerational transmission of context. *American Journal of Sociology, 113*(4), 931–969.

Silverstein, S. (1964). *The giving tree.* New York: Harper & Row.

Sleeter, C. (2001). Preparing teachers for culturally diverse schools: Research and the overwhelming presence of Whiteness. *Journal of Teacher Education, 52*(2), 94–106.

Taylor, S., and Sobel, D. (2001). Addressing the discontinuity of students' and teachers' diversity: A preliminary study of preservice teachers' beliefs and perceived skills. *Teaching and Teacher Education, 17*(4), 487–503.

U.S. Department of Education. (2009). *Race to the Top program: Executive summary.* Washington, DC: U.S. Department of Education. Retrieved from https://www2. ed.gov/programs/racetothetop/executive-summary.pdf.

U.S. Department of Education. (2014). Achievement gaps. *National Assessment of Educational Progress (NAEP).* Retrieved from https://nces.ed.gov/nationsreportcard/studies/gaps/.

Veenman, S. (1984). Perceived problems of beginning teachers. *Review of Educational Research, 54*(2), 143–178.

Wilkenfeld, B. (2009). *Does context matter? How the family, peer, school, and neighborhood contexts relate to adolescents' civic engagement* (Working paper no. 64). Medford, MA: Center for Information and Research on Civic Learning and Engagement. Retrieved from http://www.civicyouth.org/PopUps/WorkingPapers/WP64Wilkenfeld.pdf.

Winfield, A. (2013). The quest: Achieving ideological escape velocity—becoming an activist teacher. In A. Canestrari and B. Marlowe (Eds.), *Educational foundations: An anthology of critical readings* (pp. 245–249). Thousand Oaks, CA: Sage.

9

EMPOWERING PRAXIS IN OUR YOUNGEST CITIZENS

An Instructional Framework for Helping Elementary School Students Explore and Respond to Contemporary Social Issues

Ryan Colwell

In their report *America's Youngest Outcasts* (2014), the National Center on Family Homelessness calculated that nearly 2.5 million children experienced homelessness in the United States in 2013, while approximately 1.2 million homeless children in the U.S. attended public schools. Although homelessness is just one of many social issues in our world today that directly impacts the lives of the students who enter our classrooms, it is a prominent expression of economic disparity. As with most social issues, studying homelessness is controversial in that individuals and groups of people have different understandings and opinions about it (Carrington and Troyna, 1988). In addition, social issues are inherently complex and challenging. They lack a universally accepted solution or a simple one-size-fits-all response.

Since social issues directly and dramatically affect students' lives, it makes sense for students and teachers to address them in the classroom, beginning as early as the elementary grades. However, elementary school teachers may be reluctant to include such issues in their classrooms. Some teachers indicate a lack of confidence in their own background knowledge or abilities to teach about social issues, particularly those that are politically charged (Harwood, 1985). Teachers' resistance to tackling social issues with their students may also stem from a belief that young children are not developmentally ready for them. James (2008) discovered that preservice teachers employ a "discourse of protection" as part of their rationale for avoiding historically controversial issues in elementary classrooms (p. 191). These teachers claim that they are "protecting the innocence" of children who are not old enough to discuss and critically analyze concepts that could potentially be upsetting to them (p. 189).

Conversely, there are also a number of educators who believe that it is essential for elementary school teachers to help young students critically examine the social issues that surround them (Cowhey, 2006; Vasquez, 2004). Jeffs (1988) wrote: "If we seriously wish to prepare young people for a future role as a 'moral citizen' (White, 1977), or as a politically aware elector, then it is essential that the social and educational groundwork needs to commence in the primary school" (p. 39). Dulberg (2005) argued that to assume that elementary children must reach a certain stage of cognitive development before being introduced to complex and controversial issues is to misunderstand their capabilities. She noted that, when teachers provide developmentally appropriate scaffolding in their lessons, even our youngest students can engage with and think critically about important historical and contemporary social issues.

In order to feel more comfortable and confident about exploring social issues with young students, elementary school teachers could benefit from an instructional framework to guide their teaching. Grounded in the tenets of problem-posing education and building on Freire's (1970/2005, 1973, 1998) notions of conscientization, dialogue, and praxis, this chapter proposes one such instructional framework: one that empowers elementary school teachers and their youngest student-citizens to work together to critically evaluate and respond to contemporary social issues that exist in the world around them.

Freire's Critical Pedagogy

Banking versus Problem-Posing Education

In Paulo Freire's *Pedagogy of the Oppressed* (1970/2005), Freire railed against what he referred to as the banking model of education. In this model, teachers serve as all-knowing experts who make deposits of cultural information into the minds of passive, receptive young children. Meanwhile, students—who are considered to know nothing—are expected to listen and allow themselves to be "filled" with knowledge (p. 72). Their task is to store these deposits of information in order to ultimately recall and repeat them back on demand. Freire noted that in a banking model "the teacher is the Subject of the learning process, while the pupils are mere objects" (p. 73). He argued that banking classrooms are mechanical rather than creative, and that transmission of knowledge through teacher monologues silences students' voices and discounts their personal backgrounds and experiences.

In contrast to this banking approach to education, Freire (1970/2005) advocated for a problem-posing educational model, one where teachers present students with authentic problems related to their own lives and their experiences in the world, and then encourage and empower them to respond to those problems. Teachers in problem-posing classrooms are not responsible for transmitting knowledge to their students. Instead, they pursue knowledge alongside their students, through collaborative inquiry into the world and its challenges. Unlike the banking approach, in which teachers do the thinking for their students, problem-posing education challenges students to think critically and creatively in order to investigate and address the realities of their world. Students' backgrounds and their experiences serve as sources of knowledge, and their voices are valued as part of the ongoing classroom dialogue.

Conscientization through Dialogue Leads to Praxis

Freire argued that, when students engage in problem-posing education, they undergo a process of conscientization (Freire, 1988, 1998). This occurs when students develop an increased awareness of the social, economic, and political problems that impact their everyday lives. As students name these problems, describe them, and relate them to their own personal experiences, they unveil the conflicting realities of the world in which they live. Rather than viewing the world as static, and people's lives as predestined, students begin to recognize that the world is in a process of ongoing development, and that individuals are not required to fatalistically accept the hands they are dealt in life. This realization leads students to an understanding that they can—and should—play an active role in transforming their world and shaping its future. Students have a choice between passively accepting their reality—allowing it to be determined by others—and intervening in it to address social, economic, and political disparities and injustices.

Students achieve conscientization through the dialogue that they engage in, both inside and outside of the classroom (Taylor, 1993). Of consequence to students' own efforts is the way or ways in which teachers approach their teaching; their practices can serve as bridges or barriers to students' progress toward conscientization. In banking model classrooms, students' voices are silenced; they defer to the expertise of the teacher. Conversely, in problem-posing classrooms, dialogue between teachers and students, inquiry, and knowledge construction give voice to students (Freire, 1970/2005). In order for students to gain a greater awareness of the social, economic, and political problems that impact their everyday lives, they need opportunities to discuss their own personal experiences, hear about the experiences of classmates, and share knowledge that they have gained through research. Teachers and students may also have to reach beyond the walls of their classrooms and schools, extending their dialogue to include the voices of others who are experiencing problems or forms of injustice. True dialogue doesn't involve the imposing of any one specific viewpoint; rather, it critically considers multiple viewpoints and perspectives to enrich understanding. Dialogue, according to Freire (1970/2005), must be realistic, hopeful, and trusting, occurring in the context of love for the world and its people.

Conscientization emerges for students as they engage in dialogue, but ultimately the process of conscientization may lead students to take concrete actions, which represent Freire's notion of praxis. Praxis involves students producing and acting upon their own ideas in order to transform the world. Rather than assuming the roles of immobile spectators, students can propose and take action to address the social, economic, and political disparities and injustices that they have identified in the world around them.

Challenges of Implementing Freirean Pedagogy

Freire's colleagues and contemporaries have analyzed his pedagogical approach, identifying some of the challenges of implementing Freirean pedagogy in schools and classrooms. Morrow and Torres (2002) argue that many students are not used to problem-posing, dialogic learning environments, in which they are asked to analyze and offer solutions to real-world challenges. Additionally, Freirean pedagogy requires a fundamental shift in the control and development of curricular content. In standards-based educational systems, the curriculum is often directed from the top down, with school districts developing or adopting curricular content based on local, state, and national standards or high-stakes tests. As part of problem-posing education, Freire advocated for a bottom-up approach to curriculum development, in which teachers and students uncover curricular content as they critically engage with the world and with one another.

Educators also face the challenge of envisioning what Freirean pedagogy could and should look like in traditional classroom settings. Few accounts exist to provide classroom teachers with the pedagogical direction necessary to move themselves and their students from critical thought to critical practice (McLaren, 2000; McLaren and Leonard, 1993). So, while Freire argued that the process of conscientization could lead students to engage in revolutionary action with regard to the inequities and injustices in society, they are unlikely to do so without the guidance or support of capable teachers. Elementary teachers must be able to answer the following questions: What kinds of revolutionary actions are my students capable of taking? What hidden potential do they have that is yet to be made manifest? What tools do my students need to have at their disposal in order to act efficaciously? And how can I scaffold and support my students in their revolutionary endeavors?

An Instructional Framework for Evaluating and Responding to Social Issues

Building on Freire's work, this section of this chapter offers a framework to guide elementary school teachers' classroom instruction. Specifically, the framework provides five concrete steps that elementary school teachers and students can take in order to deeply investigate and take action with regard to contemporary social issues. For each of the five steps in the instructional framework, a classroom vignette is included to provide readers with an example of how an elementary school teacher might implement the framework in order to explore the issue of homelessness in his fourth grade classroom. Although the vignettes present a fictionalized account of an elementary school teacher and his students in action, they are supported by evidence-based practices.

Step 1: Activate Background Knowledge and Personal Experience

When elementary school teachers and students begin to tackle a social issue, particularly one that is controversial, as well as emotionally and politically charged, it is important for teachers to determine what students already know about it, and whether the issue has had a personal impact on students' lives. In addition, teachers and students may bring into the classroom preconceived notions, misconceptions, or stereotypes regarding a social issue of the people affected most directly by it. It is equally important to identify these beliefs and opinions prior to undertaking an in-depth exploration. Problem-posing educators build upon the personal background knowledge and lived experiences that all students bring into their classrooms.

Classroom Vignette 1

With his students gathered on the classroom rug in front of him, Terrence—a fourth grade teacher in an urban school district—began the class unit on homelessness with a single word written up on the Smart Board: HOME. He asked students to turn and talk with their classmates about what a home is and why it is important for people to have one. Terrence invited students to share what they talked about with the entire class, while he recorded their responses on the Smart Board. Terrence's students described a home as a place where you eat and sleep, and a place where you live with your family. They noted the diversity of homes that exist in the world, from houses and apartments to trailers and mud huts. When Terrence asked students to share why it is important for people to have a home, his students mentioned that people need a place to go where they can feel safe, keep their possessions, and stay warm in the winter.

After their opening discussion, Terrence moved on to a new Smart Board page where he displayed another word: HOMELESS. He talked about how the suffix "less" means "without," so people who are homeless are "without a home." Terrence informed his students that they would be studying homelessness and learning about people who are homeless over the course of their unit. He told his fourth graders that the first thing that he wanted to find out was what they already knew about homelessness and what questions they had about the topic. Terrence began developing a whole-class KWL chart (What do we *know*? What do we *want to know*? What have we *learned*?) (Vacca and Vacca, 2008) on three sheets of chart paper, and he modeled how he would fill in the first two sections of the chart.

One thing Terrence already knew was that some homeless people live on the streets, and one thing that he wanted to know was why people become homeless.

Terrence asked students to return to their desks and take out their inquiry journals (Barell, 2008). These journals provided students with a space to ask and answer questions about the world around them. Terrence had students create their own KWL charts in their journals, and fill in the first two columns, indicating what they already knew about homelessness and what they would like to find out. He ended the introductory lesson by asking students to share some of the entries from their personal KWL charts, while he scribed their responses on the whole-class chart that would remain on display throughout the unit.

Terrence wanted to see if students carried with them any preconceived notions, misconceptions, or stereotypes on the topic. During his next lesson, Terrence had his students complete an anticipation guide (Alvermann et al., 2010). This contained statements about homeless individuals, and asked students to indicate whether they agreed or disagreed with each statement. Statements included: "People are homeless because they don't work hard"; "All homeless people live in shelters"; "Homeless people don't have any friends or family"; "Homeless people want to find a new home to live in"; and "Homeless people don't want other people to know that they are homeless." After completing their anticipation guides, Terrence held a whole-class discussion, inviting students to share with classmates some of the reasons why they agreed or disagreed with each statement.

As a final introductory activity, Terrence wanted to find out if homelessness had personally impacted the lives of his students. He had his students engage in a quickwrite (Rief, 2003) in their inquiry journals. He asked students to write letters to him, letting him know if they, or anyone they knew, had ever dealt with homelessness in their lives. After the quickwrite, Terrence gave students an opportunity to share their letters, but only if they felt comfortable doing so. Many students wrote about how they had seen homeless people on the streets of their city, or they knew about homeless people from reading books or watching movies. However, several students in Terrence's class shared more personal experiences with homelessness. One student wrote about how his aunt and cousins had recently been evicted from their apartment. Another wrote about how her family had spent six months in a city shelter during the previous school year. Terrence's purpose in asking students to write about their experiences with homelessness was twofold. First, he wanted students to feel that the classroom was a safe and supportive space where they could talk about all aspects of their lives. Second, he wanted his class to understand that homelessness impacted students and families in their own school and community, making it even more relevant and worth learning about.

Step 2: Develop a Deep Understanding of the Issue

Once elementary school teachers and students have activated background knowledge and personal experiences regarding a social issue, the next step is to work collaboratively towards a deeper understanding of it. Teachers and students can co-construct a deeper understanding of a social issue by asking, and investigating the answers to, essential questions about the social issue. Essential questions (Wiggins and McTighe, 2005) lie at the heart of a particular subject or topic. They promote inquiry and often result in multiple complex answers rather than a single straightforward one. In elementary classrooms, literature offers one pathway to help students answer essential questions. Students can read, discuss, and write about a diverse collection of texts in order to uncover the complexities of a social issue.

Classroom Vignette 2

In an effort to deeply understand the issue of homelessness, Terrence and his fourth grade students examined their whole-class KWL chart, looking for essential questions to investigate and answer. Terrence explained that essential questions could be answered in many ways. They require you to use the texts you are reading and the knowledge you are gaining, along with your own thoughts, experiences, and emotions, in order to formulate answers. Terrence modeled a few examples of essential questions. Then, working through the questions on their KWL chart, Terrence and his students identified the following essential questions about homelessness:

- Why do people become homeless?
- What problems and dangers do homeless people face?
- How can people take action to help those who are homeless?
- How can people take action to help end homelessness?

Terrence and his students agreed that it was essential to answer these four questions if they were going to have an in-depth understanding of the issue of homelessness.

To assist students in their attempts to answer the essential questions, Terrence developed a classroom text set about homelessness. A text set (Cappiello and Dawes, 2012; Nichols, 2009; Ward and Young, 2008) is a multimodal and multi-genre collection of literacy resources surrounding a particular topic of study. In collaboration with the library media specialist at his school, Terrence gathered a variety of texts on homelessness, specifically designed to support the students in his classroom, who possessed a range of literacy skills, experiences, and interests. The text set included more traditional literary resources, such as picture books, chapter books, and magazine articles, but it also included a range of visual and online texts, such as photographs, video documentaries, and Internet websites.

Terrence used varied instructional approaches to scaffold students' interaction with, and comprehension of, the homelessness text set. During a whole-class lesson, Terrence read *Fly Away Home* (Bunting and Himler, 1993) to students.

This fiction picture book tells the story of a homeless father and his son, who are living at an airport. Terrence paired his reading of *Fly Away Home* with a read-aloud of a news article from the *New York Times*, entitled "Airport Homeless: A Long, Pleasant Layover" (Holloway, 1995). The article profiles several homeless individuals who have survived by living in New York City's airports. Terrence asked his students to work with their classroom literacy partners to complete a compare and contrast matrix (Alvermann et al., 2010) that directly related to the essential questions the class had identified. Students wrote about how the individuals in each text became homeless, what problems and dangers homeless people faced in each text, and how people took action to help those who were homeless.

During another series of lessons, Terrence and his students participated in small-group literature circles focused on picture books that address the issue of homelessness. Terrence selected four picture books from the homelessness text set and asked students to vote for the text that they would like to read. Once students were placed in their literature circle groups, they read their picture books independently or with a partner. Students used sticky notes to annotate the text, marking places where they discovered answers to their essential questions. When students were done reading, they met with their literature circle group to discuss how the text helps them to think about their essential questions. Terrence followed up on the initial literature circle group meetings with a second set of group meetings where he mixed students up so that each new group had at least one individual from each original literature circle group. This helped ensure that students would have the opportunity to hear about all four of the picture books that were read by their peers. In their new groups, students were asked to share what they had learned about homelessness from their respective books, and continue discussing the various causes and effects of homelessness, as well as the actions being taken by characters in the book to help people who are homeless. As Terrence and his students read, discussed, and wrote about various texts from the homelessness text set, one of the class's major goals was to problematize (McLaughlin and DeVoogd, 2004) the issue of homelessness—attempting to understand the problem and its complexity by questioning and seeking multiple explanations.

Step 3: Explore the Issue from Multiple Perspectives

In order to understand a social issue more deeply, elementary school teachers and students need to recognize that social issues can be experienced, examined, and understood from a variety of perspectives. It is important for students to hear about a social issue from multiple voices, including voices that are traditionally marginalized or silenced. Students should have opportunities to interact with individuals who are considered experts on a social issue, especially those who work closely with the social issue, and even people whose lives are deeply affected by it.

Classroom Vignette 3

Terrence wanted his fourth graders to hear a variety of perspectives on homelessness. One way he sought to accomplish this was by setting up a whole-class visit to a local homeless shelter and soup kitchen that was near the school. He contacted the director of the homeless shelter and asked if she would be willing to speak to his class, offering her expertise on homelessness, and sharing her experiences working with homeless individuals and families. Prior to their trip to the homeless shelter and soup kitchen, Terrence asked his students to brainstorm interview questions for the director in their inquiry journals. Among the things that students wanted to ask were: Where do homeless people keep their things? Can homeless people get enough to eat? What do homeless people do during the winter? How do people who have lost their homes get homes again? Although Terrence had organized the visit to the shelter, he wanted his students to generate their own questions, helping to collaboratively construct the content of the homelessness unit.

During the class visit to the shelter, the director gave students a tour and discussed the functions of a homeless shelter and soup kitchen. She described some of the reasons why people become homeless, such as the inability to pay bills because of a limited income, the loss of a job, or the death of a family member. The director spoke about the challenges that homeless individuals face, from receiving adequate medical care, to finding the clothes necessary to go on a job interview. A chef who volunteered regularly in the soup kitchen talked with the students about how the shelter seeks donations from local restaurants, grocery stores, and area farmers, to help ensure that they have enough food to feed the residents at the shelter. To wrap up the visit, the shelter director asked several willing residents of the homeless shelter to speak with the students. The students were able to ask the director and the residents many of the interview questions they had brainstormed.

When Terrence and his fourth graders returned to their classroom, he had his students reflect on what they had learned during their visit to the homeless shelter and soup kitchen. Students recorded what they had learned about homelessness while they were there in their inquiry journals, including answers to their interview questions. They wrote personal reflections about their visit, sharing the thoughts and feelings they experienced while visiting the shelter and speaking with the director, the chef, and several of the shelter residents. Terrence gathered his students on the classroom rug to debrief and discuss the homeless shelter visit. He guided the open-ended conversation, encouraging students to discuss their emotions and share what they had learned from individuals who work most closely with the homeless, and individuals who are currently struggling with homelessness.

Terrence also wanted his students to know that homelessness is a social issue that does not just impact adults, but often affects elementary-age children just like them. He wanted students to hear the voices and stories of children who have experienced homelessness firsthand. In order to provide a child's perspective on homelessness, Terrence and his students studied Hurricane Katrina, the powerful category-five hurricane that slammed the Gulf Coast of the United States during the summer of 2005. Terrence read students several *Scholastic News* articles about the hurricane, to help them develop background knowledge about the event. He then shared brief video clips from a documentary called *Katrina's Children* (Belsey, 2008), which explores the impact of Hurricane Katrina on the lives of children in New Orleans, and is told entirely from the children's point of view. Terrence pre-selected developmentally appropriate clips in which children about the same age as his students shared their experiences during Katrina. The children in the documentary described their homes being destroyed by flooding, and the roofs of their houses collapsing. They talked about the challenges they faced during and after the hurricane, including a lack of clean water, spoiled food, and no electricity. Many of the children who were interviewed told of how they found themselves suddenly homeless as a result of the hurricane.

After sharing segments of *Katrina's Children* with his students, Terrence asked classroom literacy partners to discuss how their own lives might be different if they didn't have homes to go back to because of a natural disaster. Students talked about losing all of their possessions, and how it would be a challenge to find food, clothing, new places to live, and even new schools to go to. Part of Terrence's rationale in sharing clips from *Katrina's Children* was to help his fourth graders move beyond stereotypical beliefs (McLaughlin and DeVoogd, 2004) about homelessness. As Terrence and his students explored homelessness from multiple perspectives, both teacher and students began to realize that its causes and consequences were more complex than they had initially thought.

Step 4: Brainstorm and Take Action Related to the Issue

If elementary school teachers and students devote the time to deeply explore a social issue, examining it from multiple perspectives and uncovering its complexities, the next step in this process is to begin thinking about what actions they can take to address the issue. Peterson (2012) wrote that action is a key component of teaching for social justice: "At a time when cynicism and hopelessness increasingly dominate our youth, helping students understand the world and their relationship to it by encouraging social action may be one of the few antidotes" (p. 56). Even our youngest students need opportunities to consider transformative actions that they can take to address social issues. As Pearson (2009) describes, it is important to have hope, but hope that is grounded in seriousness, not fancy. This hope can only be achieved if people have developed a sense of consciousness and the capacities to enact steps to achieve hopeful ends. Elementary school teachers play a critical role in scaffolding students' planning, action, and reflection.

Classroom Vignette 4

Two of the essential questions that Terrence and his fourth graders had identified early on in their homelessness unit were: How can people take action to help those who are homeless, and how can people take action to help end homelessness? Terrence displayed these two questions up on the Smart Board during the middle of the homelessness unit, and explained to his students that as young citizens they have the power to take action to help people who are homeless, and to help try to end homelessness. He then challenged his class to brainstorm possible actions that fourth graders could take toward these goals.

Students worked in small groups to create posters of potential actions. After they shared their posters with the whole class, Terrence asked each student to vote for an action that they felt passionate about pursuing. After compiling the votes, Terrence and his students agreed to pursue three actions in small groups. Terrence worked closely with each of the three groups to develop homelessness action plans. He had each group list the steps that they would engage in, the materials they would need, and how they thought Terrence could support them most effectively.

Leading a School-Wide Donation Drive to Help the Homeless

Terrence's first group of students was committed to collecting donations for the local homeless shelter and soup kitchen that the class had visited. The students began by sending e-mails to the director of the homeless shelter and the chef who volunteered at the soup kitchen. They asked the director what kinds of supplies the shelter residents needed most and the chef what the soup kitchen needed most. Students learned from the director that the children and adults at the shelter needed winter clothing, including hats, gloves, and warm socks, as well as toiletries, such as toothpaste and shampoo. The chef let the students know that the soup kitchen was always in need of non-perishable food items such as peanut butter, canned tuna fish, and pasta, and that fresh fruits and vegetables were always in short supply.

Armed with this information, students worked to create advertising materials for their homeless shelter donation drive. They created posters to display in the school's entryway and flyers to send home to every family in the school. They wrote up a formal announcement about the donation drive, and shared it over the loudspeaker during morning announcements. Over the course of the next month, the students took charge of collecting and sorting all of the donations that came in from students and families. They created charts and graphs to catalog the different supplies and types of food that were coming in, and to track any monetary donations as well. Terrence provided guidance with these tasks, and he also helped to deliver any fresh fruits and vegetables to the soup kitchen on a daily basis. At the end of the month-long donation drive, the director of the homeless shelter visited the school to pick up the donations during a school-wide assembly on homelessness. The donation drive group presented a report during the assembly, summarizing all of the donations that had been collected.

Recommending Policy Changes to End Homelessness

Terrence's second group of students was interested in writing letters to people to make recommendations about how to end homelessness. Terrence met with this group of students and helped them brainstorm a list of people they could contact. He provided them with access to the homelessness text set, so that they could conduct research to help them formulate their recommendations. Finally, Terrence modeled how to write a persuasive letter, to help students as they began to draft letters of their own.

Students worked collaboratively to conduct their research and write their persuasive letters. Two students chose to write to their state representative. In their letter, they described the different ways in which people become homeless, and the challenges they face. The students asked the state representative to support programs that help homeless individuals take classes at local community colleges and provide assistance with finding jobs. Another pair of students chose to write to the governor. They wrote about how many homeless people there are in the state and across the country, and discussed how many homeless individuals are young children. The students argued that the governor should fight to raise the minimum wage, so that people who have minimum wage jobs can afford to keep a home, pay their bills, and feed their families. Terrence helped the students find the appropriate addresses where they could send their letters. After the students read their letters at the school-wide assembly, Terrence mailed the letters out to their recipients.

Educating Others about Homelessness

Terrence's final group of students wanted to teach other people about homelessness. Terrence agreed that many people are generally uninformed or misinformed about the causes and consequences of homelessness. He helped the students think about who their audience might be and how they might present to them. The group decided that they wanted to teach other children their own age about homelessness. Terrence recommended several presentation methods, from creating and distributing informational pamphlets, to developing a video public service announcement. The students in the group chose to produce a digital Prezi.

Once the students had their plan of action in place, they began gathering the information that they wanted to share in their presentation. Students returned to their inquiry journals to examine what they had learned throughout the unit. They conducted additional research by diving back into the homelessness text set. Terrence helped the students organize their presentation around the essential questions that had guided their homelessness unit. He provided the group with mini-lessons on how to gather and organize research, and how to create a digital Prezi. Working collaboratively as a group, the students developed a Prezi that included a blend of text and photographs. It provided information about the various reasons why people become homeless, the challenges they face, and the ways children can take action to help those who are homeless and to try to end homelessness. The group presented their Prezi to kick off the school-wide assembly on homelessness, and the principal posted the Prezi on the school's website, in an effort to inform families and community members about the issue.

Step 5: Engage in Reflective Praxis

Elementary school teachers and students who work to deeply understand a social issue and take action to ameliorate its effects must also take time to reflect on their work. Freire (1970/2005, 1998) argued that critical reflection is an important form of action, since it encourages students to examine and change their lives. When teachers and students reflect upon a social issue, they can process what they have learned about it, discuss whether their views and beliefs have changed, and think about ongoing actions they might take in the future. In addition, elementary school teachers can help their students consider their roles and responsibilities as active citizens and participants in a democratic society.

Classroom Vignette 5

On the morning following the school-wide assembly on homelessness, Terrence gathered his students together on the classroom rug to wrap up the homelessness unit. He celebrated the actions that his students had taken in their small groups, before shifting gears to engage students in a culminating reflection. First, he displayed the whole-class KWL chart from the beginning of the unit, which contained students' background knowledge and the initial questions they had about homelessness. Terrence pointed out to his students that they had uncovered the answers to many of their initial questions, including those that they had deemed "essential." He modeled an answer to one of his own initial questions: Why do people become homeless in the first place? In the "What have we *learned*?" column of the KWL chart, Terrence wrote that people become homeless for many reasons, such as the loss of a job or a natural disaster. Terrence then sent his students back to their inquiry journals to complete the final column of their own personal KWL charts, answering any initial questions they had about homelessness. The class reconvened to share their answers, while Terrence scribed on the whole-class KWL chart. Although they had not answered every question they initially posed, they now had a much deeper understanding about homelessness as a social issue.

Along with asking his students to reflect upon what they had learned about homelessness, Terrence wanted his fourth graders to discuss whether their views and beliefs about the issue had changed at all over the course of the unit. He handed back to students the anticipation guide that they had completed during the beginning of the unit, which asked them to indicate whether they agreed or disagreed with a number of statements about homeless individuals. Terrence asked his students to look through the statements again, putting a check mark next to any statements where their opinion had remained the same, and putting a star next to any statements where their opinion had changed. During a whole-class dialogue, Terrence had students reflect on how their views about homelessness had developed over the course of the unit, and discuss why some of their beliefs had changed. Terrence's goal in asking students to return to their anticipation guides was to help them reflect on the evolution of their views and beliefs about homelessness and homeless individuals as a result of exploring and taking action regarding this social issue.

To bring closure to the homelessness unit, Terrence wanted his students to consider their roles and responsibilities as active citizens and participants in a democratic society. He showed a brief video clip from Malala Yousafzai's (2013) speech to the United Nations Youth Assembly, where she told the audience, "One child, one teacher, one pen, and one book can change the world." Terrence displayed this quote up on the Smart Board along with some final reflection questions:

- Do you think it is important for fourth graders to learn about issues like homelessness? Why or why not?
- Do you think that fourth graders can change the world, as Malala said in her speech?
- If you agree with Malala, how can fourth graders change the world? And, if you disagree with her, why can't they change the world?

Terrence gave his students time to talk about these reflection questions in small groups. Then he asked students to respond to them in writing, as a final entry in their inquiry journals. Terrence gave students an opportunity to share their responses, and the whole class discussed their thoughts and ideas about how fourth graders—and children of all ages—can take the lead in exploring social issues and acting to change the world.

Concluding Thoughts

The instructional framework proposed in this chapter offers elementary school teachers and students a series of steps that can facilitate a deep and critical exploration of contemporary social issues. As teachers and students engage in these explorations, they bring to life Freire's (1970/2005) problem-posing model of education. Teachers begin to examine social issues in their classrooms by recognizing, valuing, and building on students' background knowledge and personal experiences. Rather than taking a stance as all-knowing experts, and enlightening students about social issues, teachers pursue explorations of social issues alongside their students. Working collaboratively, teachers and students examine social issues from a variety of perspectives, uncovering the complexity of those issues and unveiling the reality of the world in which they live. Through mutual dialogue, teachers and students engage in praxis—investigating, planning, enacting, and reflecting—in an effort to address real-world problems. Finally, teachers allow students to reflect on what they've learned about social issues, how their thinking has evolved, and what their potential roles and responsibilities might be as young citizens who have the power to transform the world and shape its future.

In order to help elementary school students develop as young citizens, it is imperative for teachers to directly address social issues in their classrooms, rather than avoiding them through a "discourse of protection" (James, 2008). Social issues are certainly complex, controversial, and challenging. Yet, with the right amount of teacher planning and scaffolding, our youngest students can explore these issues deeply and critically. Terrence identified his fourth grade students' current levels of understanding about homelessness, and then helped students build upon those levels of understanding in developmentally appropriate ways. He modeled his own thinking about homelessness, selected appropriate texts to explore with his students, and guided his students through real-world experiences and actions. Elementary school teachers must support students' direct engagement with social issues, and empower our youngest citizens to respond directly to them. In the process, Terrence's grade four students were able to recognize the nuanced circumstances leading to homelessness and work toward the amelioration of this primary symptom of economic disparity in their community.

References

Alvermann, D. E., Phelps, S. F., and Gillis, V. R. (2010). *Content area reading and literacy: Succeeding in today's diverse classroom* (6th ed.). Boston, MA: Allyn & Bacon.

America's youngest outcasts: A report card on child homelessness. (2014). Waltham, MA: National Center on Family Homelessness at American Institutes for Research.

Barell, J. (2008). *Why are school buses always yellow? Teaching for inquiry, preK–5.* Thousand Oaks, CA: Corwin Press.

Belsey, L. (2008). *Katrina's children.* New York: Shadow Pictures.

Bunting, E. (text), and Himler, R. (illustrations). (1993). *Fly away home.* Boston, MA: Sandpiper.

Cappiello, M. A., and Dawes, E. (2012). *Teaching with text sets.* Huntington Beach, CA: Shell Education.

Carrington, B., and Troyna, B. (1988). *Children and controversial issues: Strategies for the early and middle years of schooling.* London: Falmer Press.

Cowhey, M. (2006). *Black ants and Buddhists: Thinking critically and teaching differently in the primary grades.* Portland, ME: Stenhouse.

Dulberg, N. (2005). "The theory behind how students learn": Applying developmental theory to research on children's historical thinking. *Theory and Research in Social Education, 33*(4), 508–531.

Freire, P. (1973). *Education for critical consciousness.* New York: Continuum.

Freire, P. (1988). The adult literacy process as cultural action for freedom and education and conscientização. In E. R. Kintgen, B. M. Kroll, and M. Rose (Eds.), *Perspectives on literacy,* (pp. 398–409). Carbondale: Southern Illinois University Press.

Freire, P. (1998). *Pedagogy of freedom: Ethics, democracy, and civic courage.* New York: Rowman & Littlefield.

Freire, P. (2005). *Pedagogy of the oppressed.* New York: Continuum. (Original work published 1970.)

Harwood, D. (1985). We need political not Political education for 5–13 year olds. *Education, 13*(1), 12–17.

Holloway, L. (1995, February 3). Airport homeless: A long, pleasant layover. *New York Times.* Retrieved from http://www.nytimes.com.

James, J. H. (2008). Teachers as protectors: Making sense of preservice teachers' resistance to interpretation in elementary history teaching. *Theory and Research in Social Education, 36*(3), 172–205.

Jeffs, T. (1988). Preparing young people for participatory democracy. In B. Carrington and B. Troyna (Eds.), *Children and controversial issues.* London: Falmer Press.

McLaren, P. (2000). *Che Guevara, Paulo Freire, and the pedagogy of revolution.* Lanham, MD: Rowman & Littlefield.

McLaren, P., and Leonard, P. (Eds.). (1993). *Paulo Freire: A critical encounter.* New York: Routledge.

McLaughlin, M., and DeVoogd, G. (2004). *Critical literacy: Enhancing students' comprehension of text.* New York: Scholastic.

Morrow, R. A., and Torres, C. A. (2002). *Reading Freire and Habermas: Critical pedagogy and transformative social change.* New York: Teachers College Press.

Nichols, M. (2009). *Expanding comprehension with multigenre text sets.* New York: Scholastic.

Pearson, N. (2009). Radical hope: Education and equality in Australia. *Quarterly Essays, 35,* 1–106.

Peterson, B. (2012). Teaching for social justice. In L. Christensen, M. Hansen, B. Peterson, E. Schlessman, and D. Watson (Eds.), *Rethinking elementary education* (pp. 49–56). Milwaukee, WI: Rethinking Schools.

Rief, L. (2003). *100 quickwrites: Fast and effective freewriting exercises that build students' confidence, develop their fluency, and bring out the writer in every student.* New York: Scholastic Teaching Resources.

Taylor, P. (1993). *The texts of Paulo Freire.* Buckingham, UK: Open University Press.

Vacca, R. T., and Vacca, J. L. (2008). *Content area reading: Literacy and learning across the curriculum* (9th ed.). Boston, MA: Allyn & Bacon.

Vasquez, V. (2004). *Negotiating critical literacies with young children.* Mahwah, NJ: Lawrence Erlbaum Associates.

Ward, B. A., and Young, T. A. (2008). Text sets: Making connections between and across books. *Reading Horizons, 48*(3), 215–226.

White, P. (1977). Political education in a democracy: The implications for teacher education. *Journal of Further and Higher Education*, *1*(3), 40–55.

Wiggins, G., and McTighe, J. (2005). *Understanding by design* (2nd ed.). Alexandria, VA: ASCD.

Yousafzai, M. (2013, July 12). Full text: Malala Yousafzai delivers defiant riposte to Taliban militants with speech to the UN General Assembly. *Independent.* Retrieved from http://www.independent.co.uk.

10

PARTICIPATORY CITIZENSHIP

A Commitment to Action Civics

Karon LeCompte and Brooke Blevins

Students who will come of voting age within the next decade have the opportunity to help ensure a vibrant and positive democratic republic. It is essential that schools and communities prepare students with the important skills and dispositions needed to become engaged and informed citizens and create opportunities for civic engagement and political participation (Ekman and Amnå, 2012). Economic disparity is a key factor that impedes civic engagement opportunities for low-income families. The widening gap of income inequality means that educational and civic resources have become increasingly unequal. A constellation of trends has led to a rapidly growing disparity in the extent to which families invest their time and money in their children's education. Indeed, high-income families now spend nearly seven times as much on their children's development as low-income families (Kornrich and Furstenberg, 2013). Thus, research reveals persistent disparities between the civic and political engagement of low-income youth and youth of color and their more affluent peers (Delli Carpini and Keeter, 1996).

For decades, scholars have expressed concerns about the lack of civic knowledge and electoral participation of all students (Dalton, 1998; Norris, 2002). Despite changes in the nature of campaigns, digital and news media, the demographics of the youth population, and voting law, changes in youth turnout and civic knowledge have been limited since 1972. The average youth turnout (for ages 18–24) in presidential years from 1972 to 2012 was 43.7 percent. The rate in 2012 was just a bit below the mean at 41.2 percent (Center for Information and Research on Civic Learning and Engagement (CIRCLE), 2013a). The most robust data on civic knowledge in the United States, the National Assessment of Education Progress (NAEP) Civics Assessment, has also shown very small changes since the 1970s. Thus in 40 years very little has changed regarding the civic knowledge and electoral participation of our youth. In particular civic knowledge and political participation are lowest in populations diverse in race, culture, and social class.

The Census Bureau projection reports that the population of children will become more diverse, with a majority–minority crossover in 2020 (Colby and Ortman, 2015). Reflected in these numbers is the recent growth of younger new minority populations including Latinos, Asians, and those identifying as "multiracial." The 2013 Report of the Commission on Youth Voting and Civic Knowledge (CIRCLE, 2013a) found that young people from disadvantaged backgrounds are less likely to be civically informed or to vote. There is a growing concern that minority youth have the least amount of civic knowledge and experience in active civic participation (Rubin et al., 2009). Civics education is much less prevalent in schools that serve low-income and minority youth (CIRCLE, 2013a). Both class and race are related to a lower likelihood of scoring in the "proficient" range on the NAEP Civics Assessment, but the gap is even larger when we compare White, wealthy students to Black or Hispanic students who come from less affluent backgrounds. Affluent White students are four to six times more likely than Hispanic or Black students who come from low-income households to exceed the "proficient" cut-off on the NAEP Civics Assessment. Unfortunately, civic education opportunities for marginalized youth are minimal, leaving those who most need empowerment the least opportunity to learn important civic knowledge and develop key values, skills, and dispositions related to citizenship. The civic gap between low-income and wealthier youth is termed the "civic empowerment gap" (Levinson, 2012, p. 32).

Despite this lack of civic knowledge and electoral participation, research also shows that youth are engaging in their communities in other ways—ways that hold promise for revitalizing communities and civic education (Levine, 2013). In Chapter 11, Kornfeld et al. discuss one such program, the Mikva Challenge. In this chapter we explore another example of the kinds of positive youth development (PYD) programs that have the propensity to support such change through intentional, pro-social approaches that engage youth within their communities, schools, organizations, peer groups, and families in a manner that is productive and constructive (Lerner, 2004). Organizations such as YouthBuild and Everyday Democracy are examples of PYD initiatives. YouthBuild programs provide support systems that unleash the positive energy of low-income young people to rebuild their communities and lives, breaking the cycle of poverty with a commitment to work, education, community, and family. Everyday Democracy is a project dedicated to strengthening deliberative democracy and improving the quality of public life in the United States. PYD initiatives such as these give youth the opportunity to connect with their community in ways that are not what one typically thinks of as conventional forms of civic engagement like voting or political campaigning.

Civic engagement can and does transcend beyond electoral participation. Civic engagement is also manifested in the actions that ordinary citizens take part in which seek to improve their respective communities (Ekman and Amnå, 2012). These actions must expand beyond those of economic citizens that Nichols describes in Chapter 2. There is an expanding recognition that, in order for students to cultivate a commitment to civic participation and to become active members of vibrant communities, they need regular opportunities to engage in civic learning activities from preschool through college (Guilfoile and Delander, 2014).

The purpose of this chapter is to provide teachers, both preservice and in-service, with a research-based understanding of civics education that is rooted in social justice, a framework for engaging in action civics, and examples of how they might create opportunities to empower students to become civic participants. We conclude the chapter by describing and providing examples of an action civics project called Building Bridges, which is designed to engage young people—particularly marginalized young people—in authentic and meaningful civic action. The National Council for the Social Studies (NCSS) (1994) suggests that "the primary purpose of social studies is to help young people make informed and reasoned decisions for the public good as citizens of a culturally diverse, democratic society in an interdependent world" (p. 3).

We acknowledge that there are multiple understandings and definitions of civic and political participation and engagement, and that these conceptions inform how we go about educating young people for civic participation. From their two-year study of ten civic education programs in the United States, Westheimer and Kahne (2004) outlined three types of citizenship orientations: the personally responsible citizen; the participatory citizen; and the justice-oriented citizen. In Chapter 3, Johnson discusses their study detail; for our purposes, we examine both participatory and social justice citizenship orientations. For the purpose of this chapter we describe civic participation as what Ekman and Amnå (2012) describe as both individual and collective forms of manifest political participation, latent political or civil participation, and anti-political active forms of non-participation. Thus participation refers to things such as taking an interest in politics and society, volunteering, working with community-based organizations, voting, signing petitions, and protesting, the goals of which are to affect authoritative decisions on different levels of political systems (Zimenkova, 2013).

Indeed, there exists a call for schools to socialize all children, particularly immigrant children, into traditionally taught patriotic knowledge and dispositions. Many educational stakeholders cite the imperative of civic education to preserve the true character of American democracy (Junn, 2004). However, from the perspective of immigrant families, discrimination is an everyday norm that is palpably felt in economic, social, and civic life. Structural inequities and inequalities color the daily lives of minority children, and their experience of concepts such as freedom, fairness, equality, justice, and even democracy are far from unambiguous. The American democratic creed, while a notable goal when one is advocating its support, does not apply equally, but instead depends on where one is situated in social and economic class. In this chapter, our vision of citizenship education seeks to further both participatory and social justice citizenship goals. In the next section, we address educational issues within the context of civic education and social justice.

Civic Education and Social Justice

Criticisms of conventional civics education include concerns about deficits in students' civic knowledge and a focus on high-stakes testing. All too often teachers are directed to focus on testing students' civic knowledge with little attention to positive youth development and civic engagement (CIRCLE, 2013a). Research also indicates that students who are part of marginalized and politically underrepresented populations have fewer opportunities for high-quality civic education (Kahne and Middaugh, 2008; Levinson, 2012). Students in higher socioeconomic groups are the ones who have more sustained access to efforts for civic learning, including a school newspaper, advanced social studies courses, student government, and other organizations (Levine, 2012). As Levine (2012) argues, "universal public schooling was established to create universal civic engagement, but it actually exacerbates inequality" (p. 41). Studies suggest differences in the civic achievement of American youth are linked to the racial and socioeconomic backgrounds of the students being tested (Baldi et al., 2001). Fine et al. (2004) argued that students from low socioeconomic backgrounds become civically alienated because of conditions of overcrowding, lack of quality teachers, and crumbling facilities. Schools serving low-income youth all fail to provide learning opportunities that promote civic engagement (Kahne and Middaugh, 2008). School systems and, most importantly, classroom teachers must take into account how student's daily experiences affect their sense of citizenship. As Arend and Cuenca point out in Chapter 12, these daily interactions are marked by racial and socioeconomic inequalities. These interactions, in turn, affect their internal perceptions of themselves as civic actors (Rubin et al., 2009).

In order to reduce the ever-widening academic and civic opportunity gaps that exist in our society, it is important that teachers embrace a social justice approach to education. They need to consider the demographics of the communities in which they teach, including the rich funds of knowledge—as described by Dolan and Kaufman in Chapter 8—students from these communities bring to their classrooms, as well as the inequities these students may face (Moll and González, 2004). As Wade (2001) argued, "Social justice education begins with children's lived experiences and then moves toward fostering a critical perspective and action directed toward social change" (p. 25). While it takes time and effort, teachers who practice their profession from a social justice perspective in which they try to provide all students with a caring learning environment that is just, fair, and—importantly—democratic help to foster students' capacities, and develop citizens who are committed to social activism (Lalas, 2007).

In social justice-oriented social studies classrooms, students are given "opportunities to act in their schools and communities—to advocate for concrete changes concerning issues that have been analyzed and critiqued in the classroom" (Wade, 2001, p. 26). In our example, elaborated below, the teacher Mrs. Brown (pseudonym) stressed the importance of a dialectical cycle of action and reflection with her students. She encouraged them to seek information and ask critical questions. She sought to empower her students by utilizing their passion to address community issues that had personal meaning. This kind of pedagogy has the propensity to dismantle traditional power structures of authority (Mirra et al., 2013). Teachers like Mrs. Brown are central to a social justice approach to civics education.

Civics education rooted in social justice should be focused on engaging students in "developing critical habits of mind, understanding and sorting out multiple perspectives, and learning to participate in and contribute to a democratic society by developing both the skill and the inclination for civic engagement" (Cochran-Smith, 2004, p. 159). Research suggests that robust engagement in civic initiatives exposes students to factors that will increase their academic achievement, allow them to develop collegial relationships with adults and peers, and boost their self-esteem (Levine, 2013; Levinson, 2012). Recent trends in civic education focus on positive youth development and civic engagement. These programs (e.g., Project Citizen and the Mikva Challenge) use an asset–strength-based approach to engage youth (Lerner et al., 2005). Referred to by Levinson (2012) as "guided experiential civic education," these types of civic education experiences are intended to bridge academic, civic learning, and community involvement (p. 236). *Action civics* is a term that refers to civic education that goes beyond textbook learning and focuses on active problem solving on real community issues. In the next section, we describe why action civics is a potentially effective strategy for engaging students in meaningful civic education that is socially justice oriented.

Action Civics

Action civics is an educational practice that holds promise for the kinds of activities whereby students understand the implications of having a "voice" in the public arena and being informed about issues that affect their lives. Action civics "is a broad term used to describe curricula and programs that go beyond traditional civics programs by combining learning and practice" (CIRCLE, 2013b, p. 2). This approach insists that "students *do* and *behave as citizens* by engaging in a cycle of research, action, and reflection about problems they care about personally while learning about deeper principles of effective civic and especially political action" (Levinson, 2012, p. 224). Action civics differs from service learning in that it is purposefully political and policy oriented (Levinson, 2012). Through action civics experiences, students are challenged "to take on a social justice orientation as they reflect upon their lived experiences and the actions they propose to take" (Levinson, 2012, p. 226). Within this frame, students are viewed as assets who possess knowledge and insight that will help them make positive contributions and act as agents of change in their communities.

While *action civics* is a relatively new term, it is rooted in a long history of research-based civics education practices. This type of community-based learning has a strong theoretical foundation in the work of John Dewey, who argued that civics engagement should be tied to community-based experiential learning linked to public problem solving (Saltmarsh, 2008). This Deweyan approach to civics education asserts that, to learn active citizenship, one must *be* an active citizen. Similarly, action civics also reflects Freire's (1970/2005) notion of problem-posing education—see Colwell, Chapter 9—in which "people develop their power to perceive critically *the way they exist* in the world *with which* and *in which* they find themselves; they come to see the world not as a static reality, but a reality in process, in transformation" (p. 83). As students discuss issues in their community, they practice democracy by learning how to listen to others, respect views different from their own, and understand why multiple perspectives are essential for democracy (Youniss, 2012).

Action civics puts students at the heart of civics learning, by providing the opportunity to participate in authentic civic activities, "from elections to advocacy, from public debates to the creation of new civic media" (Center for Action Civics, 2013). Although action civics programs vary in scope, content, and duration, they do share key elements, including that:

- student voice, experience, and decision making are valued;
- students learn by engaging in civic activities in the classroom or beyond;
- students choose an issue important to them and work to make a difference;
- students reflect on actions, successes, and challenges throughout the project.

(CIRCLE, 2013b)

In 2010, the National Action Civics Collaborative was formed to support educators and policy makers interested in providing youth with the kinds of experiences that enable them to take action and leadership on community problems. This organization made a commitment to promote and expand the practice of action civics as an evidence-based approach to creating an engaged and educated citizenry. Epstein (2014) outlines an action civics process in which students engaged in three phases of civic literacy: (1) students identify a social problem; (2) students engage in a study of the problem, paying particular attention to revealing its complexity; (3) students seek to publicly address the problem, in an effort to ameliorate or fix it.

Utilizing an action civics approach, we developed and implemented a civics education program for middle school that was designed to help engage and empower marginalized youth in civic action projects though which youth would research and act upon local community issues. We worked with the principal and teachers at Carver Academy (a pseudonym), a middle school serving gifted students from low socioeconomic backgrounds, to develop the action civics project called Building Bridges. We evoked the image of the bridge because students made active civic connections that spanned their personal lives, their communities, and their schools.

The Building Bridges Project

A C3-Compatible Process

Building Bridges is an overarching name for a project enacted in a middle school setting. Individual and small groups of students carried out action civics projects that were a result of the manifestation of the C3 framework. The Building Bridges projects adhere to C3 (NCSS, 2013) standards by providing opportunities for students to examine their community and develop questions about a community issue of interest (Dimension 1: Developing Questions and Planning Inquiries). Students were tasked with developing questions, evaluating sources, and examining evidence as they sought to examine a community issue in more detail (Dimension 2: Applying Disciplinary Tools and Concepts; Dimension 3: Evaluating Sources and Using Evidence). Students then developed an evidence-based argument for their issue and created a plan that provided a strategy for action (Dimension 2: Applying Disciplinary Tools and Concepts). Finally, as the last part of the action civics cycle, students developed a plan of action to advocate for their issue, which could include a variety of student products such as writing persuasive letters to adults with an interest in their topic, creating web-based advocacy projects, or engaging in hands-on acts of service (Dimension 4: Taking Informed Action). Each of the interconnected parts of the action civics cycle is intentionally designed to help students take ownership of a meaningful civic challenge of their choice and examine existing structural issues, while at the same time providing appropriate support to assist students in developing the knowledge and skills they need to engage as active citizens.

Identifying a Community Problem

In this first phase, students critically examined their community and identified issues they were personally interested in exploring. To begin, teachers asked students to create a list of problems in their community. To help students recognize their potential to make a difference with these community issues, students then played the iCivics.org game *Activate* (2009). In *Activate*, players are responsible for selecting and analyzing an issue and advocating from the personal to the national level. After students have completed a series of volunteer tasks related to this issue, they then advance to a level in which they must decide the focus of their campaign and determine the steps they will take to promote their cause, such as spreading awareness, raising funds, and garnering the support of local leaders. The penultimate level of the game is the national level. At this level, players are asked to decide what specific actions they will undertake to advocate for their issue. Through this simulated process, students recognized the importance of civic action in a democratic society and identified various ways in which they could participate effectively in community affairs and the political process.

By playing *Activate*, students had the opportunity to theoretically practice the steps of an action civics project, in a virtual dimension, prior to embarking upon a real project. *Activate*, much like a simulation, served as a technological springboard for discussion about the myriad ways students could make a difference in their community. Once students had brainstormed a list of community problems and played *Activate*, they then selected one community issue to focus on. Throughout this problem identification phase, teachers did not promote their own agenda; rather they facilitated student brainstorming and analysis of a variety of issues. During this phase teachers focused on asking questions such as: "Why is this so?" "What has created this issue?" "What are other ways of seeing this issue?" These questions helped students investigate the root causes of their issues, including examining structural and political factors. As Wade (2001) noted, "student voice and choice" lie at the heart of democratic social justice education (p. 25). This youth–adult partnership allowed both the students and the teacher to share in the decision-making process and equalized power amongst both parties—an important element of social justice education (Serriere, 2014).

Exploring the Problem

In the second phase, students spent time researching their issue, including developing guiding question(s) for their work, finding related historical and contemporary documents, examining social, political, and economic structures influencing their issue, and identifying advocates and community leaders who could help them effectuate change. To support students, teachers spent time helping them develop the skills necessary to effectively evaluate sources and examine evidence. In addition, they provided students with several graphic organizers that they could use to collect, organize, and synthesize information.

Developing a Plan of Action

In the third phase, students developed an evidence-based argument for their issue and created a plan of action. During this phase, students learned about effective argumentation, which was introduced through issues that were relevant to students' lives. Once students had determined their position on the issue, teachers helped them both consider counterarguments and develop rebuttals. In order to accomplish these goals, teachers focused on teaching specific skills to students such as interviewing, letter writing, effective argumentation, and researching so that they could appropriately examine and understand the nuances of their chosen issues, before developing a plan of action.

After developing an evidence-based argument about their issue based on their research and interviews, students then created plans of action. Action plans included things such as writing a persuasive letter to someone who could impact their community issue, creating an advocacy video, developing a website, writing and performing spoken word poetry, engaging in hands-on acts of service, and protesting injustices. The goal of these advocacy projects was to "engage students in local efforts to effect change with individuals or organizations as well as larger scale activities aimed at addressing the root causes of the problem" (Wade, 2001, p. 26). A key component of social justice education and action civics is reflection and critical analysis. In developing evidence-based arguments and creating plans of action, students were encouraged to question larger social issues, including examining the underlying causes of their community issue, how they are perpetuated, and what steps citizens can take—both individually and collectively—to address them.

Sharing with the Community

To celebrate, students prepared and presented their advocacy projects with members of their families, school, and community. This opportunity for celebration provided the opportunity for students to showcase their efforts as well as to publicize the project, show appreciation for those who helped along the way, and develop increased support and commitment to civic action (Wade, 2008).

Throughout this action civics process, students recognized the importance of raising awareness about social problems and advocating for possible solutions. Building Bridges projects began with students' lived experiences and then moved toward fostering critical analysis and action. These projects allowed students to explore issues that had personal meaning for them, while at the same time helping them develop the knowledge, skills, and dispositions needed to engage in civic action.

Students as Engaged Citizens

In total, over 284 middle school students participated in 115 Building Bridges projects. Examples of projects included cleaning up the local park, creating an anti-bullying public service announcement, hosting a canned food drive for the local food bank, delivering Christmas gifts to a children's home, and collecting sports equipment for the local Little League. After analysis of the data from these projects, findings indicated that students developed meaningful and personal connections to the world outside their classroom, and an increased sense of personal efficacy. They developed deep knowledge and important communication and civic skills, including researching, evaluating multiple perspectives, and weighing evidence about their topics (LeCompte and Blevins, 2015).

In addition, topics chosen by these students reveal how they embraced social justice agendas. In each case, students tackled difficult subjects that affected their lives. While these students may not have "solved" their specific issues, they did have a venue to research them, take action, and find their voices. Through this project students were empowered to recognize their rights and stand up against injustices. Here we present an example from the Building Bridges projects—a project that focused specifically on the topic of immigration. Following the description of this project we discuss student outcomes from Building Bridges as they align with the goals of social justice and action civics in fostering civic participation.

Isabella (pseudonym) chose the topic of immigration because she wanted others to know about the challenges that immigrants face. At the time of the project, she had not seen her family who lived in Mexico for 12 years. Isabella and three of her siblings had immigrated to the United States when Isabella was just a baby. Isabella lived with her mother, who was raising four children as a single parent while working two jobs to support her family. Like many other immigrant families, Isabella's family was part of the "working poor"—a term used to describe those who despite being formally employed fail to earn enough income to achieve basic economic stability. Research shows that less-educated, single immigrant mothers have a substantially higher risk of ending up in the working poor (Zuberi, 2013). Unfortunately, economic, political, and social policies in the United States continue to reinforce economic disparity for immigrant families like Isabella's.

Like others in her class, Isabella chose a topic that was personally meaningful to her. She spent time researching the issue and interviewing people who were knowledgeable about immigration. She was particularly interested in understanding why immigrants were often viewed negatively—particularly in the media. Isabella's researched-based findings showed three areas that were significant to immigrants: crime, education, and healthcare. In her post-interview she stated:

> Immigrants constantly live in fear. In fact, many immigrants are criminally abused and don't go to the authorities for fear of being deported. Unfortunately, people don't know there is a law that says if a person is hurt they can go to the authorities without having to worry about being deported. It is important that immigrants have rights and that they know about these rights.

Isabella's heart-wrenching and astute comments highlight the ways in which low-income workers, including immigrant workers, are systematically exploited by economic and employment systems in the United States. The decline of unions, the stagnation of the minimum wage, oppressive state and federal taxation policies, and incongruent welfare practices are just a few examples of systems that continue to allow employers to exploit immigrant and low-income employees (Brady et al., 2013; Hartig et al., 2014; Zuberi, 2013). According to Passel (2011), immigrant children have higher poverty rates than any other age group—a pattern that developed in the mid-1970s and has persisted since. Notably, many of these families are generally not eligible for many of the social welfare programs, because eligibility is determined by legal status and, more importantly, citizenship. Certainly, Isabella and her family felt the impact of such policies. Thus, when given the opportunity to investigate an important and meaningful issue, Isabella was compelled to investigate issues surrounding immigration.

Isabella was concerned about healthcare for immigrants. Isabella stated: "My family can't get healthcare because of the expense. If they get sick, going to a doctor is not an option because they cannot afford to pay because we can't get insurance. The only option is to get some medication from a local drug store and hope it works." Research suggests that immigrants, particularly undocumented immigrants, have consistently lower rates of health insurance coverage than U.S.-born populations, with 65 percent of undocumented immigrants lacking health insurance. In addition, this sector of the population does not have access to government safety nets such as Medicaid and Medicare, making it very difficult for them to find affordable and quality healthcare (Derose et al., 2007). Thus Isabella's final project sought to showcase the issues immigrants faced, including access to healthcare, education, and legal services. In her project, Isabella issued a call to action for those with legal citizenship status to stand up and help immigrants, particularly immigrant children. By sharing her own personal story, she hoped to help others better understand the hardships and realities immigrant families face.

In their eighth grade year and after finishing these projects, the students at Carver had the opportunity to travel to Washington, D.C. During this trip, Isabella and her friends had the opportunity to meet with their national congressman and voice their concerns about immigration policies and practices. During this meeting, Isabella spoke passionately and professionally about the challenges of immigration and what her family had to overcome to have a better life in the United States. Isabella remarked: "By sharing my experiences, maybe I can help out others who are in the same situation. I want to change immigration policy forever." Isabella's experiences reflect changes in immigration patterns in the United States. From 2000 to 2010, Latin Americans accounted for 58 percent of the growth in the immigrant population, and Mexican immigrants alone accounted for 29 percent of all immigrants (Camarota, 2011). This change in countries of origin in the 1980s and afterward was accompanied by a higher risk of poverty among immigrants and their children.

Isabella's Building Bridges project provided her with an opportunity to understand how school systems and governments work. Isabella was fearful of the risk of deportation if her family did not follow the unstated rule of

"Don't ask, don't tell" in regard to their immigration history and citizenship status and not the military policy about sexual orientation. Students came to recognize that rules, laws, and other governmental structures are not apolitical; instead they reflect and create cultural, developmental, gendered, racial, and class-based beliefs about human nature, adolescents, and the purpose of regulating a community (Raby, 2012). Second, these projects helped students become actively involved in community issues. In each of these cases students had a personal connection to the community issue. In turn, that connection made learning about the issue a powerful motivator for critical thinking. These projects provided a vehicle for learning that required students to develop skills for effective and informed civic involvement. Isabella and her peers had to research, develop arguments, and articulate their stance on community issues with detail and sophistication. This practice provided them with the kinds of critical thinking skills that are beyond mundane textbook learning. This action civics experience encouraged young citizens of the new majority to become informed and voice their opinions on crucial civic agendas that affect their lives and the lives of those in their communities. In the next section we discuss the significance of a project like Building Bridges and address why it is important to civic education and social justice.

Young People Can Make a Difference

Building Bridges and other action civics projects develop students' desire to participate in civic affairs and enhance their sense of civic efficacy. Through participation in Building Bridges students felt empowered by their actions. Visiting with political leaders was an action that required deep thought and effort. In this case a student chose a topic that related well to social justice agendas. Even though Isabella is a middle school student, she was able, with appropriate support, to identify injustices and seek to voice her experiences.

Westheimer (2015) refers to this kind of experiential learning as "critical and structural social analysis" (p. 59). Students used their own experiences and those of their classmates as a way to explore issues of human rights and social justice. In regard to Westheimer and Kahne's (2004) continuum of civic action, this example exemplified *participatory citizenship* by attempting to "solve social problems and improve society" through active leadership (p. 240). Students engaged in collective, community-based efforts to solve a problem. The Building Bridges projects helped students understand how government and community-based organizations worked, and guided them in understanding how to plan and participate in organized efforts to address public issues. The project on immigration also moved toward the *justice-oriented* citizen by seeking to "improve society and change established systems and structures and replicate patterns of injustice" (p. 241).

Throughout these projects students were encouraged to discuss topics that were *meaningful* for them. Through discussion students were encouraged to wrestle with difficult ideas, hone their thinking, and effectively articulate their ideas. Classroom environments that include these kinds of discussions are places that encourage students to engage in social justice practices (Saavedra, 2012). Wade (2008) identified a commitment to social justice as a catalyst for change. Students should analyze their experiences and then move towards a critical perspective and eventually action directed toward social change. Through this thoughtfully structured action civics, community-based, social justice experience, students were given meaningful opportunities to develop their civic knowledge, participation skills, and attitudes while simultaneously making a positive impact on their community.

Certainly, the Building Bridges projects also had several limitations. First, middle school students often struggled to identify and unpack larger structural issues influencing their community issue. Oftentimes students' initial research and analysis were fairly shallow, requiring significant teacher scaffolding to help them move towards a more justice-oriented approach. In some cases, participants never reached this stage. In Chapter 8, Dolan and Kaufman provide a framework with which to provide teachers with the skills they need to facilitate these processes. Time proved to be an issue. With pressure from administrators to prepare students for "the test," the Building Bridges project was not always given the kind of time needed to successfully engage students in a justice-oriented approach to civics education. Despite limitations, these projects served as a unique way to provide students with the opportunity to put social studies to work in their communities (Wade, 2008).

In order for teachers to be catalysts for social change and provide their students with opportunities for civic engagement, they have to undergo a cycle of reflection and deepened understanding of pedagogy. Teachers have the opportunity to do this through careful reflection on their own belief systems, open discussion about controversial issues, and a willingness to listen to others who have different life experiences. Building Bridges projects provide the opportunity for teachers and students to do just that. They provide opportunities to develop socially responsive and responsible pedagogy in which learning becomes a reciprocal process, one in which student ideas and questions are not only valued, but essential.

Action civics projects like Building Bridges represent ambitious learning goals that go beyond test-driven instruction. Students' ideas are a central resource and the starting point for instruction (Ball and Forzani, 2009). Projects like Building Bridges require teachers to know about the content students are investigating, which often means teachers themselves must spend time researching about these particular topics in order to help guide students to attain ambitious learning goals. Teachers who involve themselves in this kind of action-oriented curriculum should know that it takes time, ingenuity, and courage. They have to be willing to step back and let their students become the change agents. Teachers who do accept the challenge to embrace an action civics curriculum rooted in social justice recognize that students need the resources and space to practice active citizenship. In their hands and hearts lie the development and sustainability of an inclusive and just democracy, one where economic disparity can be named and addressed in lasting ways.

References

Activate. (2009). [Video game from iCivics.org]. Madison, WI: Filament Games.

Baldi, S., Perie, M., Skidmore, D., Greenburg, E., and Hahn, C. (2001). *What democracy means to ninth graders: U.S. results from the international IEA Civic Education Study.* Washington, DC: National Center for Education Statistics.

Ball, D., and Forzani, F. M. (2009). The work of teaching and the challenge for teacher education. *Journal of Teacher Education, 60*(5), 497–511.

Brady, D., Baker, R. S., and Finnigan, R. (2013). When unionization disappears: State-level unionization and working poverty in the United States. *American Sociological Review, 78*(5), 872–896.

Camarota, S. (2011). *A record-setting decade of immigration: 2000–2010.* [Backgrounder]. Washington, DC: Center for Immigration Studies.

Center for Action Civics. (2013). What is action civics? Retrieved from http://www.centerforactioncivics.org/what-is-action-civics/.

Center for Information and Research on Civic Learning and Engagement (CIRCLE). (2013a). All together now: Collaboration and innovation for youth engagement. [Report]. Retrieved from http://www.civicyouth.org/commission-on-youth-voting-and-civic-knowledge-releases-report/.

Center for Information and Research on Civic Learning and Engagement (CIRCLE). (2013b). Civic learning through action: The case of generation citizen. Retrieved from http://www.civicyouth.org/wp-content/uploads/2013/07/Generation-Citizen-Fact-Sheet-July-1-Final.pdf.

Cochran-Smith, M. (2004). *Walking the road: Race, diversity, and social justice in teacher education.* New York: Teachers College Press.

Colby, S., and Ortman, J. (2015). Projections of the size and composition of the U.S. population: 2014 to 2060. *Current Population Reports* (No. P25–1143). Washington, DC: U.S. Census Bureau.

Dalton, R. J. (1998). *Citizen politics in western democracies.* Chatham, NJ: Chatham.

Delli Carpini, M., and Keeter, S. (1996). *What Americans know about politics and why it matters.* New Haven, CT: Yale University Press.

Derose, K. P., Escarce, J. J., and Lurie, N. (2007). Immigrants and health care: Sources of vulnerability. *Health Affairs, 26*(5), 1258–1268.

Ekman, J., and Amnå, E. (2012). Political participation and civic engagement: Towards a new typology. *Human Affairs, 22*(3), 283–300.

Epstein, S. E. (2014). *Teaching civic literacy projects: Student engagement with social problems.* New York: Teachers College Press.

Fine, M., Burns, A., Payne, Y. A. P., and Torre, E. A. (2004). Civics lessons: The color and class of betrayal. *Teachers College Press, 106*(11), 2193–2223.

Freire, P. (2005). *Pedagogy of the oppressed.* New York: Continuum. (Original work published 1970.)

Guilfoile, L., and Delander, B. (2014). *Guidebook: Six proven practices for effective civic learning.* Denver, CO: Education Commission of the States and National Center for Learning and Civic Engagement. Retrieved from http://www.ecs.org/clearing house/01/10/48/11048.pdf.

Hartig, S. D., Skinner, C., and Ekono, M. M. (2014). *Taxing the poor: State income tax policies make a big difference to working families*. [Report]. New York: National Center for Children in Poverty.

Junn, J. (2004). Diversity, immigration, and the politics of civic education. *PSOnline*. Retrieved from http://www.apsanet.org.

Kahne, J., and Middaugh, E. (2008). High quality civic education: What is it and who gets it? *Social Education, 72*(1), 34–39.

Kornrich, S., and Furstenberg, F. (2013). Investing in children: Changes in parental spending on children, 1972 to 2007. *Demography, 50*(1), 1–23.

Lalas, J. (2007). Teaching for social justice in multicultural urban schools: Conceptualization and implication. *Multicultural Education, 13*(4), 17–21.

LeCompte, K., and Blevins, B. (2015). Building civic bridges: Community centered action civics. *Social Studies, 106*(5), 209–217.

Lerner, R. M. (2004). *Liberty: Thriving and civic engagement among America's youth.* Thousand Oaks, CA: Sage.

Lerner, R., Almerigi, J., Theokas, C., and Lerner, J. (2005). Positive youth development. *Journal of Early Adolescence, 25*(1), 10–16.

Levine, P. (2012). Education for a civil society. In D. Campbell, M. Levinson, and F. Hess (Eds.), *Making civics count: Citizenship education for a new generation* (pp. 37–56). Cambridge, MA: Harvard Education Press.

Levine, P. (2013). *We are the ones we have been waiting for: The promise of civic renewal in America.* New York: Oxford University Press.

Levinson, M. (2012). *No citizen left behind.* Cambridge, MA: Harvard Education Press.

Mirra, N., Morrell, E. D., Cain, E., Scorza, D., and Ford, A. (2013). Educating for a critical democracy: Civic participation reimagined in the Council of Youth Research. *Democracy and Education, 21*(1), 1–10.

Moll, L. C., and González, N. (2004). Engaging life: A funds of knowledge approach to multicultural education. In J. A. Banks and C. A. Banks (Eds.), *Handbook of research on multicultural education* (pp. 699–715). San Francisco, CA: Jossey-Bass.

National Council for the Social Studies (NCSS). (1994). *Expectations of excellence: Curriculum standards for social studies.* Washington, DC: NCSS.

National Council for the Social Studies (NCSS). (2013). *The college, career, and civic life (C3) framework for social studies state standards: Guidance for enhancing the rigor of K–12 civics, economics, geography, and history.* Silver Spring, MD: NCSS.

Norris, P. (2002). *Democratic phoenix: Reinventing political activism.* New York: Cambridge University Press.

Passel, J. S. (2011). Demography of immigrant youth: Past, present and future. *Future of Children, 21*(1), 19–41.

Raby, R. (2012). *School rules: Obedience, discipline and elusive democracy.* Toronto, ON: University of Toronto Press.

Rubin, B., Hayes, B., and Benson, K. (2009). "It's the worst place to live": Urban youth and the challenge of school-based civic learning. *Theory into Practice, 48*(3), 213–221.

Saavedra, A. R. (2012). Dry to dynamic civics education. In D. Campbell, M. Levinson, and F. Hess (Eds.), *Making civics count: Citizenship education for a new generation* (pp. 135–160). Cambridge, MA: Harvard Education Press.

Saltmarsh, J. (2008). Why Dewey matters. *Good Society, 17*(2), 63–68.

Serriere, S. (2014). The role of the elementary teacher in fostering civic efficacy. *Social Studies*, *105*(1), 45–56.

Wade, R. (2001). Social action in the social studies: From the ideal to the real. *Theory into Practice*, *40*(1), 23–28.

Wade, R. (2008). Service learning. In L. Levstik and C. Tyson (Eds.), *Handbook of research in social studies education* (pp. 109–123). New York: Routledge.

Westheimer, J. (2015). *What kind of citizen? Educating our children for the common good*. New York: Teachers College Press.

Westheimer, J., and Kahne, J. (2004). What kind of citizen? The politics of educating for democracy. *American Educational Research Journal*, *41*(2), 237–269.

Youniss, J. (2012). How to enrich civic education and sustain democracy. In D. Campbell, M. Levinson, and F. Hess (Eds.), *Making civics count: Citizenship education for a new generation* (pp. 115–134). Cambridge, MA: Harvard Education Press.

Zimenkova, T. (2013). Active citizenship as harmonious co-existence? About political participatory education. In R. Hedtke and T. Zimenkova (Eds.), *Education for civic and political participation: A critical approach* (pp. 36–53). New York: Routledge.

Zuberi, D. (2013). *The working poor*. In V. Smith (Ed.), *Sociology of work: An encyclopedia* (pp. 1005–1010). Thousand Oaks, CA: Sage.

11

FOSTERING YOUTH VOICE

Philosophy, Strategies, and Outcomes of the Democracy in Action Program

Emma Kornfeld, Jill Bass, and Brett L. M. Levy

> It may be an easy thing to make a republic; but it is a very laborious thing to make republicans.
>
> *(Horace Mann, 1848)*

What practices can schools employ to foster civic participation among youth with diverse perspectives? How can educators build agency and efficacy in their students? How can students develop skills needed to be powerful in a democracy? What follows in this chapter is not simple answers, because, quite honestly, answers to such questions do not exist in a vacuum of our own good intentions. Instead we offer concrete strategies for developing student voice and engagement in order to illustrate how we might begin to cultivate the agency, and therefore the power, of young people. We propose a promising practice for fostering student engagement in our classrooms and in our democracy in spite of and in conversation with systems that can sometimes disenfranchise, disempower, and discount the youth they claim to serve. This chapter will explore action civics as a framework for youth civic engagement and will discuss Mikva Challenge's Issues to Action curriculum as a promising practice for educating for democracy.

Mikva Challenge, a non-partisan non-profit organization based in Chicago, seeks to develop the next generation of civic leaders through programs that focus on electoral participation, policy-making, and community activism. Founded in 1997 in honor of former congressman, federal court judge, and White House counsel Abner Mikva and his wife Zoe Mikva, a former teacher and education activist, the organization's endeavors are built on a few core principles: (1) civic education is essential to the health of our republic;

(2) young people learn civics best when they are actively participating in democratic activities inside and outside the classroom; and (3) intentional effort must be paid to help ensure ample and equal opportunities for engagement. When Abner Mikva first visited his local ward office, prior to his esteemed career, he was abruptly turned away and told "I don't want nobody that nobody sent." The realities for engagement in our democracy, despite its necessity, are in fact bleak at times. Our youth are all too often the nobodies that nobody sent.

There is an explicit mismatch for many youth when they are taught that democracy carries values of equality, opportunity, and fairness, while they live in a world with vast wealth inequality, extreme poverty, and systematic discrimination (Rubin, 2007; Rubin et al., 2009). It is for these reasons, among others, that Iris Young's (2000) contention that democracy is hard to love is especially resonant. For some young people, official political discourse seems distant and irrelevant (Tupper et al., 2010). Furthermore, at a time when violent conflicts between police officers and citizens in minority communities are receiving tremendous attention and #BlackLivesMatter rings out on social media and in the streets (a phenomenon that Arend and Cuenca in Chapter 12 and Krutka and Carpenter in Chapter 14 explore in more detail), we as practitioners must consider what it means to embark on civic engagement work with disenfranchised youth through the promise of enhancing voice, power, and rights. We highlight this challenge at the outset to situate our discussion on how we educate for democracy while attending to the authentic challenges that many youth and communities face.

Action civics is not a quick fix that will end discrimination, income inequality, or the contradictions in our democracy. But it remains a worthy pursuit because it may provide space for young people to develop as engaged citizens and leaders in the face of those injustices. Action civics is a process driven by student interest that seeks to expand access and participation in our democracy, which might otherwise feel out of reach at best and systematically exclusive at worst. What students can learn and achieve through this process is impressive and wide-ranging. We have seen examples where: students seeking to understand truancy at their school take the reins to develop a survey of their peers to inform the policies of their administration; students concerned about the safety of the intersection outside their school propose infrastructure changes to their alderman; or in the face of budget cuts made manifest in a compromised learning environment students spoke out at the Board of Education. Students can learn how to be powerful actors in our democracy rather than internalize persistent messaging that it is either only for them in the future when they are adults or not for them at all. We offer action civics and Mikva Challenge's Issues to Action curriculum as a promising practice for bridging these disconnects and helping develop youth as leaders and citizens.

Educating for Whose Democracy?

Essential to the exploration of promising practices for educating young people for democracy is defining what type of citizenship practitioners are seeking to develop: What are the skills, knowledge, and dispositions that teachers hope to develop in their students, and consequently what curricula and teaching practices can support those goals? Joel Westheimer and Joseph Kahne (2004) illustrate a valuable paradigm, as outlined in Chapter 3, describing how civic education can help develop young people into (1) personally responsible citizens, (2) participatory citizens, or (3) justice-oriented citizens. Indeed there may be different goals and outcomes in citizenship development, so it is important for practitioners to consider and reflect on the type of citizens they hope to develop in their classes. In other words, if the goal is civic engagement, what exactly should that look like?

Various scholars and organizations have developed metrics to measure civic engagement, and these reveal widely differing perspectives on what civic engagement might look like. While certain indicators may be general enough to encompass a variety of ways to understand civic behaviors, such as holding membership in a group or engaging in community problem-solving, these standardized measures are still an outgrowth of a mainstream perspective and may exclude additional civic understandings and skills possessed by marginalized minority youth. Meira Levinson (2012) further illustrates this disconnect when she writes:

> My eighth-grade students, for example, eloquently made the case that I, a White, middle-class woman living in a middle-class Boston neighborhood— would have a hard time understanding and negotiating the politics of "the hood" in which they lived. I certainly would have flunked a test that asked me to identify members of the locally relevant power structure: who controlled what block; which housing projects I could safely enter as a resident of another project; or which social workers, police officers, and housing authority representatives could be trusted and which were to be avoided.
>
> (p. 337)

Levinson's passage highlights the shortcomings of assessing young people's civic knowledge and behaviors solely on a normative standardized tool. Doing so misses the mark and underestimates the civic prowess many young people already possess. Educators should try to ensure strategies for youth civic engagement do not discount the expertise students possess and are not blind to the contexts in which they live their lives.

Similarly, civic education does at times ask young people to connect with a series of institutions with which they may have tension or animosity. Cathy Cohen (2010) articulates that many black Americans have been "politically socialized" to have a distrust of public officials and the political system since childhood (p. 128). Perhaps not surprisingly, studies have shown that youth who have both greater trust in and knowledge of the system are engaged in more traditional forms of civic participation (Hart and Gullan, 2010). Therefore traditional forms of civic engagement, such as voting, may be ineffective on their own in engaging marginalized youth who have valid, yet often unacknowledged, distrust of the very institutions with which civic educators may be asking them to engage (Hart and Gullan, 2010, p. 69).

Because our democracy is imperfect, we should not create future citizens who unquestioningly accept systemic inequity or whose definition of civic education begins and ends with the three branches of government. It is important that we, as civic educators, be careful to avoid "asking the wrong questions regarding civic and political behavior amongst urban and suburban youth of color" (Akom et al., 2012, p. 7). We contend that the goal of civic education must be about not only participation, but also questioning, improvement, and action. It must be about working to help ensure our democracy lives up to its ideals. Mikva Challenge's slogan is "Democracy Is a Verb." In other words, democracy is voting, lobbying, questioning, researching, speaking, listening, engaging, organizing, campaigning, and problem-solving. In our view, widespread adoption of such behaviors would be a sign of a healthy democracy because of its potential for inclusivity and responsiveness to members of excluded groups whose voices have been silenced or absent. This type of citizenship development can begin with the creation of opportunities for all youth to develop civic leadership skills in their classrooms, rather than passively learning about how democracy works.

Learning Democracy by Doing Democracy

Preparing to be an active, informed citizen in a democracy requires practice. Peter Levine and Meira Levinson (2013) aptly illustrate that learning citizenship is not unlike learning to read, to do math, to dance, or to play basketball—the most fruitful learning takes place when students are actually doing what it is that they are seeking to learn. Despite this shared knowledge of how students learn best, for many youth the opportunity to have authentic opportunities to practice democracy is minimal or altogether absent; schools and society generally do not offer young people productive ways to have their voices heard. Additionally, well-intentioned educators face a variety of obstacles to creating a classroom environment that cultivates participation, leadership, and democracy. For one, the model of short, departmentalized periods, increasingly aimed at test achievement (Sondel, 2015), is built around a philosophy of teaching and learning based in knowledge transfer. Classroom environments where the expectations are for the teachers to teach (i.e., tell) and the students to listen and learn (e.g., Howard, J., 1998) allow only limited opportunities for authentic projects that are linked to students' real lives. Additionally, research shows that often the classes with the least amount of student voice are those of low-income, minority, and low-achieving students (Pace, 2008). Overcrowded classrooms, numerous standardized tests, and classroom management concerns may be some of the challenges that lead away from authentic learning experiences in classrooms (e.g., Wilson, 2003). In these circumstances, educating for democracy becomes a luxury rather than a central purpose of schooling.

Action civics offers a pedagogy that emphasizes young people's voices and experiences in ways that can leverage their development into leaders and citizens, even those students not traditionally identified as leaders. It can be broadly understood as "guided experiential civic education—whether it be serving on a mock trial jury, engaging in community organizing, participating in Model United Nations, or interning with a nonprofit" (Levinson, 2012, p. 216). The National Action Civics Collaborative (NACC), a coalition of 21 organizations and 49 individuals, elaborates that action civics requires an authentic and experiential approach that is guided by four tenets: (1) collective action; (2) youth voice; (3) youth agency; and (4) reflection (National Action Civics Collaborative, n.d.). Action civics can allow students to have a participatory role in their own learning, pursue topics of interest and relevance, develop and express their opinions, and share their expertise with others. Teachers may use a variety of strategies, big and small, to develop an open, democratic classroom environment (Levy et al., 2015). The layout of the room (i.e., in a U-shape as opposed to traditional rows of seats), the tone of the classroom (i.e., co-creating class norms), and the way the class is organized (i.e., voting on certain class procedures) all attend to the centrality of youth voice, collaboration, and thoughtful and reflective engagement.

Action civics is built on the idea that the best way to learn democracy is by doing it. One can think of action civics as an answer to Horace Mann's assertion about the importance of spaces for youth to engage civically in order to help ensure that they can take the reins of leading this country in the future. Ultimately, an important premise of action civics is the idea that policies and decisions impacting young people would be better informed and more effective if youth were involved in their design ("Mikva Challenge," 2015). This approach fosters opportunities to assess student growth as students apply their developing skills in real-world and practical contexts (e.g., lobbying a decision maker on an issue of importance or speaking in a public forum) rather than through a simulation or a test (Kirshner, 2006). Furthermore, scholars have suggested that action civics opportunities may help boost students' self-efficacy and engagement (Levy, 2011, 2013), which consequently could improve not only their civic knowledge but perhaps also their academic performance (Pope et al., 2011).

Scholarship pertaining to practices like action civics is also complemented by scholarship exploring implementation of civic education specifically with youth living in communities with limited resources. Ben Kirshner, Karen Strobel, and Maria Fernandez (2003) assert that civic education with marginalized youth must be viewed through a critical lens, thereby allowing and encouraging young people's participation in civic realms to be motivated by their own experiences with injustice. In fact, students enter educational spaces already having a civic identity—whether it is one they have intentionally developed or one that has been given to them by institutions or individuals (Levinson, 2012; Wilkenfeld et al., 2010). Civic educational spaces like those created in action civics pedagogy and programming provide an opportunity to redefine the civic identity young people may have been given and reconstruct one informed by their voice, expertise, and active participation.

Putting Action Civics into Practice

The value of action civics lies in its ability to be implemented in meaningful ways in the classroom to provide transformative and relevant experiences for students. Perhaps most importantly, action civics defies the misnomer that citizenship development is solely the responsibility of civics teachers. Rather, the four tenets of action civics—youth voice, youth expertise, learning by doing, and reflection—can be employed in any number of disciplines in a manner that can have a lasting impact on students. Action civics is a malleable pedagogical practice, not bound by subject, but rather driven by its approach and philosophy. It defies a traditional classroom model of teacher as dispenser of knowledge, since it facilitates youth voice, expertise, and peer-to-peer collaboration. We offer the following suggestions for laying down an action civics foundation in a classroom.

Develop a Democratic Classroom Environment

When students feel that the classroom is a space where they can openly share and discuss ideas without pressure to conform to others' views, they may be more likely to practice self-expression and learn from each other (Holley and Steiner, 2005). Community-building activities, student participation in decision-making, and procedures to resolve conflicts can all contribute to the kind of environment in which students are more likely to speak and write freely and be willing to take risks, which is similar to the kind of environment that Engebretson and Hollett describe as a necessary feature of feminist pedagogy in Chapter 7. Classrooms that move from measures of individual success to communal success contribute to developing a democratic ethic. It is within this classroom environment that students can participate in their learning rather than seeing it as something that is done to them. Furthermore, evidence indicates that such open classroom environments support young people's development of political voice and efficacy (Hahn, 1998).

As a Teacher, Reflect on Voice and Identity

Even in classrooms where youth voice is cultivated, the teacher can still be consciously and unconsciously influential. We recommend practitioners reflect deeply on who they are, and what assumptions, biases, and points of view they bring into the classroom. Reflective questions may include: What do I, the teacher, think and feel about an issue? Why? Should I tell students at the outset what my views are so that they can allow for possible biases? Or should I not tell them, but guard against any inclinations to influence students' perspectives? Am I leading them to follow my interests? Am I giving my students space to explore issues and/or positions on issues I disagree with? To what extent might my gender, racial, religious, and cultural background(s) impact the topics and discussion in class? Hess (2009) argues that teachers should be aware of how their own political perspectives could affect students' learning, but she also acknowledges that most adolescents will develop their own opinions regardless of their teachers' views. That said, instead of ignoring who we are or what we think, we encourage practitioners to recognize that we are not value neutral. As Gary Howard (1999) explains, knowing oneself, one's background, and one's experience is as important as knowing one's students and knowing one's practice.

Build on Students' Expertise and Avoid Assumptions

Although most teachers acknowledge that students enter the classroom with prior knowledge, it can be a challenge to successfully access and build upon student experience and expertise in the classroom. Additionally, we as adults should be careful not to make assumptions about what young people may or may not know, as these generalizations may be insulting or offensive. The simplest way to find out what students know is to ask and listen. Direct questioning, surveys, group discussions, and journal writing can be effective strategies to find out what students know. An important component of utilizing student expertise is not to stop at solely soliciting it, but also to use it to inform future class work and assignments.

Illustrating Action Civics: Mikva Challenge's Issues to Action Curriculum

Mikva Challenge's Issues to Action curriculum provides a promising practice for educating for democracy and an illustration of the impact of action civics pedagogy. Issues to Action is the curricular support for Mikva Challenge's Democracy in Action program, which engaged nearly 3,000 students and 50 teachers from 37 schools throughout the city of Chicago in the 2014–15 school year. Our alumni evaluation data demonstrate that when students are given the opportunity to participate in civic life they are more likely to participate in the future. Of our alumni, 88 percent are registered voters, compared to only 53 percent of 18- to 29-year-olds nationwide, and equally many alumni report that they feel a responsibility to get involved to make things better for society, compared to 39 percent of their peers nationwide. These statistics are significant because they precisely defy a broadly held misconception of young people as apathetic and/or disengaged. Unfortunately, too often young people are simply not invited to participate meaningfully in democratic processes that directly affect their lives—the Issues to Action curriculum aims to disrupt this pattern.

The Issues to Action curriculum (ITA) provides a six-step framework to facilitate youth voice, choice, and participation in community issues. Developed over the past decade by teachers, the curriculum is by no means one-size-fits-all. It was expressly designed for educators to pick and choose lessons that best suit their needs and the needs of their students. Teachers use the curriculum in a variety of different contexts, including integrating it into content areas, in advisory, as an elective course, or in an after-school club. Steps can vary in length and be adapted based on class scheduling, student learning, and teacher preferences. Action projects may be completed over the course of a few weeks or throughout the entire school year. Given this range, the lessons are designed to allow for maximum flexibility and adaptability. Teachers may find the need to modify lessons in order to differentiate for the needs of their students by providing more challenge or additional scaffolding. The curriculum provides suggestions for adaptations while relying on the fact that teachers already possess a host of strategies. Reflective prompts are woven into most lessons to facilitate reflection as a regular practice so students can continually take stock of what they have learned.

To that end, the six-step process that appears below more accurately represents the process and its regular integration of reflection throughout. Below are illustrative summaries of each step of the Issues to Action curriculum.[1]

Examine Community

In this step, students begin to develop a working definition for the word "community" and explore their own communities with an asset-based approach. Once they have an idea what community means in general, they will be able to start thinking about the traits of their community in particular. Students may create community maps, conduct a community scavenger hunt, create a civic footprint for themselves that identifies their elected representatives, and consider what, if any, responsibility they have to their community.

Choose an Issue

In this step students identify issues that they care about within their communities. First, each student stands up and speaks out on an issue that he or she cares about through Project Soapbox, a series of public speaking lessons which concludes with every student delivering a two-minute speech. Once all the students have shared the issue that is most important to them, the class goes through a series of civic deliberations to choose an issue to work on for their group civic action project. (Usually there is one issue per class, but some teachers may allow for several.) During the decision-making, the students consider their interest or passion for the issue as well as the degree of impact they could have.

Research the Issue

Students first analyze their issue and determine its underlying root causes so as to break it into component parts. They examine the root causes through primary and secondary research. Students survey the community for input about their issue and meet with experts. Based on their research, students set a preliminary goal (or goals) for action.

Analyze Power

This step focuses on locating the key decision makers who possess power over the class's issue. For example, they identify who has power to help them accomplish the goals established in the previous step. Once decision makers are identified, students analyze the motivations of targeted decision makers so as to develop a strategy to connect their goals to the motivations of the decision makers in question. Students also prepare and practice for a meeting with a decision maker.

Decide on a Strategy and Develop a Plan

Once students have chosen a goal for their issue and know who has the power to make that goal happen, this step facilitates brainstorming possible plans of action, analyzing the pros and cons of multiple strategies, and developing a comprehensive action plan.

Take Action and Reflect

By this point students have likely been taking action throughout the process, but this step tends to include a big action that involves a large-scale effort in service to their goals, such as organizing a petition drive, holding a town-hall meeting, or attempting to influence an elected official. This step may involve getting media attention for the students' action, a social media campaign, or a celebratory showcase of some kind. The best way to truly see this practice is through observing the work of students and teachers. Included below are some examples of how teachers and students chose to tackle a community issue.

Youth Voice in School Policy

After conducting a survey with the student body, Issues to Action students identified a recurring concern over the lack of student voice in school decision-making.

The students presented a proposal to the local school council and the instructional leadership team to have youth involved in the filling of the principal vacancy. Both bodies approved the proposal, and students were involved in the interviewing and hiring of the new principal. The school now involves students in all new hires through an interview and feedback process.

Improving Arts Education in the Face of School Budget Cuts

Concerned about the increasing lack of arts education for students in their district, students sought to create a program that would allow high school students to bolster arts education programs at elementary schools in their school's neighborhood. They wrote a proposal, presented it to their principal, and are now collaborating with the district's Office of Arts Education to pilot their program at a local elementary school.

Young Male Achievement

After identifying that young men at the school were earning lower grades and test scores than their female counterparts, a group of students convened a town-hall meeting of female students to address what young women could do to support their male classmates. This project was the catalyst for gender-specific programming at the school to support the various needs of students.

Links to Local History

After learning that Martin Luther King, Jr. led marches in their own neighborhood, students wanted to make sure members of their community and others were aware of their connection to an important historical event. Students worked with various city agencies, museums, and technology developers to create a digital kiosk in their community to commemorate the march and educate others.

Empty Space Full of Opportunity

When students saw a vacant lot near their school on the city's southwest side, they also saw an opportunity for change. After researching the history of how Chicago neighborhoods have changed in the past, they developed a plan to start a community garden and possibly even a community center in the vacant lot.

Conclusion

These examples highlight how young people can drive sustainable change in their schools and communities when given the space and the tools to do so. By asking young people to leverage their expertise and become the primary facilitators of their own solutions, we can create active and engaged citizens. It is what Meira Levinson (2012) describes as employing youth expertise as a vehicle for civic development and what John Dewey (1916) identifies as a critical job for our schools. Employing an action civics framework that is justice oriented and rooted in youth voice and authentic democratic experiences is critical not only to developing civic agency and efficacy in youth, but to ensuring the health and integrity of our democracy (Westheimer and Kahne, 2004).

Note

1 Visit www.mikvachallenge.org for more information.

References

Akom, A. A., Cammarota, J., and Ginwright, S. (2012). Youthtopias: Towards a new paradigm of critical youth studies. *Youth Media Reporter: Professional Journal of the Youth Media Field*, 2(4), 1–30.

Cohen, C. J. (2010). *Democracy remixed*. Oxford: Oxford University Press.

Dewey, J. (1916). *Democracy and education*. New York: Free Press.

Hahn, C. L. (1998). *Becoming political: Comparative perspectives on citizenship education*. Albany, NY: SUNY Press.

Hart, D., and Gullan, R. L. (2010). The sources of adolescent activism: Historical and contemporary findings. In L. R. Sherrod, J. Torney-Purta, and C. A. Flanagan (Eds.), *Handbook of research on civic engagement of youth* (pp. 67–90). Hoboken, NJ: John Wiley & Sons.

Hess, D. E. (2009). *Controversy in the classroom: The democratic power of discussion*. New York: Routledge.

Holley, L. C., and Steiner, S. (2005). Safe space: Student perspectives on classroom environment. *Journal of Social Work Education*, 41(1), 49–64.

Howard, G. (1999). *We can't teach what we don't know: White teachers, multiracial schools*. New York: Teachers College Press.

Howard, J. P. F. (1998). Academic service learning: A counternormative pedagogy. *New Directions for Teaching and Learning*, 73, 21–29.

Kirshner, B. (2006). Apprenticeship learning in youth activism. In S. Ginwright, P. Noguera, and J. Cammarota (Eds.), *Beyond resistance! Youth activism and community change: New democratic possibilities for practice and policy for America's youth* (pp. 37–57). New York: Routledge.

Kirshner, B., Strobel, K., and Fernandez, M. (2003). Critical civic engagement among urban youth. *PennGSE Perspectives on Urban Education*, 2(1). Retrieved from http://www.urbanedjournal.org/archive/volume-2-issue-1-spring-2003/critical-civic-engagement-among-urban-youth.

Levine, P., and Levinson, M. (2013). Taking informed action to engage students in civic life. *Social Education*, 77(6), 339–341.

Levinson, M. (2012). *No citizen left behind*. Cambridge, MA: Harvard University Press.

Levy, B. L. M. (2011). Fostering cautious political efficacy through civic advocacy projects: A mixed methods case study of an innovative high school class. *Theory and Research in Social Education*, 39(2), 238–277.

Levy, B. L. M. (2013). An empirical exploration of factors related to adolescents' political efficacy. *Educational Psychology, 33*(3), 357–390.

Levy, B. L. M., Ramakrishnan, V., Gibbs, B., and Cross, A. (2015). Democratic practices in classrooms and schools. In W. G. Scarlett (Ed.), *Sage encyclopedia of classroom management*. Thousand Oaks, CA: Sage.

Mann, H. (1848). Twelfth annual report of Horace Mann as secretary of Massachusetts State Board of Education. Retrieved from http://usa.usembassy.de/etexts/democrac/16.htm.

"Mikva Challenge." (2015). Retrieved from http://www.mikvachallenge.org/.

National Action Civics Collaborative. (n.d.). Why action civics? Retrieved from http://actioncivicscollaborative.org/why-action-civics/framework/.

Pace, J. L. (2008). *Educating democratic citizens in troubled times: Qualitative studies of current efforts*. Albany, NY: SUNY Press.

Pope, A., Stolte, L., and Cohen, A. K. (2011). Closing the civic empowerment gap: The potential of action civics. *Social Education, 75*(5), 267–270.

Rubin, B. C. (2007). "There's still not justice": Youth civic identity development amid distinct school and community contexts. *Teachers College Record, 109*(2), 449–481.

Rubin, B. C., Hayes, B., and Benson, K. (2009). "It's the worst place to live": Urban youth and the challenge of school-based civic learning. *Theory into Practice, 48*(3), 213–221.

Sondel, B. (2015). Raising citizens or raising test scores? Teach for America, "no excuses" charters, and the development of the neoliberal citizen. *Theory and Research in Social Education, 43*(3), 289–313.

Tupper, J., Cappello, M., and Sevigny, P. (2010). Locating citizenship: Curriculum, social class and the "good" citizen. *Theory and Research in Social Education, 38*(3), 336–365.

Westheimer, J., and Kahne, J. (2004). What kind of citizen? The politics of educating for democracy. *American Educational Research Journal, 41*(2), 237–269.

Wilkenfeld, B., Lauckhardt, J., and Torney-Purta, J. (2010). The relation between developmental theory and measures of civic engagement in research on adolescents. In L. R. Sherrod, J. Torney-Purta, and C. A. Flanagan (Eds.), *Handbook of research on civic engagement of youth* (pp. 193–220). Hoboken, NJ: John Wiley & Sons.

Wilson, S. M. (2003). *California dreaming: Reforming mathematics education*. New Haven, CT: Yale University Press.

Young, I. M. (2000). *Inclusion and democracy*. Oxford: Oxford University Press.

New Fronts in the Fight for Democracy

12

INTERROGATING DEMOCRACY

Lessons from Ferguson, Missouri

Lauren Arend and Alexander Cuenca

Ostensibly, the permanence of a democracy is maintained through the preparation of youth to assume the thought patterns, values, and responsibilities consistent with democratic life. In the United States, public schools are the spaces where democratic ideals are cultivated. As Parker (2003) argues, public schools are "the only public spaces encountered by virtually all children, and this makes them, if not ideal sites ... promising sites for a genuine civic apprenticeship" (pp. 10–11). This arrangement between schools and society is what makes education for democracy an uncontroversial public trope. Often embedded within the ideology and rhetoric of public discussions about schools are claims of the importance of preserving ideals consistent with a democracy. Within schools, subjects like social studies, civics, history, and government are dedicated curricular spaces to prepare youth for civic life. Although this arrangement serves to perpetuate democracy, it is a unidirectional arrangement where schools are intentionally designed to serve society—a point that Nichols makes so powerfully in Chapter 2.

What is problematic about the schools-serving-society arrangement is that the preservation of democracy comes with a cost; rather than interrogating society and the democratic order in schools, it is presupposed that these domains will be taken for granted by both teachers and students. The discursive forces of history, politics, and economics shape the norms of democratic participation, expression, and engagement being cultivated in schools. Under this unidirectional arrangement, these norms are simply appropriated for reproduction. But, in order for democracy to be dynamic, it must constantly be questioned by those living within it.

Today, a predominant influence on the idea of democracy is neoliberalism (Chomsky, 1999), which reframes citizenship through the lens of the economic.

As Nichols (Chapter 2) elucidated, market values become proxies for democratic values within this frame. The behavior of the consumer is confounded with the behavior of the citizen. In schools, the language of accountability and the endless initiatives and reforms that lie in its wake have continued to entrench citizens as consumers. As Biesta (2004) contends, neoliberal logic has reconfigured the relationship between the state and its citizens. Essentially it "has become less a political relationship—that is, a relationship between government and citizens, who together, are concerned about the common good—and more an economic relationship—that is, a relationship between the state as provider and the taxpayer as consumer of public services" (p. 237). With accountability as an external pressure, schools have succumbed to the rationalization that economic prosperity determines self-worth. Thus the latent and explicit curriculum in schools is constructed in response to the question of how schools can best create capital and economic growth. According to the neoliberal rationale, the most viable goal for education is the production of the rational individual able to act as a free and autonomous agent, mediated by financial independence. Consequently, the expressions of democratic life that flow from this goal are personally responsible acts such as voting, obeying the law, and maintaining a good character, while pursuing economic ends.

Hyperfocused on the individual, neoliberal logic gives schools alibis to turn away from the issues that sustain the mutuality needed in a democracy. Questions of justice, inequity, and social welfare are diminished in response to the calls to replace the behaviors of citizens with those of consumers. As Hursh (2008) describes, under neoliberalism, "inequality is the product of individual choice and should not be remedied by social welfare programs, but by individuals taking more responsibility and striving to become productive members of the workforce" (p. 155). Thus, without the mandate to interrogate the arrangement of citizens to society, this logic instead asks schools simply to replicate a thin democratic life bent towards individualism and consumerism. Societal disparities will continue to widen because we have abdicated our responsibilities as citizens to address them.

Under the neoliberal gaze, preparing youth for superficial expressions of public engagement further exacerbates the inequality that neoliberalism refuses to consider. The civic efficacy of personally responsible acts is tilted in the favor of individuals who have greater civic and economic resources, positions of influence, power, and the social and cultural capital to manipulate political structures to achieve desired outcomes (Castro and Knowles, in press). In other words, democracy as a personally responsible act is a predominantly white and middle-class performance of deference to the status quo (Schutz, 2008). Thus, the forms of participation in a democracy that schools peddle continue to exacerbate inequality. Given these realities, schools must find ways to rewrite democracy and not simply accept the norms of participation that echo individualistic pursuits that do not permit engagement with questions of inequity beyond the individual failings described by Nichols (Chapter 2).

Because the aspirations central to the ethos of democracy are best articulated by the voices marginalized within a democracy, in this chapter we turn our attention to the people and movements that called into question the hypocrisy of inequality in America in the aftermath of the death of Mike Brown[1] in Ferguson, Missouri. The social interrogation that emerged in Ferguson provides unique lessons on ways to expose, challenge, and recast democracy. Thus the response to Ferguson is a powerful counter-narrative to the neoliberal ideal that promotes a demure democracy, because the activists in Ferguson rejected accepted norms for expressing—or not expressing—political dissent. For those looking to educate for democracy in an age of economic disparity, the Ferguson activists and their acts of resistance and public inquest exemplify how to engage in a democracy undergirded by the search for justice.

We begin this chapter by briefly sketching the events in Ferguson and highlighting some of the historical, social, political, and economic factors that conditioned this civic uprising. Drawing from the various people and movements that emerged in the wake of Ferguson, we discuss three acts that interrogate democracy: spontaneous resolve, solidarity, and disruption of protected spaces. These three acts are then illustrated across three vehicles of communication deployed in Ferguson: hip-hop, visual art, and social media. We then give some suggestions on how to validate the interrogation of democracy in the classroom, before concluding. Given the neoliberal demand that schools, classrooms, and curricula cultivate citizens who turn away from inequity, Ferguson is a critical example of not just the necessity for interrogation but also the means to accomplish it.

Ferguson, Missouri

On August 9th, 2014 Mike Brown, an unarmed black teenager, was shot and killed by white police officer Darren Wilson. Ferguson residents began to gather almost immediately as Mike Brown's body lay in the street for over four hours. This immediacy spoke to the timeliness of the scenario for black residents in North St. Louis County, and foreshadowed events that were to come. Social media led to instantaneous virtual and on-the-ground community gatherings. The growing crowds over the weekend triggered a response from police including riot gear and K-9 units, which culminated in a night of violence and the infamous burning of the Quick Trip gas station on August 10th. The following week saw police release tear gas in residential black neighborhoods in Ferguson, and the emergence of an array of movements calling for justice, not just for Mike Brown, but also for the persistent inequities that surrounded his life. In the ensuing months we witnessed a grand jury that failed to indict Wilson, more nights of uprising in Ferguson, and the release of a Department of Justice (DOJ) report documenting a history of race-based and racist policing practices by the Ferguson Police Department.

The killing of Mike Brown is situated in the context of growing attention to police shootings of black men. Yet Ferguson became a flashpoint for the mobilization of movements in ways that the deaths of other black men such as Trayvon Martin, John Crawford, and Eric Garner did not. The historical, political, and economic conditions that shaped the intensity and persistence of the Ferguson protests, and the movements that followed in its aftermath, spoke to a unique confluence of localized inequity. People in Ferguson were responding not only to the historical harassment of black residents at the hands of area police—which was verified by the DOJ investigation—but to a system of local municipalities that subsist on predatory court fines paid almost exclusively by poor black people. ArchCity Defenders, a local legal organization, wrote a detailed report outlining how the fragmented municipality structure in St. Louis County, resulting from decades of white flight and racist zoning policies, led to over-policing and fining of black communities to support the governing municipal bodies, which represent sometimes as few as 600 residents. The report cited that "the amount collected through the municipal courts seems to be inversely proportional to the wealth of the municipality" (Harvey et al., 2014, p. 9). The use of warrants and threatened jail time for unpaid fines largely levied for low-level misdemeanors like traffic stops further exacerbates the economic disparities in North St. Louis County. If you are poor and black in St. Louis you don't have to be reaching for an officer's gun to be subjected to the consequences of institutional racism, disproportionate taxation, surveillance, or incarceration; they are all the daily realities of the people living in these communities (Harvey et al., 2014).

The economic reality for residents in Ferguson and neighboring municipalities is housed within a cruel system of resource depletion from a lack of access to jobs, poorly funded school districts, and illegal taxing through aggressive levying of court fines. Beyond the dubious policing and court practices, there are both tacit and explicit exclusions of blacks from citizenship and commerce in the St. Louis metro region. For example, the continued rejection of the public light rail's expansion, linking these communities to commercial areas, has been supported by outwardly expressed fears of increases in crime.

It would be a disservice to diminish the experiences of the Ferguson community in the wake of Mike Brown's death to a singular concern about their economic reality. Ferguson and the people in communities like it have multifaceted lives that matter; black lives matter. But the movements in Ferguson have been centered on the humanity and lives of black people through the varied aspects of what it is to have a life that matters in contemporary society: a person who is alive, a citizen participating in a democracy, and a consumer participating in an economy. The municipality of Ferguson in particular is a poignant example of the intersection of racist and aggressive—in this case deadly—policing practices, constitutionally questionable court practices, and disproportionate appropriating of poor people's assets through fines and fees. It is out of this context that the uprising in Ferguson provides a framework to challenge traditional versions of what it means to participate in a democracy.

The various movements that emerged in response to the death of Mike Brown provide opportunities to explore in context what it means to interrogate rather than merely participate in a democracy. In our estimation, a few distinct acts of interrogation materialized from these movements. First is the spontaneous resolve exhibited in Ferguson. The call to organize was immediate, but also reso-lute in its end goal: the search for justice. Like political philosopher Gus DiZerega (2000), we see the movements in Ferguson as an illustration of how democracy is an ongoing spontaneous organization and reorganization of people expressing their values. Through the immediacy of the demonstrations, protests, and staged actions, Ferguson provides a lens to see not only the spontaneity of organization in a democracy, but also how this spontaneity calls into question the power of the state. Second, these acts of solidarity bound people and voices together to leverage democratic action and change. The death of Mike Brown galvanized not just the local community of Ferguson but other individuals across the globe with the common interest of confronting the depravity of inequity through a mass interrogation of democracy. Third, the demands for justice worked to disrupt protected spaces such as streets, venues of entertainment, and places of com-merce. Entering protected spaces invalidated the personal and social alibis that failed to address questions of equity within our democracy. Disruption also chal-lenged where, when, and how democratic action was allowed to be expressed.

To illustrate how this interrogation of democracy was conducted in Ferguson, we will describe three modes of communication that were utilized by the peo-ple and organizations demanding justice for Mike Brown. The first mode is hip-hop, which has roots in resistant and subversive expressions of antagonism towards establishment systems of governance. The second is visual art, used both as an individual medium for activism and as a collective response to politics through uncommissioned public art. Finally, social media was a mode of com-munication that influenced, informed, and inspired a critical interrogation of democracy. Each of these modes illustrates the inherent rejection of effete modes of democratic engagement that refuse to stand against the tyranny of injustice. In articulating just three modes, we don't mean to suggest that other modes of communication, such as organized protests or civil disobedience, are invalid or ineffective, nor do we desire to suggest that the forms of civic communication are limited to these three modes. We do, however, see the communicative modes of hip-hop, visual art, and social media as representative of the contemporary ways in which democracy was being expressed in Ferguson.

Hip-Hop: Not Your Father's Civil Rights Movement

In the weeks following Mike Brown's death, there was a continued call for a response from hip-hop. Rap music listeners and critics questioned the silence from top producing rappers on the Black Lives Matter movement in general and the death of Mike Brown in particular. The responses that hip-hop artists made publicly were then subjected to a high level of scrutiny, with critiques of "too little, too late," and dismay at language that ranged from tepid to potentially self-loathing. These conversations, which played out through multiple modalities (Twitter, music websites, mainstream media) about the role of hip-hop as an industry in activism, highlights the power that is inherent in the genre to interrogate. In Ferguson, there was condemnation of both the silence and the intrusion of inauthentic, uncommitted non-local rappers. Local rapper and activist Tef Poe became a symbol of the antithesis of this trepidatious response. Tef Poe's work will be the lens through which we frame the expressions of democratic interrogation. His local knowledge allowed him to be intimately tied to the place of Ferguson. "Place is both a commodity and sign value in hip-hop, as artists from specific locales have glorified their proximity to physical—and symbolic—spaces in order to reify their claims of authenticity" (Sigler and Balaji, 2013, p. 339).

Tef Poe typified the spontaneity inherent in democratic interrogation. His response was immediate on Twitter, documenting the community response, and inserting his own narrative condemning the Ferguson police. His op-ed in *Time* appeared a little more than a month after Brown's death, demonstrating his timeliness and his ability to traverse the streets of Ferguson, the hip-hop arena, and the established vehicles for expression of political opinion. Yet he also used the *Time* publishing opportunity to undermine traditional expressions of democracy, lamenting: "I decided it is possible I'll never vote for another American president for as long as I live" (Jackson, 2014). His voice was omnipresent at local protest events. At a mass meeting at Saint Louis University, he and others in the local movement demonstrated their disillusionment with traditional civil rights actors when they stood and turned their backs as NAACP president Cornell William Brooks addressed the meeting. The spontaneity of this action challenged the moderator, Reverend Traci Blackmon, to either ignore or embrace unplanned demonstrations of democratic voice. Ultimately, she embraced spontaneity and handed Tef Poe and other young activists the microphone, stating "This is what democracy looks like," a rallying cry of the local movement.

Tef Poe created hip-hop tracks that were reactive and representative of the movement. "War Cry" (Poe, 2014b), released just days before the Darren Wilson grand jury announcement, was free and available to fans immediately for streaming on SoundCloud. It received a spontaneous distribution via Twitter, where the song experienced an underground series of "releases" through SoundCloud links and sparked a flurry of informal critical conversations. "Gas Mask" (Poe, 2014a), released a month after the indictment announcement and in the midst of continued uprising in Ferguson, was a second example of Tef Poe's commitment to creating responsive and timely hip-hop. The hip-hop news website *AllHipHop* wrote: "This song is a perfect soundtrack for the times we live in" (AHH Staff, 2015).

"War Cry" and "Gas Mask" embody the critical consciousness that hip-hop tracks were founded on. In "War Cry," Tef Poe counters traditional narratives even within his own genre, unapologetically defining the solidarity needed for an interrogation of the systemic oppressions manifested in Ferguson: "My voice is like a shotgun/I speak for my lesbian and transgender sisters that ain't got one" (Poe, 2014b). This track is filled with similar lines that critique a marginalization of women and the LGBTQ community found in much of the genre. Tef Poe's calls for mass solidarity among "black and brown people" reflects what Schutz (2008) outlines as an expression of "democratic solidarity" among the working class. "Their visceral experiences of oppression and poverty and their traditions of mutualism made it clear to them that their only strength lay in solidarity" (p. 423). For Tef Poe, his solidarity with the citizens of Ferguson is manifested most powerfully not through editorials or speeches, but when he gets a gas mask (Poe, 2014a). On "Gas Mask," Tef Poe suggests that solidarity is found in shared experience, in this case being teargassed on the residential streets of Ferguson.

These tracks are musically disruptive, with intensifying beats and vocals. Tef Poe's voice, which is rough and shouting in both tracks, forces the listener to sit down and hear the lyrics. Beyond that, Tef Poe's release of the tracks for free streaming on SoundCloud troubles the accepted commercial spaces that promote the commodification of music. This is truly activist hip-hop, and Tef Poe heralds a call for relentless disruption of the comfort found in middle-class city spaces: "Chicago, Milwaukee, you could be next" (Poe, 2014a). In "War Cry," Tef Poe (2014b) dismisses participation in traditional democratic spaces, calling for an amassing of individuals to disrupt the status quo.

Hip-hop in Ferguson was both a pronouncement of the democratic values that a community was exerting, and a call to question undemocratic values situated within a supposed democracy. The ability of artists such as Tef Poe to mobilize hip-hop to call out these ironies, amplify voices through the creation of alliances, and interrupt the commodification of voice provides critical insights into the power of interrogation. As Cornel West (2004) argued, hip-hop provides avenues to tell the truth about black struggle and political resistance. Its poetry is able to directly "indict the American empire for its mendacity and hypocrisy" (p. 184). The rhapsodies that aurally occupied the streets in Ferguson and continue to flow through headphones, car radios, and mobile devices serve as a reminder of the necessity to unleash and mobilize democratic energies to question democratic life.

Visual Art: Creative Black Artist Battling Ignorance

Similar to the genre of hip-hop within music, there exists a subset of activist visual art that not only challenges mainstream aesthetics, but also seeks to interrogate democratic ideals. Maxine Greene (1995), a champion of social justice teaching in the context of aesthetics education, wrote: "participatory involvement with the many forms of art does enable us, at the very least, to see more in our experience, to hear more on normally unheard frequencies, to become conscious of what daily routines, habits, and conventions have obscured" (p. 379). The responses of individual and collective artists to the events in Ferguson provide a framework to see how visual art can be used as a medium to interrogate democracy.

Cbabi Bayoc, a local St. Louis artist whose first name is an acronym that stands for "Creative black artist battling ignorance," emerged in the wake of Ferguson as a critical example of the transformative potential for visual art to challenge transformative participation in democracy. Brown's death came on the heels of a two-year project where Bayoc (2014) committed to painting 365 images of black fatherhood. His *365 Days with Dad* challenged prevailing narratives about what it is to have or to be a black father in America. As Bayoc was an established local and revolutionary artist in the St. Louis area, his response to Ferguson would be important in identifying what the role of visual artists could or should be in the struggle for justice.

Bayoc is known for the instantaneous release of images of his art through Facebook, Instagram, and Twitter (e.g., n.d., b). His art is community inspired, and he disseminates it en masse and in the moment. Two weeks after Brown's death, Bayoc set up an easel on Canfield Drive where Brown was killed and returned for several nights. The painting created on Canfield was initially titled "Scary to You, Daddy to Me" and portrayed a young Mike Brown with his father, accompanied by a young Trayvon Martin. The piece and its framing emerged from Bayoc's work over the last two years in concert with the immediate context of the St. Louis community. The project then morphed into a more deliberate political act when the piece was retitled "R.I.P. Son" and Bayoc (n.d., a) launched a GoFundMe campaign to support wide distribution of prints of the piece. Both Bayoc's art and the dissemination of his art exemplified the ways in which spontaneous and contextual responses are endemic in movements seeking to interrogate democracy. Bayoc wrote: "This painting literally received life under the streetlights at West Florissant and Canfield Drive. It was near midnight, a week after the streets had been live with chaos" (Bayoc, n.d., a).

For an example of expressions of solidarity through art, we shift our focus to uncommissioned public art, which within the Ferguson movement was manifested as both visual art and performance art. Since August 2014 there have been isolated evenings that ended with damage to local businesses. The community at large, and the protest community in particular, responded to this damage within days (hours in some instances) by re-appropriating the plywood covering shattered windows with art. This artistic claiming of damaged spaces was done throughout the St. Louis region in concert with business owners in a unique show of solidarity between local businesses that had experienced property loss and residents and members of the movement who were important in framing the acts of destruction. An example of this is the All Hands on Deck project, a collaboration between local artist Damon Davis and *GlobalGrind* editor Michael Skolnik, which was conceived during an activist meeting in Ferguson. Davis described how his art documents the "people's movement. It is our right to be seen—to be heard ... to be validated. It is our collective responsibility" (Davis, n.d.). The project includes taking pictures of people's hands and blowing up the images for display in public spaces and, in the case of Ferguson, on boarded-up businesses (Figure 12.1). The message delivered through Davis's art is that relationships in communities are highly complex and the state's claim that business property needed protection from the people was flawed. Re-appropriating business facades to express solidarity with the movement in Ferguson was a powerful demonstration of democratic solidarity that transcends economic stability.

Artists responding to Ferguson, both individually and as a community collective, repeatedly challenged and disrupted traditional democratic spaces. Bayoc (n.d., b) created and showcased his series *Young Cornrows of America* in the months following the no-indictment grand jury decision. The series disrupted notions of patriotism through an appropriation of the image of the American flag. The paintings in this series portray images of black youth, mainly from behind or in profile to highlight their hairstyles, against the backdrop of segments of the flag, re-oriented and re-designed, aptly representing the ways in which black participation in American democracy is in itself disruptive in traditional spaces. The series highlighted ways in which public space can be disrupted, not only through claiming a public street as studio space, but through visually challenging

FIGURE 12.1 "Sam's Meat Market & More on West Florissant Avenue" Photographed on May 8, 2015 by the author.

the sanctity of the most cherished symbol of American democracy, the flag. In the protest movement, performance art such as the project #ChalkedUnarmed, where social media organized meet-ups at area malls or restaurants to chalk outlines of bodies and then stage group "die-ins," used artistic expression as a way to disrupt casual consumerism and reclaim spaces traditionally considered apolitical (Heuer, 2014).

Regardless of the canvas—easel, plywood, concrete, or sidewalk—the artistic responses to Ferguson illustrate how creative resistance can interrogate democracy. Because visual art is a dialogic exchange between the artist and spectator, the simple contoured lines of a body being traced on the ground demand a response. Art anticipates an answer, allowing this medium to pose questions, expose hypocrisy, and challenge false virtues. Through this interrogation we are also able to see the aspirations of democracy. Cbabi Bayoc in his introduction to the *Young Cornrows of America* series poses the following question: "The flag is such a loved and celebrated symbol, would it still be seen with the undeniable symbol of black youth and culture weaved into the composition?" (Bayoc, n.d., b). This question certainly serves as a contemporary critique, but the answer it demands casts a vision for a future without present-day dissonance. It is the potential embedded in this kind of exchange that accentuates the power of art within a democracy.

Social Media: #ShutItDown

Social media has emerged as a powerful tool in activist work focused on interrogating democracies. The Arab Spring in 2011 demonstrated to the world the powerful potential that resided in social media environments which facilitated people's efforts to disseminate spontaneous, uncensored information to local and global audiences alike. In particular, sites such as Twitter have been integral to supporting activist movements in politically repressive nations or amongst traditionally marginalized populations. The capacity for social media to facilitate subversive conversations and plan actions to challenge inequities offers a fruitful resource for the movement in Ferguson.

Several important Twitter voices emerged in the days and months following Brown's death. Three prominent online voices were local residents and activists Ashley Yates, Brittany Ferrell, and Alexis Templeton. The three women, co-founders of the group Millennial Activists United, are widely recognized for mobilizing not only local activists, but movements nationally as well. These activists utilized social media to organize area protestors quickly and covertly, challenged the definitions of solidarity within the movement itself, and unapologetically "intruded" into traditionally protected spaces. These online voices are particularly important cases to study because they are women, black, and queer. Tef Poe's nod to sisterhood in "War Cry" (2014b) may be speaking to these women. Templeton and Ferrell's wedding at St. Louis City Hall amidst protests in the fall demonstrated the intersectionality of these women's resistance.

Millennial Activists United as an organization, and Yates, Ferrell, and Templeton individually, utilized social media to mobilize, direct, and then document grassroots protest actions. The immediate broadcast of information allowed for protesters to strategize, respond, and regroup in ways that paralleled the organization traditionally reserved for agents of the state. Additionally, the use of social media to document the protests and the police reactions in the moment became a powerful force of citizen journalism, with imagery that further mobilized people, who in turn generated a movement.

As women who are part of the LGBTQ community, these activists bridge solidarity with marginalized groups, which models the intersectional feminist pedagogy described by Engebretson and Hollett in Chapter 7. They use their visibility (each woman has over 10,000 followers on Twitter) to proclaim solidarity with the Black Lives Matter movement. Moreover, they use their social media platforms to continually call for a broad recognition of the diverse identities of black lives. The online conversations about the role of women and transgender or queer folk in the movement read like intimate debates at a family dinner, the subtext always that, outside of this dually public and intimate space of social media, they are unquestionably united in the task of continued disruption of the state.

Social media as a medium for diffuse communication and spontaneous mobilization of individuals in unity makes it an ideal force for disruption of space, particularly spaces typically protected for middle-class leisure and commerce. Organized protests in the fall were galvanized around #ShutItDown, which was associated with protest actions that specifically disrupted these places. The hashtag was used to organize and document protests at area malls, Target, WalMart, highly utilized street intersections, and a St. Louis Symphony concert. #ShutItDown rested on the premise that it would not be business as usual until and unless systemic inequities were addressed and remedied. A particular action of the #ShutItDown movement that continues to witness resurgence not only locally but nationally is #BlackBrunch. Supporting the overall drive to shut down spaces of commerce, this action sought to interrupt a cultural ritual specific to middle-class (and arguably white) communities as an example of the luxury of leisure afforded to those who are privileged. Reactions to #BlackBrunch, documented on Twitter, included an overwhelming outrage at the disruption of families, particularly children, who might be inconvenienced or scared merely for eating out at a restaurant. The message that black children and families are subjected to spaces in which oppression and fear are persistent realities made the disruption of #BlackBrunch an extraordinary example of the disruption of "normal" spaces in our society that interrupted the leisurely oblivion of those privileged enough not to notice or recognize the disparity in lives of American citizens.

The ubiquitous nature of social media in the movement is illustrated in the difficulty of identifying when a particular protest action was conceived or initiated. It is challenging to pinpoint, for example, when #BlackBrunch started. The spontaneity of social media disrupts the traditionally linear narratives emblematic of established institutions of meaning making. Although this chapter focuses on three particularly important voices related to interrogating democracy, the social media movement truly is a chorus of voices with no clear conductor, which echoes the democratic solidarity needed to undo systems of inequity. Finally, social media as a forum challenges the conventional conversation space (character limits, public broadcast) and acts as a vehicle for mass organization to disrupt typically unchallenged physical spaces.

Interrogating Democracy in the Classroom

The response to the death of Mike Brown through hip-hop, visual art, and social media offers a true reflection of what democracy looks like. Each of these forms of communication interrogated democracy through spontaneous resolve, solidarity, and disruption of protected space, creating dissonance between the norms and aspirations of a democracy. In essence, democracy was placed in conflict with itself. What the movements in Ferguson demanded was a democratization of democracy. As Balibar (2008) suggests, democracy "is not an established reality or a constitution in the material sense of the term, but it is also not a mere ideal: it is rather a permanent struggle for its own democratization and against its own reversal into oligarchy and monopoly of power" (p. 528). The voices behind the protests, creative disruptions, and demonstrations each spoke to the necessity to see democracy in a continual state of becoming.

While neoliberal influences have continued to frame civic preparation in schools as passive participation, the movement started in Ferguson offers a vision of civic preparation predicated on dissent in the form of action and organization. In order to unpack the nature and implications of this dissent for the classroom, it is important to remember that the movement in Ferguson interrogated democracy through its very existence. Collective action by those marginalized in a democratic society that purports equity and delivers injustice is itself interrogative. Ferguson teaches us that active dissent is a legitimate and powerful mode of inquiry in a democracy.

The responses to the injustice of the persistent vulnerability of black bodies through microphones, canvases, and digital platforms frame citizenship as active and moral. This is the first lesson from Ferguson in an age of economic disparity. In order to interrogate democracy, teachers must validate and legitimize the modes of civic communication within social uprisings. The modes of communication used in Ferguson—hip-hop, visual art, and social media—are not the traditional vehicles of civic expression. The social, economic, and political oppression of the black citizens of Ferguson exists because the traditional mechanisms of democracy failed. Challenging racism as a society will never appear as a ballot measure. The systemic marginalization of black families is not up for deliberation.

For the citizens responding to Ferguson, hip-hop, visual art, and social media are the ways in which people can raise questions about the hypocrisy of inequity within a democracy. The expansion and validation of civic voice through hip-hop, visual art, and social media represent a shift that rejects the notion that there are only a few prescribed ways of communicating displeasure within a democracy. Further they interrupt the proscription of those actions that fall outside of these sanctioned activities. In the classroom, teachers should validate and legitimize the various ways in which actors in social uprisings express their civic voices. Students should explore the seemingly "unconventional" modes of communication in order to see democracy as expansive. What these unconventional modes look like is contingent upon the context of students' lives. Therefore, teachers must constantly take a critical stance toward their own perceptions of what constitutes acceptable norms of communication and participation in a classroom. The interrogation of democracy in a neoliberal era must come from the periphery of "accepted" communication and participation.

A second lesson is that the use of bodies is an important tool for democratic interrogation. In Ferguson, bodies were used to make civic statements to close down streets, disrupt commerce, and make poignant statements. Although the use of the body in civic protest is not a new phenomenon, the activists in Ferguson utilized their bodies in ways that were unique to their search for justice. For example, the "die-in" movement was particular to the death of Mike Brown. Each instantiation of the die-in across the country was a reminder of the senselessness of Brown's death. The silence that followed each die-in was indicative of the needless snuffing of another black life—an interrogation itself of the conditions within a democracy that devalues black lives. Teachers must be willing to help students see their bodies as part of their civic selves. Admittedly, this is difficult in a profession that prioritizes the regulation of bodies. Classroom management is often a project in confining bodies into limited spaces. However, as the movements generated by Ferguson illustrate, bodies are equal to voice as modes of civic expression. Thus the civic performativity of students must be carefully considered in classroom spaces.

We borrow the term *performativity* from Judith Butler (1990), who argued that gender is a performance constructed through the stylized repetition of acts: "The effect of gender is produced through the stylization of the body and, hence, must be understood as the mundane way in which bodily gestures, movements, and styles of various kinds constitute the illusion of an abiding gendered self" (p. 140). Likewise, we see the construction of the performativity of citizenship in schools as constraining acts of bodily control. By constantly suppressing how students use their bodies in classroom spaces, we are controlling and limiting the civic agency of our students. In order to further interrogate democracy, teachers must be able to subvert these messages about the proper role of the body in the classroom and within a democratic society. Encouraging students to use their bodies is an important way of challenging the decorum of democracy in order to question neoliberalism.

A third lesson for the classroom from Ferguson is that, in order to interrogate democracy, traditional temporal considerations about the democratic process must be reconsidered. The death of Mike Brown caused an immediate reaction from the local black community in Ferguson. Over time, this initial reaction led to a series of movements working toward justice. The expeditiousness of the resolve for justice through different mediums and venues in Ferguson counters the traditional temporal nature of civic participation and democratic action. When oppression and marginalization are constant realities, the election cycle becomes effectively moot. Deliberation alone unequivocally fails to meet the urgency conditioned by a history of systemic inequality.

For teachers, the responses to Ferguson are lessons that the interrogation of democracy requires immediate and rhizomatic responses to the hypocritical acts that sustain inequality. Ferguson elucidates the spontaneity of democracy. Teachers must recognize and support discussion of and action on the critical issues of injustice and inequality that students believe demand a response. This recognition, however, is contingent upon the teacher recognizing that students are not pre-democratic, but are already democratic beings. Democratic education is not an exercise into which children, youth, and adolescents should be incorporated or initiated—they already come to teachers with democratic ideas, values, virtues, and convictions. Democratic education ought to be the facilitation of these predilections directed toward the transformation of our democracy into one that fosters a more just society. As Biesta (2010) contended, the main problem with democracy is that it is premised on the idea that it requires:

> nothing more than bringing more people into the existing democratic order. This is basically a colonial way to understand democratization and it is precisely the logic behind . . . a certain definition of democracy. The main problem with this approach is that . . . democracy in which others are being included, is taken for granted; it is the starting point that itself cannot be questioned.
>
> *(p. 124)*

Acting "in the moment" for justice validates the democratic impulses of students and validates their subjective experience, which directly contradicts the typical narratives promoted by traditional civics curricula. Teachers must come alongside these impulses and support their emerging citizen-selves. In Ferguson, the expressions of individuals were varied, but the response was immediate. Classrooms should provide similar spaces for students to respond immediately to local, national, and global matters of injustice, and also to provide them with multiple points of entry into which they may insert—and assert—themselves. If we as teachers fall into the colonial fallacy that we are the ones democratizing students, we risk disabling rather than empowering them to interrogate democracy in the future.

Undoubtedly, the lessons from Ferguson are bound by the civic identities that students bring with them into the classroom. As Rubin (2007) suggests, students' daily experiences with their social, political, economic, and institutional realities frame how they make sense of civic lessons in the classroom. For affluent students, interrogating democracy may seem unwarranted because of the congruence between their lived experiences and the fact that civic institutions have mostly worked in their favor. However, for traditionally marginalized students, interrogating democracy in the classroom may be experienced quite differently, because it validates the disjuncture they experience between the typical promises and failures of civic institutions.

Although it is important to acknowledge the situated realities that shape students' civic identities, the interrogation of power, systems, and structures benefits all students. Injustice in a democracy is pernicious; we must come to recognize that "injustice anywhere is a threat to justice everywhere" and that "whatever affects one directly affects all indirectly" (King, 2012, p. 178). Therefore, engendering further engagement of marginalized students and rendering the injustice inherent in our society visible to students who have had the privilege not to see them are both critical goals for classrooms operating in an age of economic disparity. Teachers must be active in helping all students recognize, explore, and interrogate how disparity interrupts democracy through civic action. In Ferguson, we witnessed an interrogation occur through spontaneous resolve, solidarity, and disruption. Classrooms must be the spaces where these interrogative actions are cultivated.

Conclusion

Classrooms and curricula must move beyond teaching about democracy and toward engaging students in interrogations of democracy. This work requires teachers to actively resist neoliberal definitions of the formal knowledge and action needed in a democracy. Admittedly, resistance is challenging in an era of accountability, which has made teaching a spectacle that the public is allowed to discipline. For example, a recent high school student art exhibit in Westfield, New Jersey titled "Law Enforcement—Police Brutality" offered an aesthetic challenge to power (Lieberman, 2015). One image in the exhibit featured a gun pointed at black silhouettes, with the following artist statement below the image:

> This picture represents corruption in law enforcement seen recently in today's society. The hands holding a gun represent the police aiming at silhouettes running away from corruption. The power of the police is clearly displayed in this picture showing the choice to shoot or not to shoot. I believe police have recently abused their power and the police need to reassess their position in society.
>
> *(Lieberman, 2015)*

The teacher who encouraged the critical artwork received significant media attention, local scrutiny, and ultimately public shaming by the district superintendent. These responses serve to strengthen the perception that teaching is a public spectacle that requires public discipline.

Given this example, it would be easy to simply fall into a spiraling cycle of discipline, deterrence, and conformity (Vinson and Ross, 2007). Yet this is what the activists demanding justice in Ferguson are asking us to resist—conformity. Conformity is how we got to a place in which civic passivity and malaise are normal, even preferable to the alternative we present here. Conformity as a civic virtue does not belong in our classrooms if we are to promote a vibrant democratic society. Like the art teacher in Westfield, we must acknowledge mediums of expression that question power but are often underutilized in contemporary classrooms such as hip-hop, art, and social media. Moreover, the power, agency, and resistance exerted by the activists in Ferguson provide a template for teachers to expand their pedagogic repertoire to include and allow for student expressions of spontaneous resolve, solidarity, and the creative use of their bodies to interrogate democracy. Perhaps through such collective and continuous interrogation we may find ourselves in the future more capable of identifying miscarriages of justice, instances of disparity, and systems of inequality, and with the capacities to address them immediately and effectively through multiple modes of expression, participation that further democratizes how we seek to redress them.

Note

1 We refer to Michael Brown as Mike throughout the chapter because this is how friends, family, and activists in Ferguson refer to him. Using his nickname is a purposeful act in honoring his humanity.

References

AHH Staff. (2015, September 3). Tef Poe—"Gas mask" (produced by Duke Rellington). *AllHipHop*. Retrieved from http://allhiphop.com/2015/01/03/tef-poe-gas-mask-produced-by-duke-rellington/.

Balibar, E. (2008). Historical dilemmas of democracy and their contemporary relevance for citizenship. *Rethinking Marxism, 20*(4), 522–538.

Bayoc, C. (n.d., a). R.I.P. son printing costs. Retrieved from http://www.gofundme.com/ripsonprints.

Bayoc, C. (n.d., b). *Young cornrows of America* series. Retrieved from https://www.facebook.com/media/set/?set=a.867160909973149.1073741827.328298620526050&type=1.

Bayoc, C. (2014). *365 days with dad*. Retrieved from http://cbabibayoc.com/index.php/365.

Biesta, G. (2004). Education, accountability, and ethical demand: Can the democratic potential of accountability be regained? *Educational Theory, 54*(3), 233–250.

Biesta, G. (2010). *Good education in an age of measurement: Ethics, politics, democracy*. New York: Paradigm.

Butler, J. (1990). *Gender trouble*. New York: Routledge.

Castro, A. J., and Knowles, R. T. (In press). Democratic citizenship education: Research across multiple landscapes and contexts. In M. Manfra and C. Bolick (Eds.), *Handbook of social studies research*. New York: Wiley-Blackwell.

Chomsky, N. (1999). *Profit over people: Neoliberalism and global order.* New York: Seven Stories Press.

Davis, D. (n.d.). About All Hands on Deck. Retrieved from http://www.allhandson deckproject.org/about.

DiZerega, G. (2000). *Persuasion, power, and polity: A theory of democratic self-organization.* Cresskill, NJ: Hampton Press.

Greene, M. (1995). Art and imagination: Reclaiming the sense of possibility. *Phi Delta Kappan, 76*(5), 378–382.

Harvey, T., McAnnar, J., Voss, M. J., Conn, M., Janda, S., and Keskey, S. (2014). ArchCity Defenders: Municipal courts white paper. Retrieved from http://www. archcitydefenders.org/wp-content/uploads/2014/11/ArchCity-Defenders-Municipal-Courts-Whitepaper.pdf.

Heuer, A. (2014, August 22). St. Louis artists respond to Ferguson with chalk. *St. Louis Public Radio.* Retrieved from http://news.stlpublicradio.org/post/st-louis-artists-respond-ferguson-chalk.

Hursh, D. (2008). Beyond the justice of the market: Combating neoliberal educational discourse and promoting deliberative democracy and economic equality. In W. Ayers, T. M. Quinn, and D. Stovall (Eds.), *Handbook of social justice in education* (pp. 152–164). New York: Routledge.

Jackson, K. (2014, September 16). Ferguson rapper Tef Poe: Barack Obama has forsaken us, but we will not stop fighting injustice. *Time.* Retrieved from http://time.com/.

King, M. L., Jr. (2012). Letter from Birmingham Jail. In R. Gottlieb (Ed.). *Liberating faith: Religious voices for justice, peace, and ecological wisdom* (pp. 177–187). Lanham, MD: Rowman & Littlefield.

Lieberman, J. (2015, May 14). Art exhibit at Westfield High School draws criticism from cops. Retrieved from https://www.tapinto.net/towns/westfield/articles/art-exhibit-at-westfield-high-school-draws-critic.

Parker, W. C. (2003). *Teaching democracy: Unity and diversity in public life.* New York: Teachers College Press.

Poe, T. (2014a, December 30). Gas mask (produced by Duke Rellington). SoundCloud. Delmar Records, St. Louis, MO.

Poe, T. (2014b, November). War cry (produced by DJ Smitty). SoundCloud. Delmar Records, St. Louis, MO.

Rubin, B. (2007). "There's still not justice": Youth civic identity development amid distinct school and community contexts. *Teachers College Record, 109*(2), 449–481.

Schutz, A. (2008). Social class and social action: The middle-class bias of democratic theory in education. *Teachers College Record, 110*(4), 405–442.

Sigler, T., and Balaji, M. (2013). Regional identity in contemporary hip-hop music: (Re) presenting the notion of place. *Communication, Culture, and Critique, 6*(2), 336–352.

Vinson, K. D., and Ross, E. W. (2007). Education and the new disciplinarity: Surveillance, spectacle and the case of SBER. In E. W. Ross and R. Gibson (Eds.), *Neoliberalism and education reform* (pp. 59–86). New York: Hampton Press.

West, C. (2004). *Democracy matters: Winning the fight against imperialism.* New York: Penguin Books.

13

NARRATIVE POSSIBILITIES OF THE RADICAL HUMANITIES

Shaping Participatory and Justice-Oriented Citizens for Democracy

Tara Hyland-Russell and Corinne Syrnyk

> The course taught me about myself . . . the meaning of life, the purpose of life. That basically is that we are here [and] we can find ourselves through the culture, through the arts.[1]

As Richard Shaull (2000) points out in the foreword to the 30th anniversary edition of Paulo Freire's influential *Pedagogy of the Oppressed*, "there is no such thing as a *neutral* educational process" (p. 34). If our aim is to shape citizens to participate in meaningful ways in democratic society and, indeed, to work toward a society in which all persons have equal voice, then we need to consider carefully not only the content and processes of what we teach but, more importantly, our rationale for doing so. What is the goal of our educative endeavors and what kinds of citizens are we trying to shape? This chapter offers Humanities 101 as a case study and a model through which to consider the content and praxis that can be used across educational contexts for building citizens for democracy.

Although the narrative arts of the humanities are at the heart of Humanities 101, such content alone is not sufficient to develop active citizens for democracy. Westheimer and Kahne (2004) provide a framework of citizenship that helps us think through *what kinds* of citizens we are trying to shape through education and *why*. Freire's emphasis on purposeful dialogical encounters with others in order to reveal and shift patterns of oppression informs both the program's pedagogical processes and the content. We are mindful of what Paula Allman (2009, p. 418) terms "the necessary dialectical unity between process and content" within any site of radical education practice, and of her caution that Freirean principles cannot be applied in any methodological manner without losing the tissue of Freire's argument. This is an interwoven process of action and reflection at the heart of developing a critical/dialectical perception. Agreeing with Allman that content and methodology are thoroughly interwoven, yet recognizing the benefits of learning about pedagogical applications through real examples, in what follows we outline the essential components of the Radical Humanities program, permeated by our reflections and insights gleaned from over a decade of work within Humanities 101. The elements which are necessary foundations to this project of shaping participatory and justice-oriented citizens include:

- a profoundly safe and trauma-informed learning environment;
- purposeful dialogic encounters oriented toward untangling strands of privilege, oppression, marginalization, and power;
- access to diverse cultural spaces;
- close reading and critical reflection;
- modeling practices of change.

Radical Humanities: Individual and Social Change

In 1995, based on his research into intergenerational poverty in the United States, journalist and social critic Earl Shorris launched the Clemente Program, a humanities program modeled on the liberal arts education typically offered to the moneyed and elite. Shorris's model "begins with the idea that the poor are human and that the proper celebration of their humanity is in the public world, as citizens" (Shorris, 2000, p. 11). Inspired by Shorris's vision, by 2008 ten such humanities programs operated across Canada, with many more in the US. All sought to use the unique insights and reflective capacities of the humanities to positively impact the lives of people whose lives were marked by poverty and an inability to access education.[2] Using a notion of "Socratic humanism" (Shorris, 2000, p. 10), he believed that courses in the humanities offered adults a unique reflective opportunity to reframe their worldviews and their relationships to themselves, others, and the world around them: "the humanities have great appeal to give people a sense of self, to see the world and themselves differently in the Greek sense of reflective thinking, of autonomy. . . . People who know the humanities . . . become active, not acted upon" (Shorris, as cited in Reichers, 2001, p. 29). The ancient notion of a *viva activa*, an active life, drawn from Greek philosophy, undergirds humanities courses and implies the ability to critically examine and engage in one's life, making informed choices. The humanities offers accounts of people's aspirations, fears, and understandings in ways that are thick, detailed, and layered with meaning.

The term "Radical Humanities" (Groen and Hyland-Russell, 2010) highlights the ways in which programs moved beyond Shorris's model of offering an elite education to the poor to a vision that insists on the equal worth of all and critiques Shorris's "great books" curriculum. As Martha Nussbaum (1997) claims:

> It is always radical, in any society, to insist on the equal worth of all human beings, and people find all sorts of ways to avoid the claim of that ideal, much though they may pay it lip service. . . . We should defend that radical agenda as the only one worthy of our conception of democracy and worthy of guiding its future.
>
> *(p. 112)*

Humanities 101 at St. Mary's University in Calgary views the university, and by extension any learning space, as a rich potential site of change and social justice if its teachers are prepared to engage in the difficult work of identifying and addressing discourses and systems of privilege and oppression: "the university itself must not be overlooked as a site of praxis, a site where issues of difference, representation and social justice, and even what constitutes legitimate academic work are being contested" (Wright, 2003, p. 808). In practical terms, we apply a radical pedagogy by shaping the syllabi to represent the vast diversity of students' lived experience, and juxtapose canonical and non-canonical works in an effort to understand ways in which the dominant social class have maintained their power and position. In this way we also align ourselves with Nemiroff's (1992) pedagogy of critical humanism. We seek not to replicate an "elite" education for "the poor" in order to further inscribe hegemonic ideals, but to examine how ideology is transmitted and can be interrogated and resisted for the purposes of effecting change in those very social structures.

Central to the Humanities 101 program is an emphasis on utilizing accomplished teachers who are both highly knowledgeable in their disciplines and able to engage in dialectical inquiry with students. Here our insistence is on pedagogical excellence that incorporates deep content knowledge intertwined with a sensitivity to, and adept ability in, pulling students into relationship and dialogue with each other that is marked by a profound respect for each and every student. Essential traits of what we consider brilliant teaching for the Radical Humanities include deep authenticity, passion for the subject matter, humility, and a belief in students' ability to engage in the dialogic work of the course and a concomitant belief in the efficacy of the humanities to engage the students in transformative narratives of self and other.

Each four-month course includes classroom instruction, dialogue, tutorials, and academic skills seminars such as grammar, research, and critical writing. Courses trace themes and forge connections through integrated material from humanities disciplines, including literature, art history, philosophy, cultural studies, history, and music, which "complement each other as they reflect on the human enterprise" (Humanities 101, 2014). Students study texts "not only to understand how meaning resides within these texts but also to grapple with the ways in which people find significant, sustaining, and personal meaning" (Humanities 101, 2014) through oral and written traditions that portray a variety of cultural perspectives.[3]

Humanities 101 is attentive not only to *how* the program facilitates greater democratic engagement but also to the *nature* of the citizenship desired.

Westheimer and Kahne (2004) highlight that three kinds of citizenship underpin educational programs; each has differing political implications that significantly impact educational program design. Furthermore, they find that the need for citizens to adhere to notions of character-building like obedience and loyalty "works against the kind of critical reflection and action that many assume are essential in a democratic society" (Westheimer and Kahne, 2004, p. 244).

Indeed, a dialectical critical reflection is at the heart of Humanities 101, and its vision of democratic citizenship is what the program seeks to develop. This type of dialogue has been found to be central in teaching students about democracy and social justice (Laman et al., 2012; Mayhew and Fernandez, 2007; Nagda and Gurin, 2007; Nagda et al., 2009). Specifically, Humanities 101's goal is to shape citizens to contribute to community issues through "the development of cognitive and interpersonal skills that enable [participants] to negotiate social and economic differences, and confidently embrace a wide range of perspectives . . . to long standing social problems" (Engberg and Hurtado, 2011, p. 417).

It is important to note that, although Humanities 101 is not a mental health program, the prevalence of trauma in students' lives demands attentiveness to the impact of trauma on learning (Horsman, 1999). Therefore, intentionally moving beyond a deficit model of "the poor," instead this program's content and pedagogy involve understanding and critiquing the complex webs of privilege, oppression, marginalization, and opportunity that function at societal levels. Moving beyond critique, but wholly dependent on such analysis, the program seeks to effect both individual and social change, as evidenced in its official vision statement: "Igniting Personal and Social Transformation" (Humanities 101, 2014). In its emphasis on societal change and effecting awareness of not only the program participants, but also the program staff and people at the host institution, Humanities 101 moves away from Shorris's "understanding of poverty as it overlooks and/or minimizes the reality of poverty's structural effects, thereby limiting the critical and transformative input this course might have on the existing class structure" (Ng, 2006, p. 42).

Humanities 101 seeks to foster the capacities of adult learners "who have experienced marginalization, social exclusion, and multiple educative barriers" (Hyland-Russell and Syrnyk, 2015, p. 515) such as poverty, violence, racism, interrupted or negative experiences with education, substance abuse, homelessness, immigration, or war. Its goals align with the Hamburg Declaration on Adult Learning (1997) that "the informed and effective participation of men and women in every sphere of life is needed if humanity is to survive and meet the challenges of the future" (p. 1).

Profoundly Safe and Trauma-Informed Learning Environment

Humanities 101 provided a safe place to interact with others . . . to find ways to relate to others.

The majority of Humanities 101 students report past and current emotional, psychological, spiritual, and/or physical distress as a result of negative life experiences (Hyland-Russell and Syrnyk, 2014, 2015). It has been well established that such trauma can have a significant impact on our brains (see van der Kolk, 2014). Indeed, brain scans of children who have experienced profound abuse show little frontal lobe activation (e.g., McCrory et al., 2011), as these children primarily depend on their hindbrains to work through their world. As a result, they often react to problems instead of "thinking through" them. The outcomes of trauma worsen with intensity and duration of exposure, accumulating over a lifetime to manifest themselves as maladaptive long-term cognitive, physical, and behavioral outcomes (Anda et al., 2006; Shonkoff et al., 2012). Research reveals that adults exposed to trauma, particularly in early life, are more likely to have memory and learning deficits and poor academic achievement (e.g., Majer et al., 2010). Living in a state of constant stress can also result in individuals behaving in the most adaptive way they know when faced with threat: by appearing aggressive, manipulative, or even bored (Kerka, 2002). Trauma's legacy is pervasive. Knowing how to recognize and support traumatized learners is therefore central to the design and implementation of the Humanities 101 program. Through training and experience, our educators are sensitive to learners' definitions of safety (Mackenzie, 2012), subjective manifestations of trauma (Perry and Szalavitz, 2006), and the fact that trauma can be easily misinterpreted (Horsman, 2004). The program's trauma-informed approach helps ensure student safety and builds trust and predictability.

Building safety in Humanities 101 begins with deliberate transparency about the program's philosophy and pedagogy. Students understand that they are signing up for courses based on the democratic values of human rights and equity—where all human beings have the capacity to realize their potential in their own way—and emancipatory content is used to challenge perceptions and build psychological insight and academic capacity. It is not unusual for the content to trigger a reactionary, and often emotional, response. Our educators attend to such disorienting content and help students navigate into wider conceptual waters through dialogue with each other and the deepening of critical reflective skills. Piaget (1975) long ago recognized that cognitive conflict, or disequilibrium, is a natural and powerful part of learning that requires learners to reorganize their worldviews. Students can only engage in this process if they feel safe—our educators are trained to be aware of how to guide students when content triggers trauma (see Table 13.1).

Safety is also nurtured through the program relationships. In their study of domestic trauma victims returning to adult education, Muro and Mein (2010) found that emotional trauma resurfaced when these women felt unsupported in their studies. Thus, educator attentiveness is important, as it lends students the confidence to explore beyond the limits of their knowledge. Such communication also allows educators to provide feedback, to shine a light on cognitive footholds

TABLE 13.1 Managing Content-Induced Learner Conflict

Remain calm and patient at all times.

Do not dismiss student views.

Engage students in role-modeling constructive discussion.

Challenge students to identify the source(s) of the conflict (Why do you think you think that . . . ?).

Actively challenge students to empathize with others.

Individually debrief with conflicted students outside of the classroom.

Conduct basic literacy assessments to tailor support.

Be assertive in not tolerating prejudice. Remind students of this frequently.

Note: Educators (ideally anyone interacting with students) are strongly encouraged to participate in a specially designed training course on trauma-informed teaching. Additionally, educators must have good emotional awareness so that they can read the "emotional thermostat" of the room.

to help students find their way through disequilibrium. Safety is also found in the community students co-create with their peers. Reciprocity experienced through shared presence, intent, and storytelling welds learners together to form a protective, almost familial, community (Weinstein, 2004). Our program strives to catalyze community-building through group lunches, where breaking bread denotes our common humanity and brings participants together to confront and quell fears through the power of collective experience.

Predictability also nurtures safety. When we know what to expect, we can make sense of our situation and shape suitable plans for the future. Like relationships, stability in the classroom allows students the security to problem-solve. When students can't make informed decisions about the future, they don't feel safe. If they don't feel safe, they don't learn. However, if the learning space is consistent and friendly, students' energy isn't put into worrying about what to expect, but can be employed towards regulating thoughts, feelings, and actions. To support students' development of a sense of safety, trust, and dependability, our program is transparent and consistent in its norms of interaction, structure, and administration. This calls for great attention to logistical detail. For example, group lunches not only allow for relationships, but provide students with hot and nutritious meals. Great care is taken when planning in-class events such as transitions and small-group tutoring. We also take care to provide childcare and transportation. To encourage stability, educators manage the program in minutiae, understanding that effective oversight of the "small things" gives students the space to tackle the "big things" like academic content.

Purposeful Dialogic Encounters: Untangling Strands of Privilege, Oppression, Marginalization, and Power

Reading Paulo Freire helped to give voice to some of my feelings/thoughts—why I dislike myself so much. How complex the forms of oppression are.

With the firm foundation of a profoundly safe learning space and a teacher attentively focused on facilitating students' emerging capacities, the participants of Humanities 101 are ready to delve into the academic coursework. We bring an anticipation that all participants are able to engage in dialogue into every portion of the course, placing a notion of "*maieutic* or mid-wifely dialogue" (Leigh, 2007, p. 319) at the heart of our pedagogy in which the instructor guides and supports students to "birth" new ideas.

Maieutic dialogue derives from the Socratic method and encourages positive, active learning and indirectly teaches "critical thinking and active open-mindedness to students" (Leigh, 2007, p. 319). The principles of the method Leigh (2007) identifies in Plato's *Sophist* and which we adapt for use in Humanities 101 are as follows:

1. Initiate a dialogue to involve the student as active participant in the learning process.
2. Induce the student to join in critical dialogue by encouraging or inducing her to reflect upon and evaluate evidence or reasons for a claim or theory being presented.
3. Stimulate and accustom the student to engage in active open-minded thinking (pp. 319–320).

We deliberately position teachers and tutors as co-learners alongside the students: everyone in the learning space functions as a midwife to thought through active, open-minded engagement with texts and ideas. The instructor takes responsibility for leadership and academic expertise, facilitating time and space for participants to try out ideas aloud, to form responses tentatively, all while getting feedback from their peers and input from the instructor.

We begin the first course, Humanities 103: Story and Meaning, by exploring prevailing notions of formal education and participants' expectations, fears, and hopes for the Radical Humanities program. We play the opening clip from the movie *Educating Rita* (Lewis, 1983), in which a hairdresser's desire to find herself through taking an Open University course is contrasted with the professor's cynical dismissal of education. Humanities 101 students laugh when Rita literally kicks open the door to learning, a symbolic act that emboldens them to offer their observations and assumptions about university and its professors, systems, and content. They offer a variety of prior educational experiences which collectively we probe for what they illuminate about intersections of class, opportunity, and privilege. In the first class we present an overview of Humanities 101's philosophy of learning as a tool to examine relationships of power and a potential way to liberate ourselves from unexamined assumptions and to begin to engage with and impact personal and social beliefs and structures.

Learning is valuable for its own sake, just as the students are uniquely worthy just as they are, not because of what they earn. Sharing our experience working in the Radical Humanities for over a decade, we identify dynamics of trauma and resilience and how they may surface during the course. A short-course PowerPoint, "Deep Down We're All Lizards," engages brain structure and the relationships between learning and prior experience. Sharing the physiology of the fight-or-flight response as well as Horsman's (1999) work on the impact of prior experience with violence or trauma on learning acknowledges a range of potential responses to the class material and processes. The instructor humorously acts out moments from her learning journey when she retreated to a "lizard brain" under stress, followed by modeling some practical strategies for coping with the challenges and possible triggers of learning.

The opportunity to practice the trauma-informed strategies comes the same day that we read through the assigned reading from Paulo Freire's (1970/2005) *Pedagogy of the Oppressed*. We offer the reading as the means to gain language and a conceptual framework through which to begin identifying and untangling intersected elements of power, prestige, marginalization, and oppression. When students are daunted by the reading's density and their own feelings of inadequacy for the material and learning in general (prompting the very dynamic of flight or fight we have just discussed), we patiently draw out their feelings and responses, opening the space to the most tentative of contributions, with the goal of making the conversation inviting enough for each student to have found a way to break the silence by the end of the first class. Tutors, some of whom are Humanities 101 alumni, model how to underline key passages, look up unfamiliar words in the dictionary, and write questions in the margins. Throughout, we both name and model what it means to be "agents of curiosity" (Freire, 1970/2005), infusing the dialogue with a sense of wonder, humor, and delight at the act of learning.

Access to Diverse Cultural Spaces

> I was in my own world and not aware of what was going on around me. I knew about forms of oppression within the domestic violence field, but managed to stay in that realm. Oppression is bigger than I realized.

Cultural spaces and events are crucial to extending students' emerging analysis of what Elizabeth Tisdell (1993) calls "interlocking systems of privilege and oppression" (p. 204). Henry Giroux (1993) suggests that it is the role of education to afford individuals the resources necessary to think democratically, just as it is democracy's responsibility to provide access to such education. Course content serves as a reflecting pool where learners may come to understand the roots of social inequality and its dynamics and think across the lines of dominance and oppression. Attending cultural events that resonate with course material facilitates understanding *how* those interlocking systems play out in society. Live drama, performance, or art potently stories people's experiences, but in such a way as to reduce the viewer's vulnerability. Thus, the play *Kim's Convenience* (Choi, 2012) invited students to consider the experience of two generations of Korean immigrants to Canada and the intergenerational tensions of assimilation, cultural competence, and language use. One of the many strengths of Humanities 101 is its cultural, racial, sex, and age diversity, which allows the group to develop its own culture, based on the shared facet of marginalization, while simultaneously probing for the differences in their social positionings and experiences with interlocking systems of privilege and oppression. *Kim's Convenience* was chosen to reflect the course's themes of belonging, place, identity, and history. Students were able to refract their experiences through the characters, inhabiting more than one perspective to gain a deeper understanding of multiple and sometimes conflicting subject positions.

Access to cultural events can also serve as a holistic, healing avenue for learning (Rosenwasser, 2000), especially when prior experiences are re-examined through a lens of interlocking privilege and oppression. A pressing area of social injustice that we address is the colonization and genocide of Canada's Indigenous peoples, a highly sensitive topic to Indigenous and non-Indigenous students and teachers alike. In one class, following a discourse analysis of the Indian Act to reveal its patriarchal and disempowering language and assimilationist policies, a white student became defensive, and argued that "The past is over—they should get over it!," unaware of the hurt and anger he was causing to the Indigenous students in the class. This was an acutely uncomfortable and emotional moment, but also a powerful moment of learning that wove together practice and theory (Freire, 1996). The educator rooted the following class in an Indigenous worldview by arranging for an Indigenous student to lead a sweetgrass ceremony followed by a talking-circle. Modeling Indigenous ceremony and bringing students into relationships of equality around the circle minimized the "othering" distance between students and countered the racism of the previous class. Such "enhance[ment of] their pluralistic orientation" (Engberg and Hurtado, 2011, p. 437) provoked a number of students to interrogate how they had been unwittingly shaped by privilege, opening the way to a more nuanced dialogue about various dynamics of oppression and privilege, including gender and race. For instance, one student recalled her mother's racism: "I couldn't sit on a toilet seat in public, because an Indian may have sat on it." The class helped her revise her stereotypes: "That's gone because it just isn't even relevant anymore [and instead I have] the openness and the willingness to learn."

Such conflict, if managed well, can be a powerful learning tool. Mayhew and Fernandez (2007) found that "students exposed to course content dealing with systematic oppression, the societal structures and inequalities that cause and sustain it, and how individuals perpetuate and/or discourage its reproduction were more likely to achieve social justice-related outcome" (p. 74). We believe the learning experiences that Humanities 101 offers both in and out of the classroom affirms Inglis's (1997) statement that "empowerment involves people developing capacities to act successfully within the existing system and structures of power, with emancipation concerns critically analyzing, resisting, and challenging structures of power" (p. 4). Educators should be attentive to the influence of authority and power upon learners, and have a responsibility to nurture this culture in a manner that does not "empower some learners and silence others" (Alfred, 2002, p. 11). One of the ways to empower learners and to initiate dialogue about sensitive but essential aspects of oppression is to attend cultural events that enact the stories that we know are typically shared by many of our students as well as those that depict lives and cultures that are beyond their knowledge.

Close Reading and Critical Reflection

> The first time I read that story ["Powder" (Wolff, 1996)] I thought what a careless dad, but when we read it again and you encouraged us to see, to understand more of the meaning of the story, we found out that the father was actually a caring dad, and one of the students said "Don't judge him that hard because I was like him too."

Developing close reading skills is an essential aspect of students' ability to engage in meaningful dialogue, informed analysis, and clear communication. Close reading is attentive to both surface and deep meaning, including ways in which symbols, images, and figures of speech interact with generic forms to produce meaning and, in turn, the surface and deep ideologies evidenced in the texts. These texts take a variety of forms, including philosophy, history and historiography, autobiography, narrative prose, poetry, movies, art, and theatrical performance (see Table 13.2).

Literary texts play an essential role in developing students' abilities as participatory and justice-oriented citizens, particularly in unmasking and critiquing the ways in which people are constituted as subjects, and thus revealing how change is possible. The task of the educator teaching for democracy is to examine how people are constructed as subjects in language and discourse and thus how they can act agentially as consciously aware beings. Change arises from awareness of the *very real and material* conditions of our lives as well as the ways in which *we can imagine differences* for ourselves and others.

We choose texts that illuminate the contradictory subject positions prompted by class structure, race, and culture. Close reading of texts that contain multiple perspectives or sites of ambiguity offers a contained yet powerful way to engage in these often opposing forces. For example, Joan Fern Shaw's "The People Upstairs" (1995) explores a rigidly gendered and classed world of Toronto in the early 1940s in which the young female narrator learns to fear the mysterious people upstairs and not touch library books because "Mother said the books were handled by so many dirty Toronto people" (p. 28). However, when she and her mother are delirious with the measles and tended to gently by the

TABLE 13.2 Readings from Two Humanities 101 Courses

Prose*	Poetry	Performance art: drama, visual art, storytelling**
Humanities 103: Story and Meaning		
Plato, Allegory of the Cave	Leonard Cohen,	Sophocles, *Oedipus*
Chris Offutt, Sawdust	Dance Me to the	Marie Clements, *Copper*
Aristotle, *Nichomachean Ethics*	End of Love	*Thunderbird*
Sandra Cisneros, My Lucy	Anne Sexton,	Ubuntu: The Capetown
Friend who Smells like	*Transformations*	Project
Corn	Ovid, *Metamorphoses*	Group of Seven,
Jane Yolen, *Briar Rose*		Morrisseau, and Carr
Paulo Freire, excerpts from		paintings
Pedagogy of the Oppressed		*Liberation Days*
Guy de Maupassant, The		Ins Choi, *Kim's*
Necklace		*Convenience*
Edgar Allan Poe, The Cask		Michelle Scott, Telling
of Amontillado		Home
Margaret Atwood, Death by		Tobias Wolff, Powder
Landscape		
Jamaica Kincaid, Girl		
Katherine Mansfield, The		
Doll's House		
Charlotte Perkins Gilman,		
The Yellow Wallpaper		
Shaun Tan, Grandpa's Story		
Humanities 105: Different Stories, Different Meanings		
Alice Walker, Everyday Use	b.p. nichol, a pome is	*Educating Rita* (movie)
Joan Fern Shaw, The People	a poem	Shakespeare, *King Lear*
Upstairs	Duke Redbird, I Am	*What the Thunder Said*
Ruby Slipperjack, Blueberry	Canadian	*Redblood*
Days	Marilyn Dumont,	Michelle Thrush,
Raymond Carver, A Small,	Not Just a Platform	Finding Your Inner
Good Thing	for My Dance	Elder
Viktor Frankl, *Man's Search*	Seamus Heaney,	
for Meaning	Digging	
Ngũgĩ wa Thiong'o,	Rita Joe, I Lost My	
Decolonising the Mind	Talk	
Neil Gaiman, *Anansi Boys*	Vivian Hansen,	
Thomas King, *One Good*	Leylines of My	
Story, That One	Flesh	
Daniel Francis, *The Imaginary*	Ed Sanders, The	
Indian	Cutting Prow	
The Indian Act		

Notes:
* Includes short stories, fiction novels, autobiographies, philosophical treatises, and oral history.
** Includes live and print drama, movies, and images of visual art.

"evil wom[e]n" upstairs, the narrator is given the opportunity to question the ways in which society and her mother marginalize and dismiss women based on preconceptions of what it is to be a prostitute rather than knowing the neighbors upstairs as individuals. "I didn't learn the meaning of prostitute until years later; I'd lost interest in it as a word. Their actions had defined it for me: they were beautiful, rich ladies who wore filmy evening gowns all day long. And brought joy into my life" (p. 33). Through close reading and attention to the surface and deep meanings of the text, readers are able to decode the ideology that allows the mother to feel superior to the prostitutes despite the prostitutes' relative financial wealth, and revealed ways in which community can form despite existing oppressive regimes. Students who had experienced discrimination and judgment were delighted by the narrator's joy in her friendship with the women living upstairs and felt vicarious affirmation of their worth as human beings.

The humanities, through their storying of the grist of people's lives, evoke empathy (Greene, 1995) and desire to come alongside and really know the people whose lives are being told, an essential prelude to the formation of participatory and justice-oriented citizenship. Martha Nussbaum (1997) asserts that it is the arts' "narrative imagination [that] is an essential preparation for moral interaction" (p. 90) through its "power to make us see the lives of the different with more than a casual tourist's interest—with involvement and sympathetic understanding, with anger at our society's refusals of visibility" (p. 88). Students have repeatedly shared that the texts studied in Humanities 101 not only bring them to know a diverse range of people and experience, but also model ways that language and narrative can powerfully shape possibility and change.

Modeling Practices of Change

> I am more interested in participating in society, with a belief that I *do* have something to offer.

Humanities 101 braids a diverse range of narratives suggested by the lives and experiences of its participants with the critical work of thinkers to bring attention to the imbricated strands of race, gender, class, and cultural location in creating and sustaining social inequity. Humanities 101 responds to social inequality, as it sees "the need to address the holistic nature of adult learning for people from culturally diverse backgrounds in order to contribute to the development of sustaining social capital for individuals, families and communities" (Townsend, 2008, p. 71). The program continually moves between theoretical and practical constructs as students practice what they are learning and dialogue with each other about how to effect change. We intentionally model various forms of social activism and change through orature, storytelling, videos, art, and performance. As we read and study texts, we reflect on their ability to promote change and their potential as viable models. Some of the texts we have used include: Martin Luther King's (2012) "Letter from Birmingham Jail" as an example of oratory to promote non-violent protest against racism; and Ngũgĩ wa Thiong'o's (1986) *Decolonising the Mind* as a reminder of the importance of language in representing culture and ways to decolonize the self. The life of Indigenous painter Norval Morrisseau, represented through his art and the play *Copper Thunderbird* (Clements, 2007), offers insight into the complex intersections of race/racism, colonialism, and addiction while affirming the power of the creative imagination.

One class used Shane Koyczan's (n.d.) anti-bullying video *To This Day* to understand figures of speech and ways in which language is used to marginalize. Discussion of the video led to students naming specific words that had been used to oppress them: "welfare bum," "loser," "fag," "nigger," "uneducated," "poor," and "low-class." Students were invited to reflect on their experiences, to use language to critique the ways in which they had been oppressed, and to create a call to action. Collectively they wrote a powerful poem entitled "I Want You to See Me" that captured their growing awareness of social inequality and their determination to effect change. Detailing all the ways in which they wanted others to regard them, the speakers recorded their experience of oppression before challenging society to see them in a new light:

> I am not what you call me
> I am not what you think you see
> You don't get to tell my story
> I want you to see me for me!
> *(Humanities 101, 2014)*

At their Celebration of Learning, the class performed their poem for the community and incited a stirring response. This type of community expression often gives rise to complex emotions in students as they are forced to "encounter" their own identity (e.g., Hanson, 2012; Zucker et al., 2010). Events and expression can act as portals to agency: students can feel and, most importantly, imagine what it is to be in control. Such agency is the provenance of resilience and self-acceptance, both of which are required for greater awareness of citizenship and democracy. Students are encouraged to think beyond their personal reality to engage in what Parker termed "oppositional imagination" (2003, p. 30) to access their identity through the relationship they have with literature. As Colin and Heaney (2001) state, "the challenge to create a participatory practice with the higher education classroom inevitably involves pushing the borders, anticipating and countering resistance. It is through engagement with this struggle that genuine participation and democracy are attained" (pp. 29–30).

Being effective midwives of emerging participatory and justice-oriented citizens entails being open to moments of potential resistance and struggle, while welcoming them into the learning space. Such a moment emerged with the installation of a "soupkah" on the grounds of our university: a booth (*sukkah*) to honor the Jewish Festival of Booths, a celebration of freedom from slavery while expressing the vulnerability of people who are homeless. The structure was named the "soupkah" in honor of the holes in its walls where people could place food cans to feed people in need. The Humanities 101 class used the soupkah to engage in storytelling and to participate in a public panel with the local rabbi about their experiences with home and homelessness. One student presented a cogent critique of the systems preventing homeless people living in a city shelter from finding employment or housing, while a Humanities 101 alumnus presented a snapshot of current food insecurities issues in the city. Willingness to respond to such opportunities as they arise often provides unexpectedly rich responses.

Conclusion

The impossibility of separating education and political thought has been well asserted (Allman, 2009; Freire, 1970/2005; Giroux, 2013). Torres (1998) goes so far as to claim that "questions about citizenship, the connections between education and democracy, or the problem of multiculturalism affect *most of the decisions* that we face in dealing with the challenges of contemporary education" (p. 421, emphasis added). As this chapter has shown, the humanities as a broad field are rich in possibility for a truly democratic and liberatory education, but only if we deliberately and consciously use them to such ends and with a deep awareness of both their content and their dynamic potential.

Freire asserts that the critical perception of reality is the right of every person. At the same time, the vast majority of people are alienated from decision-making and critical thinking, a situation that is only worsening in the contemporary reality of neoliberalism and economic division. People who have been marginalized by socio-economic factors and other forms of social discrimination and exclusion are often so isolated and alienated that they cannot imagine alternative ways of being and acting, let alone take action to impel changes in their lives or in the society in which they live. Against such a paralyzing view, the work of Freire (1970/2005) suggests that every human being, no matter how unaware or submerged in a "culture of silence," is capable of looking at the world in dialogical encounters with others (p. 30). Through such encounters, people can gradually perceive personal and social realities as well as their contradictions, become aware of their own perceptions of that reality, and deal critically with them. The narrative arts of the humanities are the means through which people can discover themselves and their potential to re-shape the world into a more equitable and just place for all.

Notes

1 This and all other quotations found at the start of sections are the words of Humanities 101 participants and are used with their permission.

2 When the program was founded in 2003 as a pilot project, it was called Storefront 101. By 2009 the program was re-named Humanities 101 and located on the campus of St. Mary's University.
3 See Humanities 101 website for complete syllabi for two courses: http://www.stmu. ca/programs-and-courses/humanities-101/.

References

Alfred, M. V. (2002). The promise of sociocultural theory in democratizing adult education. *New Directions for Adult and Continuing Education, 96*, 3–13.

Allman, P. (2009). Paulo Freire's contributions to radical adult education. In A. Darder, M. Baltodano, and R. Torres (Eds.), *The critical pedagogy reader* (2nd ed., pp. 417–430). New York: Routledge.

Anda, R. F., Felitti, V. J., Bremner, J. D., Walker, J. D., Whitfield, C., Perry, B. D., Dube, S. R., and Giles, W. H. (2006). The enduring effects of abuse and related adverse experiences in childhood: A convergence of evidence from neurobiology and epidemiology. *European Archives of Psychiatry and Clinical Neuroscience, 256*(3), 174–186.

Choi, I. (2012). *Kim's convenience*. Toronto, ON: House of Anansi Press.

Clements, M. (2007). *Copper thunderbird*. Vancouver, BC: Talonbooks.

Colin, S. A. J., and Heaney, T. (2001). Negotiating the democratic classroom. *New Directions for Adult and Continuing Education, 91*, 29–37.

Engberg, M., and Hurtado, S. (2011). Developing pluralistic skills and dispositions in college: Examining racial/ethnic group differences. *Journal of Higher Education, 82*(4), 416–443.

Freire, P. (1996). *Letters to Cristina*. New York: Routledge.

Freire, P. (2005). *Pedagogy of the oppressed*. New York: Continuum. (Original work published 1970.)

Giroux, H. A. (1993). *Living dangerously: Multiculturalism and politics of difference*. New York: Peter Lang.

Giroux, H. A. (2013). Teachers as transformative intellectuals. In A. Canestrari and B. Marlowe (Eds.), *Educational foundations: An anthology of critical readings* (pp. 189–198). Thousand Oaks, CA: Sage.

Greene, M. (1995). *Releasing the imagination: Essays of education, the arts, and social change*. San Francisco, CA: Jossey-Bass.

Groen, J., and Hyland-Russell, T. (2010). Radical Humanities: A pathway toward transformational learning for marginalized non-traditional adult learners. Retrieved from www.cclca.ca/CCL/ResearchFundedResearch/201009GroenHyland-Russell RadicalHumanities.html.

Hamburg Declaration on Adult Learning. (1997). Fifth International Conference on Adult Education. Retrieved from http://www.unesco.org/education/uie/confintea/declaeng.htm.

Hanson, J. (2012). Extending the humanistic vision: Toward a humanities foundation for the counseling profession. *Journal of Humanistic Counselling, 51*(2), 133–144.

Horsman, J. (1999). *Too scared to learn: Women, violence and education*. Toronto, ON: McGilligan Books.

Horsman, J. (2004). "But is it education?": The challenge of creating effective learning for survivors of trauma. *Women's Studies Quarterly, 32*(1/2), 130–146.

Humanities 101. (2014). Humanities in action: Adventures in curiosity and learning igniting personal and social change. Retrieved from http:// http://www.stmu.ca/programs-and-courses/humanities-101/.

Hyland-Russell, T., and Syrnyk, C. (2014). Transforming the margins: Increasing well-being and agency among marginalized non-traditional adult learners. Proceedings of the Transformative Learning Network, Columbia University, New York.

Hyland-Russell, T., and Syrnyk, C. (2015). Challenging change: Transformative education for economically disadvantaged adult learners. International Journal of Lifelong Education, 34(5), 514–529.

Inglis, T. (1997). Empowerment and emancipation. Adult Education Quarterly, 48(1), 3–17.

Kerka, S. (2002). Trauma and adult learning. ERIC Clearinghouse on Adult Career and Vocational Education.

King, M. L., Jr. (2012). Letter from Birmingham Jail. In R. Gottlieb (Ed.), Liberating faith: Religious voices for justice, peace, and ecological wisdom (pp. 177–187). Lanham, MD: Rowman & Littlefield.

Kolk, B. van der (2014). The body keeps the score. New York: Penguin Group.

Koyczan, S. (n.d). To this day. Retrieved from http://www.tothisdayproject.com/.

Laman, T., Jewett, P., Jennings, L., Wilson, J., and Souto-Manning, M. (2012). Supporting critical dialogue across educational contexts. Equity and Excellence in Education, 45(1), 197–216.

Leigh, F. (2007). Platonic dialogue, maieutic method and critical thinking. Journal of Philosophy of Education, 41(3), 309–323.

Lewis, D. (Producer, Director). (1983). Educating Rita. [Motion picture]. United Kingdom: Acorn Studios.

Mackenzie, B. (2012). Seeking refuge in the classroom. Oxford Monitor on Forced Migration, 2(2), 70–73.

Majer, M., Nater, U. M., Lin, J.-M., Capuron, L., and Reeves, W. (2010). Association of childhood trauma with cognitive function in healthy adults: A pilot study. BMC Neurology, 10, 61–70.

Mayhew, M., and Fernandez, S. (2007). Pedagogical practices that contribute to social justice outcomes. Review of Higher Education, 31(1), 55–80.

McCrory, E., De Brito, S. A., and Viding, E. (2011). The impact of childhood maltreatment: A review of neurobiological and genetic factors. Frontiers in Psychiatry, 2, 48.

Muro, A., and Mein, E. (2010). Domestic trauma and adult education on the United States–Mexico border. Adult Basic Education and Literacy Journal, 4(3), 140–150.

Nagda, B. A., and Gurin, P. (2007). Intergroup dialogue: A critical-dialogic approach to learning about difference, inequality and social justice. New Directions for Teaching and Learning, 111, 35–45.

Nagda, B. A., Gurin, P., Sorensen, N., and Zúñiga, X. (2009). Evaluating intergroup dialogues: Engaging diversity for personal and social responsibility. Diversity and Democracy, 12(1), 3–6.

Nemiroff, G. F. (1992). Reconstructing education: Toward a pedagogy of critical humanism. Toronto, ON: OISE Press.

Ng, J. (2006). Antipoverty policy perspectives: A historical examination of the transference of social scientific thought and a situated critique of the Clemente course. Educational Studies, 39(1), 41–60.

Nussbaum, M. (1997). Cultivating humanity: A classical defense of reform in liberal education. Cambridge, MA: Harvard University Press.

Parker, E. (2003). Trouble don't last always: Emancipatory hope among African American adolescents. Cleveland, OH: Pilgrim.

Perry, B. D., and Szalavitz, M. (2006). The boy who was raised a dog and other stories from a child psychiatrist's notebook: What traumatized children teach us about loss, love, and healing. New York: Basic Books.

Piaget, J. (1975). *The development of thought: Equilibrium of cognitive structures*. New York: Viking Press.

Reichers, M. (2001). Making a difference: Plato in action. *Humanities, 22*(1), 29–30.

Rosenwasser, P. (2000). Tool for transformation: Cooperative inquiry as a process for healing from internalized oppression. Proceedings of the 41st Annual Adult Education Research Conference, Vancouver, BC.

Shaull, R. (2000). Foreword. In P. Freire, *Pedagogy of the oppressed* (pp. 29–34). New York: Continuum.

Shaw, J. F. (1995). *Raspberry vinegar*. Toronto, ON: HarperCollins.

Shonkoff, J. P., Gardner, A., and Committee on Psychosocial Aspects of Child and Family Health, Committee on Early Childhood, Adoption, and Dependent Care, and Section on Developmental and Behavioral Pediatrics. (2012). The lifelong effects of early childhood adversity and toxic stress. *Pediatrics, 129*(1), 232–246.

Shorris, E. (2000). *Riches for the poor: The Clemente course in the humanities*. New York: W. W. Norton.

Thiong'o, N. w. (1986). *Decolonising the mind: The politics of language in African literature*. Oxford: James Currey.

Tisdell, E. J. (1993). Interlocking systems of power, privilege, and oppression in adult higher education classes. *Adult Education Quarterly, 43*(4), 203–226.

Torres, C. A. (1998). Democracy, education, and multiculturalism: Dilemmas of citizenship in a global world. *Comparative Education Review, 42*(4), 421.

Townsend, R. (2008). Adult education, social inclusion and cultural diversity in regional communities. *Australian Journal of Adult Learning, 48(1),* 71–92.

Weinstein, G. (2004). Learner-centered teaching in the age of accountability. *CATESOL Journal, 16*(1), 97–110.

Westheimer, J., and Kahne, J. (2004). What kind of citizen? The politics of educating for democracy. *American Educational Research Journal, 41*(2), 237–269.

Wolff, T. (1996). *The night in question: Stories*. New York: Vintage Contemporaries.

Wright, H. (2003). Cultural studies as praxis: (Making) an autobiographical case. *Cultural Studies, 17*(6), 805–822.

Zucker, M., Spinazzola, J., Pollack, A., Pepe, L., Barry, S., Zhang, L., and Kolk, B. van der. (2010). Getting teachers in on the act: Evaluation of a theater- and classroom-based youth violence prevention program. *Journal of School Violence, 9*(2), 117–135.

14

MEDIATING DEMOCRACY

Social Media as Curriculum

Daniel G. Krutka and Jeffrey P. Carpenter

Social media is a conundrum of modern life. A blip on our communication and civic radars a mere decade ago, it is now ubiquitous. Facebook arrived in 2004 as an exclusive network for college students, but within a few years became an almost mandatory means for family and friends to stay in touch, businesses to attract customers, and politicians to connect with constituents. Historically, societies are afforded generations, or at least decades, to adapt to major technological inventions (e.g., printing press, industrial machinery) and their associated effects. However, the speed with which social media has come to be a fixture of modern life challenges our collective ability for meaningful consideration of its purposes, opportunities, and challenges. Rheingold (2012) argued that reflection upon these emerging media is critical, because "the ways people use new media in the first years of an emerging communication regime can influence the way those media end up being used and misused for decades to come" (p. 1). Unfortunately, schools as institutions have long struggled to adapt to technological change.

Even though social media use is increasingly pervasive, and specifically integral to young people's social lives (boyd, 2014), many schools have yet to effectively adjust to these new media. Journell et al. (2013) asserted that "American K–12 education . . . has largely ignored social media as an outlet for civic engagement" (p. 467), and it is common for school and teacher policies concerning social media to ignore or ban their use. Yet social media merits intentional consideration and scrutiny, as many of the challenges surrounding these technologies reflect larger societal issues. These media are part of our lived social experiences, and if schools are to be responsive educators must consider how to effectively and intelligently engage with them. In this chapter, we will consider social media as curriculum. We use the term *social media* to refer to platforms like Twitter or

Facebook that facilitate networking through the creation of, and interaction with, media content. After considering social studies curricula and the relevance of social media, we will discuss social media forms and how such platforms can enhance or diminish democracy in an age of economic disparity, and then deliberate on how educators might use social media towards the democratic purposes of examining and responding to this and other social problems.

(Re)considering Social Studies Curricula

Since the rise of the social studies a century ago, a stated responsibility of the field has been to educate students for democratic citizenship. Social studies curricula have, however, been criticized regularly as irrelevant, boring, and disconnected from the experiences of students and the needs of society (Evans, 2004). Traditional curricula have long been blamed for shortcomings, and numerous solutions have been proposed over the last century. At the same time, courses organized to address problems of democracy (Singleton, 1980; Thornton, 2005), issues-centered or thematic instruction (Ochoa-Becker, 2007), and curricula that investigate controversial topics have struggled to find a place in schools (Hess, 2009), particularly in an era of standardized testing. This raises the question: where might the unique and emergent social problems of our day gain curricular attention?

We agree with Kahne et al. (2006) that civics and government classes make up "the part of the formal high school curriculum that is most explicitly linked to the democratic purposes of education" (p. 391). Therefore, government teachers should—as several authors in this volume have argued—move beyond simply learning about civic institutions, and also cultivate spaces for democratic education that address current events, controversies, and social problems (Hess, 2009; Kahne and Middaugh, 2008). Social media free speech controversies could, for example, offer a way to investigate civil liberties, and analyzing the in/effectiveness of social media activism might offer a point of departure concerning civil rights topics. Net neutrality laws and the Federal Communications Commission (FCC) could provide a means to study legislative processes, interest groups, and bureaucracy. Social media uses by political candidates, along with the convergence of old and new media, could dovetail lessons on elections, governance, and media. Unfortunately, research has indicated that the primary focus of study in many government classes is on the acquisition of factual knowledge rather than exploration of citizens' roles (Levine and Lopez, 2004). Moreover, government teachers often abdicate responsibility to explore current events because of pressures associated with high-stakes tests (Journell, 2010), and many students do not identify with the political aims of government curricula even when current events and social issues are embedded (Krutka, 2012). Yet social studies educators must continue to find spaces for the exploration of social issues, problems, and phenomena that are critical to democratic society.

Why Study Social Media?

We believe it imperative that social studies curricula address social problems unique to an era of unprecedented technological change (Thomas and Brown, 2011). Some issues associated with new media are manifestations of long-standing problems, while others are unique to these twenty-first century environments. For example, while rebellious groups have long sought to undermine those with power and fight for various causes, online hacker groups like Anonymous now wage cyberwar against groups like the Ku Klux Klan and Islamic State (IS). The surrender of political decision-making to special interests and corporations has been a persistent problem, but it is now mostly manifested in online spaces through legislation concerning net neutrality. Institutional and systemic big-otry against numerous groups has long existed, but we must now consider how marginalization and privilege influence interactions in digital spaces, where ano-nymity or geographic distance complicates social relations. American democracy is threatened, and the challenges are a mix of both relatively new and familiar issues. Even though almost all students and teachers spend time online, they need opportunities to investigate and address issues, develop democratic dispositions, and create solutions for the twenty-first century.

One particular challenge facing democratic life concerns how citizens can learn to benefit from, challenge, and adapt to social media that are influenc-ing communication, politics, and community (Rheingold, 2008). As social media use has grown rapidly, social relations are increasingly enacted in online spaces. Recent research indicated that 58 percent of the entire U.S. adult population used Facebook, and the majority of online adults accessed mul-tiple social media services (Duggan et al., 2015). Social media presents not only opportunities for communication and engagement, but also opportuni-ties for "connected learning" (Ito et al., 2013) and occasions for (re-)creation of identities and selves (boyd, 2014). Furthermore, social media has become an important political domain in democracies (Bennett and Segerberg, 2012), with candidates, parties, and governments actively using these tools to spread their messages. Citizenship education that does not consider the digital realm will fail to address a major component of modern life. Educators must help stu-dents navigate online spaces so they may grow as netizens at the local, national, and international levels.

We believe social media to be an appropriate topic for deliberation because it is likely to be of interest to students and of importance to society. Social media use by young people has grown immensely over the past decade to the point that 92 percent of U.S. youth use social media on at least a daily basis (Lenhart, 2015). However, oversimplifications of youth as digital natives who intuitively know how to use technology intelligently, and thus have little to learn from their digital immigrant teachers, might have unwittingly distracted teachers from their responsibilities to educate. Other than New Jersey becoming the first state to require a class on social media and the Internet in middle school starting in 2014 (DeNisco, 2014), there is scant evidence that many schools are teaching students how to be mindful and critical about their social media practices (Rheingold, 2010; Stoddard, 2014). In our recent study, approximately half of the educators who used the social media platform Twitter professionally, and thus might be inclined to help students investigate online mediums, reported that their schools blocked these sites for students (Carpenter and Krutka, 2014). Instead of addressing the challenges technology inevitably creates, schools often practice what Foucault (1977) called "enclosure" by attempting to control technology use through limiting the physical spaces where the Internet can be accessed on school grounds.

Yet classrooms offer spaces where students might learn to ask critical questions about social media. As Rheingold (2012) put it, people must consider whether "Google is making us stupid, Facebook is commoditizing our privacy, or Twitter is chopping our attention into microslices" (p. 1). Citizens must also examine how the affordances of social media might be leveraged for good. Numerous theorists have argued that social media can transcend temporal and spatial bounds to connect people around interests in online affinity spaces (Gee, 2004) where participatory cultures thrive (Jenkins et al., 2009). Jenkins (2009) even pondered how the enthusiasm and creativity present in online communities of youth might be transferred towards "geeking out for democracy" (para. 11), but there is little evidence that such activities have come to fruition. What does social media do and undo in our lives? Answers to such questions will not come without time, focus, deliberation, and the consideration of various viewpoints.

Social Media as Curriculum

We will offer an initial examination into several questions about social media by first considering varying contexts of social media platforms and content that contribute to our understanding of what we know about uses in democratic society. Major questions include: What types of experiences do social media platforms afford? How might citizens' uses of social media enhance or diminish democracy? We will also address sub-questions concerning how social media might serve to privilege or marginalize various groups, and how capitalist motives might constrain social media's democratic potential. Finally, we will consider what educators should do to prepare students to use social media towards democratic purposes. We believe that teachers could use these questions as a basis for a lesson, unit, or semester dedicated to the study of social media. Although some social studies teachers may lack the curricular flexibility to put social media at the center of their courses, we will identify connections to civics and government curricula that might provide a way to investigate the topic through established courses. We will lay the groundwork for deliberating on these questions by drawing from the empirical evidence and theoretical arguments of scholars. We aim to help citizens and educators contemplate the role social media does, can, and should play in our democracy.

Contexts

What Types of Experiences Do Social Media Platforms Afford? How Do Platforms Differ?

Before considering how social media might enhance or diminish democratic experiences, we must first consider to what degree, as media theorist Marshall McLuhan (1964) put it, "the medium is the message" (p. 23). McLuhan contended that media forms (i.e., orality, print, telegraph, television, social media) serve as parts of the environment that influence how people understand media messages. Considering how any medium influences messages can help people consider how those mediums can be used and misused. Teachers might challenge students to consider how new mediums for communication (e.g., books, radio, television, computers) have influenced interactions, understandings, and social institutions in the past and present. For instance, students might be asked: What is different about learning about the recent events of Ferguson, Missouri via print, radio, television, Instagram, Facebook, Twitter, or Periscope? What is aesthetically different about reading, watching a livestream, listening to a professionally packaged radio story, or reading first-hand tweets about interactions between police and protesters? In each case, the medium of communication can contribute to dissimilar understandings of the same events. Part of using any media thoughtfully is to "first have a basic epistemological view of media representations as constructed and their delivery technologies as designed for particular purposes and not as neutral tools" (Stoddard, 2014, p. 6). The best way to understand various platforms is to ask good questions about them.

In an effort to turn a critical eye towards critiquing a social media platform specifically, or mediums in general, citizens should ask questions like:

- Who created the medium(s) and for what purpose(s)?
- How does the medium influence the message?
- How has the medium changed over time?
- How does the medium use algorithms or formulas to tailor content to users?
- What data do the mediums collect and how is it used?
- In what ways does this medium encourage or inhibit communication?
- What voices are privileged or marginalized via this medium?
- How is the medium similar to and different from other mediums of communication, and in particular other social media platforms?

Questions like these can help young people unpack financial, political, social, or corporate aims associated with these technologies. Mason (2015) argued that the most effective way to encourage such critical reflection on media "is to start with students' own life experiences, including the devices and real-life situations that students regularly encounter outside of the classroom" (p. 2). A pedagogically sound approach thus might be for youth to first critique, analyze, and use the platforms with which they are familiar.

After appraising social media platforms, young citizens might then evaluate the motives and positioning of authors of content, while also considering other contextual factors that could influence messages. Students could also ponder the cultures, norms, and practices that are common in different digital spaces. How do race, nationality, gender, or other factors encourage or discourage dialogues or actions? A government class might explore how civil liberties, civil rights, political beliefs and behaviors, elections, and media coverage are addressed in various online spaces. A history class could compare and contrast historical public shaming practices with online shaming behavior that occurs via social media (Ronson, 2015). Teachers might even address instances of free speech conflicts that have arisen in the recent past related to teachers' and students' uses of social media (Russo et al., 2010). In short, when contemplating how social media might influence democracy, it is wise to start by discussing, both generally and specifically, structures of platform(s) and how and why they are used.

Content

What Do Democracy, Citizenship, and Social Media Mean?

When considering whether social media may enhance or diminish democracy it is necessary to define these terms, starting with "democracy." Barton and Levstik (2013) contended, and we agree, that democratic citizens should be deliberative, participatory, and pluralistic. Furthermore, various scholars have argued that digital media literacy requires netizens to translate such characteristics to online environments (Lan, 2013; Mihailidis, 2014). Lan (2013) asserted that citizens should be skilled in: evaluating the reliability and credibility of online sources; communicating with diverse groups and peoples; understanding how cultures or groups are privileged or marginalized in various digital spaces; developing and maintaining relationships in online communities; and coordinating and organizing civic projects while advocating for social justice. There are, of course, many competing visions of democracy (Parker, 1996; Westheimer and Kahne, 2004), and democratic citizenship can also highlight ecology (Houser, 2009), diversity (Banks, 2004), and more. Students and teachers should intentionally define these terms when evaluating social media. This is particularly true considering Westheimer and Kahne's contention that of three visions of citizenship—personally responsible, participatory, and justice-oriented—schools tend to promote the first—and weakest—vision.

Furthermore, citizens should consider: What is *social media*? Social media is not easily defined (Mandiberg, 2012), and the term has been used both broadly and specifically. The Internet through the 1990s—later dubbed Web 1.0—primarily consisted of static sites created by experts. The arrival of Web 2.0 sites signaled a shift to a cyberspace more built upon an architecture of participation where platforms like blogs and video sharing sites (e.g., Blogger, YouTube) made it easier for common citizens to create web content. Social media like MySpace and Facebook offered platforms that further enabled interactions around content. The term *social media* is broad enough to be inclusive of various definitions, and it can generally be "characterized by digital platforms where users can create, share, and interact with content and each other in online collaborative spaces" (Carpenter and Krutka, 2015, p. 29). However, citizens should consider whether this definition is sufficient for understanding and appraising the platforms under consideration.

How Might Citizens' Uses of Social Media Enhance Democracy?

Technology enthusiasts and education reformers have imagined potential benefits of new technologies for democratic processes since long before the advent of social media. In the specific case of social media, many scholars argue for the democratizing potential of these tools (e.g., Gazali, 2014). For example, Jenkins (2006) asserted that many social media environments lend themselves towards participatory experiences, and different scholars have coined a variety of phrases to try to capture this relationship, including *new media democracy*, *social media democracy*, and *networking democracy* (Loader and Mercea, 2011). New interactive media are thought to have the potential to give voice, encourage participation, and help build coalitions. Shirky (2011) suggested that social media could "help loosely coordinated publics demand change" (p. 29). Citizens who might previously have been reduced to passive consumption of political messages are enabled by new media "to challenge discourses, share alternative perspectives and publish their own opinions" (Loader and Mercea, 2011, p. 759). For example, as Arend and Cuenca describe in Chapter 12, social media played an important role in the activism that followed in the wake of Michael Brown's death in Ferguson, Missouri, facilitating the mobilization, direction, and documentation of grassroots protests.

Social media is understood to lower the costs of various forms of engagement and provide new ways to discover and become involved with issues, both mobilizing and broadening political participation. Government students might consider how new media can influence citizens' political behaviors and the election and governing habits of public officials. New media can make it easier for users to engage in political acts online, from simple participation in political discussions to various forms of online activism. While there seems to be evidence that elites have bolstered privilege and power in online spaces (Stoddard, 2014), members of groups whose perspectives are often marginalized have used hashtags on mediums like Twitter to raise awareness and solidarity (e.g., #BlackLivesMatter), bring forth current events—or perspectives of events—ignored by the mainstream media (e.g., #CharlestonShooting), critique corporate sexism (e.g., #notbuyingit), or share educational ideas (e.g., #HipHopEd, #FergusonSyllabus, #educolor). Furthermore, social media news-feeds can expose users to political information and perspectives that they may not have actively sought (Messing and Westwood, 2012; Morris and Morris, 2013). Educators might ask students to compare and contrast how perspectives, information, and news are spread via activist hashtags and consider the implications for civic activity or contrast the feed with mainstream media.

Numerous highly publicized reports from various world events have high-lighted how social media might assist democratic efforts. While the influence and role of social media in the Arab Spring is debated (Khondker, 2011; Wolfsfeld et al., 2013), Ghonim (2013) credited social media platforms Facebook and Twitter for helping to rally public sentiment and coordinate activities against an oppressive regime during the 2011 Egyptian revolution. In reflecting on a 2013 protest that was not typical of the top-down protests common to Turkey in the past, Tufekci (2013) contended that there might even be a unique style of protest particular to instances when social media plays a role in organization. She argued that mediated communication via Twitter and Facebook ignited spontaneous demonstrations that consisted of porous leadership, non-activist participation, and a certain degree of pluralism.

Scholars have also emphasized the potential for social media to attract young people towards political activities (Loader and Mercea, 2011). Although some youth may be increasingly disenchanted with, or indifferent to, mainstream politi-cal parties, technologies such as social media may provide opportunities for forms of civic engagement and citizenship that are different than those typically associ-ated with political party membership (Bennett, 2008). Xenos et al.'s (2014) study of young people in three countries reported a "strong positive relationship between social media use and political engagement" (p. 151). Loader et al. (2014) offered the term "networked young citizen" (p. 145) to describe the online political engage-ment of youth. They suggested "the possible displacement of traditional models of representative democracy as the dominant cultural form of engagement by alterna-tive approaches increasingly characterized through networking practices" (p. 143). Newsom and Dickey (2013) suggested that politicians should be using social media to involve citizens in decision-making and to make government more transparent, not just to campaign for elections. Furthermore, young people might also be able to transfer online skills to more conventional political activities, and engage in both traditional and alternative approaches (Bennett, 2008).

How Might Citizens' Uses of Social Media Diminish Democracy?

Despite enthusiasm for social media's democratizing potential, there are both empirical studies and theoretical arguments that should give educators pause as they seek to determine the roles for social media in democratic life (e.g., Zuckerman, 2013). Shirky (2011) noted cases in which political actions that sought to leverage social media failed to overcome existing hierarchies or power structures, such as Iran's 2009 Green Movement. Although social media is praised by some for lowering participation costs, others have expressed concerns that political activity that requires limited commitment risks "falling prey to unreflective groupthink, often shaped by the dominant prejudices of agenda-setting mass media" (Moss and Coleman, 2014, p. 415). Critics also contend that social media enables frivolous, low-commitment online political activity known as "slacktivism," which can potentially displace more meaningful activism (Morozov, 2009, para. 1). Students might analyze personal social media uses, investigate forms of political participation common to citizens, and then evaluate or propose civic activities that might move beyond slacktivism.

It remains unclear under what conditions social media can foster the dedication and coherence often necessary to create positive political change. It is possible that most active social media users engaging in political activism and discourse are simply those people who are already fully committed to their political cause (Loader and Mercea, 2011; Xenos et al., 2014). Furthermore, individuals and groups with clearly undemocratic aims utilize social media as well. Consider, for example, the use of social media by Islamic State (IS) to intimidate opponents with images and videos displaying their acts of violence (Andrews and Schwartz, 2014). Educators could investigate with students the ways and conditions under which social media can influence civic change that is democratic, participatory, and pluralistic.

While some scholars have reported on the possibilities for social media activity to contribute to "incidental" (Morris and Morris, 2013) learning resulting from exposure to content and perspectives users might not have actively sought out, others have expressed concern regarding how technologies, including social media, might instead limit access to diverse perspectives (Pariser, 2011; Stoddard, 2014; Thelwall, 2009). People using social media platforms might fall prey to the tendency in some other online forums for political conversations to become echo chambers where homogeneous opinions are expressed (Sunstein, 2001). The potential for competition between political discourses may be restricted by mechanisms such as algorithms which select what information appears in users' news feeds. In contrast to the notion of the *networked young citizen* are the concepts of *networked individualism* (Wellman et al., 2003) and *atomized individualism* (Mason and Metzger, 2012), which suggest that, although new technologies may connect people at one level, the connections can lack the depth and strength to support real collaboration and collective action. However, the research of Bennett and Segerberg (2012), comparing political protest mobilization efforts targeting the 2009 G20 London Summit, suggested that the more personalized political activity supported by social media contributed to collective action that maintained high levels of engagement, agenda focus, and network strength.

Several studies have challenged the notion that social media enables political or citizenship activities among young people (e.g., Ekström et al., 2014). Thorson's (2014) research indicated that, depending on the nature of their networks, some youth suppressed their opinions because of the perceived risks associated with talking about politics. The permanence of posts on some social media platforms might also cause people to be unwilling to take risks in posting unpopular opinions. Weinstein's (2014) research on the online civic expression patterns of civically engaged youth found that among these young people approximately 20 percent refrained from civic expression online, while another 20 percent only engaged in civic expression on certain platforms. For example, the anonymous nature of Twitter encouraged one individual who perceived her own views as radical to express herself more freely, while for another person the self-promotional stigma of Twitter made her avoid civic expression on the platform. While the majority of her subjects did engage in civic activities via social media, "the potential for online expression to have unwanted implications for their off-line lives crystallizes the risks for some youth and leads them to mask their civic identities online" (Weinstein, 2014, p. 228).

Does Social Media Empower Those Who Are Marginalized or Further Empower the Privileged?

Another strain of optimism regarding social media's democratic potential relates to these tools' capacities to empower marginalized or subordinated groups. It has been suggested that social media provides opportunities to disrupt traditional communicative power relations (Shirky, 2011). For example, prior research in the medical arena suggests that online forums can empower patients to ask more questions, demand more information, and challenge their doctors (Cohen and Raymond, 2011). In relation to democracy, social media could provide an "arena for political participation for people who are otherwise unengaged in politics" (Loader and Mercea, 2011 p. 764). Students might even research organizations particular to their interests and determine whether there are social media or digital outlets through which anyone may connect and participate in the groups' activities.

Established organizations and groups can effectively coordinate their actions to pursue political goals, but social media could compensate for the disadvantages of less-organized and/or under-resourced groups by reducing the costs of coordination (Ghonim, 2013; Morris and Morris, 2013; Shirky, 2011). Because "tools in broad use become much harder to censor without risking politicizing the larger group of otherwise apolitical actors," opinions that challenge the status quo and those in power can achieve a broader reach via social media (Shirky, 2011, p. 37). Xenos et al.'s (2014) multi-country research on patterns of social media use and youth political engagement found "reasons to be optimistic concerning the overall influence of this popular new form of digital media on longstanding patterns of political inequality" (p. 151).

However, the kind of access to social and cultural capital that social media can afford has in the past frequently been used to maintain or even exacerbate inequalities (Bourdieu, 1984). The disparities that exist in face-to-face contexts could easily be reproduced or even amplified in virtual settings; social media could merely help those already privileged with strong networks and connections to further their advantages (boyd, 2014; Hargittai, 2008; Schlozman et al., 2012). Unequal access, use, and leveraging of social media's affordances might negate the potential of these new technologies. In the case of young people, Xenos et al. (2014) asserted that "the mobilizing power of social media will not affect all young people in the same way" (p. 154). Left to their own devices, some young people will be savvier than others regarding how to leverage the affordances of these platforms.

How Do Capitalist Motives Constrain the Democratic Potential of Social Media?

The concentration of social media activity in a few hugely popular services is potentially problematic in that these companies' profit-seeking behaviors could constrain public discourse and exacerbate inequality. Many companies gather data from users' social media interactions, sell it to third-party marketers, and align advertisements with users' previous online activities. Corporate influence should remind users to consider both how they use and are used by social media. For example, in order to maintain access to markets, Facebook regularly complies with requests to censor posts from governments (Pagliery, 2015). Friesen and Lowe (2012) have warned that the commercial motives that impact the design of social media services may not align with what are wise practices for teaching and learning. Furthermore, it is likely that different social media platforms are more or less effective as tools of inclusion or exclusion. Facebook, for example, has been criticized for limiting how various members of LBGTQ communities (Nichols, 2014), indigenous peoples (Holpuch, 2015), and other individuals identify themselves when their identities do not conform to social norms. There are cases in which social media corporations have done little to prevent cyberbullying, verbal abuse, and even repeated physical threats (e.g., Greenhouse, 2013).

Social media also can function as a tool of surveillance (Fuchs et al., 2013; Trottier, 2012) that allows corporations to exploit users (e.g., Andrejevic, 2009; Fuchs, 2011), employers to invade the private lives of workers or potential hires (McDonald and Thompson, 2015), and universities to snoop on prospective admits (boyd, 2014). Given these uses, students might benefit from investigating how social media companies make profits as a way of analyzing economic systems, and/or consider ethical issues associated with the massive amounts of personal information collected and sold on by social media corporations. Students may delve into civil liberties issues associated with government monitoring of social media posts, particularly those that are critical of government policies (Nakashima, 2012).

While social media may well offer affordances compatible with democratic principles, and hold potential to combat inequality, young people do not inevitably make use of those affordances. Access to technology with certain potentialities does not ensure their use for civic purposes (Carr, 2013; Shirky, 2011), and thus, as boyd (2014) noted, "the mere existence of new technology neither creates nor magically solves cultural problems" (p. 156). Moreover, the digital divide in access to technologies can lead to technological skills gaps that create disparities in opportunities that fall along socioeconomic lines. Educators may be able to make it more likely that the promise of social media platforms, rather than their perils, is realized. Schools could be settings in which young people learn how to leverage social media for social, civic, and personal good.

Pedagogy

What Should Educators Do to Prepare Students to Use Social Media towards Democratic Purposes?

Educators and educational systems have been slow to define social media's place in schools (Nowell, 2014). Although some educators have begun to use social media for their own professional learning, it appears to be less common that teachers utilize these technologies with their students (Carpenter and Krutka, 2014). Levine (2015) argued that one reason that teachers have failed to meaningfully integrate social media into curricula is because it is very difficult to remain current, owing to the constantly changing digital landscape. He warned that educating youth for civic or political engagement presents several challenges, including the difficulties of teaching complex, fluid online skills that many educators themselves do not possess, and the need to motivate young people to engage with civic content when they have the option to refuse. Despite such challenges, teachers frankly do not have much choice given social media's emergent place "at the heart of contemporary culture" (boyd, 2014, p. 6). Whether educators are ready for it or not, the young people they are preparing for citizenship will likely enact a significant portion of their social, civic, political, and communal activities via social media platforms.

It is important to acknowledge past instances of exuberant optimism regarding new technologies, which were then followed by disappointment (Cuban, 1986, 2001), such as the supposedly transformative educational potential of the radio or television. However, it does appear that many social media platforms may be capable of encouraging the types of discussion, reflection, peer feedback, and mentoring that are often valued in educational settings (Carpenter and Krutka, 2015). In the past, education technology advocates have tended to focus "on using the Internet for greater accessibility to information, which could then be used as a conduit for civic action," instead of conceiving of technology like social media itself being "a medium for civic participation and political interaction with others" (Journell et al., 2013, p. 468). Yet Shirky (2011) has asserted that "access to information is far less important, politically, than access to conversation" (p. 35), and social media can potentially provide young people access to a variety of political conversations. Xenos et al. (2014) reported that civic education experiences which mixed digital media literacy with civic or political discussion topics were significantly and positively related to individual (p<0.000) and collective (p<0.01) political engagement in Australia. In terms of social media's potential educational benefits in the classroom, research suggests it can provide "an outlet for students, who are typically excluded from the political process, to have their voices heard within a larger political arena than what they would typically find at home or at school" (Journell et al., 2013, p. 476). Social media has the potential to support what has been called "social reading" (Vlieghe et al., 2014), a process through which students co-construct their understanding of texts through active questioning, commentary, and discussion during the reading process. And social media tools that support digital backchanneling—online discussion that occurs in parallel to live spoken remarks—can also encourage wider participation and contributions from students, including those who do not typically speak their minds in traditional classroom discussion formats (Carpenter, 2015; Hunter and Caraway, 2014).

Finally, Sleeter (2008) warned of the difficulties inherent in teaching for democracy in an era of standardization and accountability, which she asserted is "rooted much more firmly in corporatocracy than democracy" (p. 139). Such a situation presents educators with two challenges: "negotiating increasingly undemocratic systems in order to find space for democratic teaching, and critically examining what democracy is, including gaps between its ideals and actual practice" (p. 139). The participatory nature of social media may not sit comfortably within school systems based upon hierarchies and control, but it remains important for educators to consider whether school policies and practices prepare students more for democratic citizenship or obedience to authority.

Belying the digital native myth that youth have natural dispositions and skills that allow them to use technology effectively, many young people do not recognize and/or utilize the educational or civic affordances of these technologies. For example, Luckin et al.'s (2009) research on the use of Web 2.0 technologies found that students were not taking full advantage of their learning benefits, as few used the technologies to engage in deep collaboration or to create original content. In the case of social media use in civics education, Journell et al. (2013) described students who received little guidance on how to use social media for civic engagement and who commonly made "comments that spoke in generalities about candidates without providing support for those positions" (p. 475). The researchers also found little evidence that students "listened" to others on social media; instead "it seemed as though the students were mostly talking at each other rather than with each other" (p. 477). If teachers and schools stick their collective heads in the sand regarding social media, we suspect that there will be relatively more of a "culture of meanness and cruelty" dominated by "jockeying for social status" in young people's lives than the potential salutary effects of social media (boyd, 2014, p. 151).

What Are Possible Ways Educators Can Teach with and about Social Media?

The requirements of teaching, idiosyncrasies of youth, complexity of social media, and challenges of democracy present significant obstacles for classroom study of the use of social media as curriculum. We are not suggesting that educators can or should single-handedly determine how young people use social media, but that teaching for today's and tomorrow's democracies requires that educators take on some role in influencing that use. Teachers need to define what knowledge and skills are required by students to successfully use social media.

Communities of teachers can tackle various aspects of the problems and possibilities associated with social media uses in democratic society. The dangers of students moving through school without becoming more deliberate, pluralistic, and participatory digital citizens are concerning. Social media has infiltrated, enhanced, and changed the ways so many of us live, and educators cannot ignore the world around us. We hope that the questions and initial explorations we have presented might assist teachers investigating topics like social media.

The information in this chapter can be used in a multitude of ways. In an effort to help teachers consider key components of investigating social media we have identified the following elements that might be addressed.

Define Terms

What do *democracy* and *citizenship* mean in general (e.g., Barton and Levstik, 2004; Parker, 1996; Westheimer and Kahne, 2004), and how do these terms apply to social media? Are additional or different skills needed for digital citizenship (e.g., Lan, 2013; Rheingold, 2010)? What does *social media* mean? What platforms should be considered social media and why?

Analyze and Appraise Mediums

How do social media platforms influence messages? What are the affordances and limitations of various mediums? Do certain platforms privilege or marginalize certain groups in theory or practice? How do corporations use data from social media? Do profit motives inhibit democratic possibilities of social media? Are students' personal and/or civic uses of different platforms mindful and responsible?

Consider, Evaluate, and Research Questions

While discussing, deliberating upon, and/or researching questions or case studies in this chapter, consider what is, and what should be, the relationship between democratic citizenship and social media.

Create Plans for Democratic Social Media Use

How can social media be used more democratically in our personal and communal or civic lives? How can students use hashtags and other social media affordances to engage in dialogues about current events and social problems? Houser (2005) suggested that educators help students explore multiple avenues for civic solutions in daily, intermediate, and grand realms. Educators could ask students to consider: How might citizens change their daily uses of social media to be more democratic? How might citizens seek intermediate solutions like raising awareness about ways social media can enhance or threaten democracy? And how can we use social media to seek grand solutions that require changing policies, laws, or widespread practices that threaten democracy?

Conclusion

In an age of economic disparity educators must be mindful of not only the digital divide concerning technological access, but also the skills gap and corporate influences that affect social media uses and misuses. We believe that a critical approach, taking account of these, can help students (re)consider social media in ways that will strengthen how these media operate in our democracy.

References

Andrejevic, M. (2009). Critical media studies 2.0: An interactive upgrade. *Interactions: Studies in Communication and Culture, 1*(1), 35–51.

Andrews, N., and Schwartz, F. (2014, August 22). Islamic State pushes social media battle with West. *Wall Street Journal*. Retrieved from http://www.wsj.com/articles/isis-pushes-social-media-battle-with-west-1408725614.

Banks, J. A. (2004). Teaching for social justice, diversity, and citizenship in a global world. *Educational Forum, 68*(4), 296–305.

Barton, K. C., and Levstik, L. S. (2004). *Teaching history for the common good*. Mahwah, NJ: Lawrence Erlbaum Associates.

Barton, K. C., and Levstik, L. S. (2013). *Teaching history for the common good*. Mahwah, NJ: Lawrence Erlbaum Associates.

Bennett, W. L. (2008). Changing citizenship in the digital age. In W. L. Bennett (Ed.), *Civic life online: Learning how digital media can engage youth* (pp. 1–24). Cambridge, MA: MIT Press.

Bennett, W. L., and Segerberg, A. (2012). The logic of connective action: Digital media and the personalization of contentious politics. *Information, Communication and Society, 15*(5), 739–768.

Bourdieu, P. (1984). *Distinction: A social critique of the judgement of taste.* Cambridge, MA: Harvard University Press.

boyd, d. (2014). *It's complicated: The social lives of networked teens.* New Haven, CT: Yale University Press.

Carpenter, J. P. (2015). Digital backchannels: Giving every student a voice. *Educational Leadership, 72*(8), 54–58.

Carpenter, J. P., and Krutka, D. G. (2014). How and why educators use Twitter: A survey of the field. *Journal of Research on Technology in Education, 46*(4), 414–434.

Carpenter, J. P., and Krutka, D. G. (2015). Social media in teacher education. In M. Neiss and H. Gillow-Wiles (Eds.), *Handbook of research on teacher education in the digital age* (pp. 28–54). Hershey, PA: IGI Global.

Carr, P. R. (2013). The mediatization of democracy, and the specter of critical media engagement. In L. Shultz and T. Kajner (Eds.), *Engaged scholarship: The politics of engagement and disengagement* (pp. 163–181). Rotterdam: Sense.

Cohen, J. H., and Raymond, J. M. (2011). How the Internet is giving birth (to) a new social order. *Information, Communication and Society, 14*(6), 937–957.

Cuban, L. (1986). *Teachers and machines: The classroom use of technology since 1920.* New York: Teachers College Press.

Cuban, L. (2001). *Oversold and underused: Computers in schools 1980–2000.* Cambridge, MA: Harvard University Press.

DeNisco, A. (2014, March). New Jersey schools to teach social media. *District Administration.* Retrieved from http://www.districtadministration.com/article/new-jersey-schools-teach-social-media.

Duggan, M., Ellison, N. B., Lampe, C., Lenhart, A., and Madden, M. (2015, January). *Social media update 2014.* Pew Research Center. Retrieved from http://www.pewinternet.org/files/2015/01/PI_SocialMediaUpdate20144.pdf.

Ekström, M., Olsson, T., and Shehata, A. (2014). Spaces for public orientation? Longitudinal effects of Internet use in adolescence. *Information, Communication and Society, 17*(2), 168–183.

Evans, R. W. (2004). *The social studies wars: What should we teach the children?* New York: Teachers College Press.

Foucault, M. (1977). *Discipline and punish: The birth of the prison.* London: Allen Lane.

Friesen, N., and Lowe, S. (2012). The questionable promise of social media for education: Connective learning and the commercial imperative. *Journal of Computer Assisted Learning, 28*(3), 183–194.

Fuchs, C. (2011). *Foundations of critical media and information studies.* New York: Routledge.

Fuchs, C., Boersma, K., Albrechtslund, A., and Sandoval, M. (2013). *Internet and surveillance: The challenges of Web 2.0 and social media* (vol. 16). New York: Routledge.

Gazali, E. (2014). Learning by clicking: An experiment with social media democracy in Indonesia. *International Communication Gazette, 76*(4–5), 425–439.

Gee, J. P. (2004). *Situated language and learning: A critique of traditional schooling.* New York: Routledge.

Ghonim, W. (2013). *Revolution 2.0: The power of the people is greater than the people in power.* New York: HarperCollins.

Greenhouse, E. (2013, August 1). Twitter's free-speech problem. *New Yorker.* Retrieved from http://www.newyorker.com/tech/elements/twitters-free-speech-problem.

Hargittai, E. (2008). The digital reproduction of inequality. In D. Grusky (Ed.), *Social stratification* (pp. 936–944). Boulder, CO: Westview Press.

Hess, D. (2009). *Controversy in the classroom: The democratic power of discussion.* New York: Routledge.

Holpuch, A. (2015, February 19). Native American activist to sue Facebook over site's "real name" policy. *Guardian.* Retrieved from http://www.theguardian.com/technology/2015/feb/19/native-american-activist-facebook-lawsuit-real-name.

Houser, N. O. (2005). Inquiry island: Social responsibility and ecological sustainability in the twenty-first century. *Social Studies, 96*(3), 127–132.

Houser, N. O. (2009). Ecological democracy: An environmental approach to citizenship education. *Theory and Research in Social Education, 37*(2), 192–214.

Hunter, J. D., and Caraway, H. J. (2014). Urban youth use Twitter to transform learning and engagement. *English Journal, 103*(4), 76–82.

Ito, M., Gutierrez, K., Livingstone, S., Penuel, B., Rhodes, J., Salen, K., Schor, J., Sefton-Green, J., and Watkins, S. C. (2013). Connected learning: An agenda for research and design. [Report]. *Digital Media and Learning Research Hub.* Retrieved from http://dmlhub.net/publications/connected-learning-agenda-for-research-and-design/.

Jenkins, H. (2006). *Convergence culture: Where old and new media collide.* New York: New York University Press.

Jenkins, H. (2009, May 1). "Geeking out" for democracy (part one). *Confessions of an aca-fan: The official weblog of Henry Jenkins.* Retrieved from http://henryjenkins.org/2009/05/geeking_out_for_democracy_part.html.

Jenkins, H., Purushotma, R., Weigel, M., Clinton, K., and Robison, A. J. (2009). *Confronting the challenges of participatory culture: Media education for the 21st century.* Cambridge, MA: MIT Press.

Journell, W. (2010). The influence of high-stakes testing on high school teachers' willingness to incorporate current political events into the curriculum. *High School Journal, 93*(3), 111–125.

Journell, W., Ayers, C. A., and Beeson, M. W. (2013). Joining the conversation: Twitter as a tool for student political engagement. *Educational Forum, 77*(4), 466–480.

Kahne, J., and Middaugh, E. (2008). High quality civic education: What is it and who gets it? *Social Education, 72*(1), 34.

Kahne, J., Chi, B., and Middaugh, E. (2006). Building social capital for civic and political engagement: The potential of high-school civics courses. *Canadian Journal of Education/Revue canadienne de l'éducation, 29*(2), 387–409.

Khondker, H. H. (2011). Role of the new media in the Arab Spring. *Globalizations, 8*(5), 675–679.

Krutka, D. G. (2012). "Shouldn't everyone know about their government?" An exploration of curricular values in Advanced Placement government classes. [Unpublished doctoral dissertation]. University of Oklahoma, Norman.

Lan, C. F. (2013). Democratic education in the new media era: Toward a framework of democratic media literacy. *Ohio Social Studies Review, 50*(1), 51–62.

Lenhart, A. (2015, April). *Teens, social media and technology: Overview 2015.* Pew Research Center. Retrieved from http://www.pewinternet.org/files/2015/04/PI_TeensandTech_Update2015_0409151.pdf.

Levine, P. (2015). Media literacy for the 21st century. A response to "The need for media education in democratic education." *Democracy and Education, 23*(1), Article 15.

Levine, P., and Lopez, M. H. (2004). Themes emphasized in social studies and civics classes: New evidence. [CIRCLE fact sheet]. Center for Information and Research on Civic Learning and Engagement. Retrieved from http://www.civicyouth.org/PopUps/fact_sheet_civic_ed.pdf.

Loader, B. D., and Mercea, D. (2011). Networking democracy? Social media innovations and participatory politics. *Information, Communication and Society, 14*(6), 757–769.

Loader, B. D., Vromen, A., and Xenos, M. A. (2014). The networked young citizen: Social media, political participation and civic engagement. *Information, Communication and Society, 17*(2), 143–150.

Luckin, R., Clark, W., Graber, R., Logan, K., Mee, A., and Oliver, M. (2009). Do Web 2.0 tools really open the door to learning? Practices, perceptions and profiles of 11–16 year old students. *Learning, Media and Technology, 34*(2), 87–104.

Mandiberg, M. (2012). Introduction. In M. Mandiberg (Ed.), *The social media reader.* New York: New York University Press.

Mason, L. E. (2015). Media and education. A response to "The need for media education in democratic education." *Democracy and Education, 23*(1), Article 14.

Mason, L., and Metzger, S. A. (2012). Reconceptualizing media literacy in the social studies: A pragmatist critique of the NCSS position statement on media literacy. *Theory and Research in Social Education, 40*(4), 436–455.

McDonald, P., and Thompson, P. (2015). Social media(tion) and the reshaping of public/private boundaries in employment relations. *International Journal of Management Reviews, 18*(1), 69–84.

McLuhan, M. (1964). *Understanding media: The extensions of man.* New York: McGraw-Hill.

Messing, S., and Westwood, S. J. (2012). Selective exposure in the age of social media: Endorsements trump partisan source affiliation when selecting news online. *Communication Research, 41*(8), 1042–1063.

Mihailidis, P. (2014). *Media literacy and the emerging citizen: Youth, engagement and participation in digital culture.* New York: Peter Lang.

Morozov, E. (2009, May 19). The brave new world of slacktivism. *National Public Radio.* Retrieved from http://www.npr.org/templates/story/story.php?storyId=104302141.

Morris, D. S., and Morris, J. S. (2013). Digital inequality and participation in the political process: Real or imagined? *Social Science Computer Review, 31*(5), 589–600.

Moss, G., and Coleman, S. (2014). Deliberative manoeuvres in the digital darkness: E-democracy policy in the UK. *British Journal of Politics and International Relations, 16*(3), 410–427.

Nakashima, E. (2012, January 13). DHS monitoring of social media worries civil liberties advocates. *Washington Post.* Retrieved from https://www.washingtonpost.com/world/national-security/dhs-monitoring-of-social-media-worries-civil-liberties-advocates/2012/01/13/gIQANPO7wP_story.html.

Newsom, G., and Dickey, L. (2013). *Citizenville: How to take the town square digital and reinvent government.* New York: Penguin.

Nichols, J. (2014, September 15). Facebook "name change" policy disproportionately affecting LGBT community. *Huffington Post.* Retrieved from http://www.huffingtonpost.com/2014/09/15/facebook-name-change_n_5824836.html.

Nowell, S. D. (2014). Using disruptive technologies to make digital connections: Stories of media use and digital literacy in secondary classrooms. *Educational Media International, 51*(2), 109–123.

Ochoa-Becker, A. S. (2007). *Democratic education for social studies: An issues-centered decision making curriculum.* Greenwich, CT: IAP.

Pagliery, J. (2015, February 6). The 3 places where Facebook censors you most. *CNN Money*. Retrieved from http://money.cnn.com/2015/02/06/technology/facebook-censorship/.

Pariser, E. (2011). *The filter bubble: What the Internet is hiding from you*. London: Penguin.

Parker, W. C. (1996). Curriculum for democracy. In R. Sodor (Ed.), *Democracy, education, and the schools* (pp. 182–210). San Francisco, CA: Jossey-Bass.

Rheingold, H. (2008). Using participatory media and public voice to encourage civic engagement. In W. L. Bennett (Ed.), *Civic life online: Learning how digital media can engage youth* (pp. 1–24). Cambridge, MA: MIT Press.

Rheingold, H. (2010). Attention, and other 21st-century social media literacies. *EDUCAUSE Review*, *45*(5), 14–24.

Rheingold, H. (2012). *Net smart: How to thrive online*. Cambridge, MA: MIT Press.

Ronson, J. (2015). *So you've been publicly shamed*. New York: Penguin.

Russo, C. J., Squelch, J., and Varnham, S. (2010). Teachers and social networking sites: Think before you post. *Public Space: Journal of Law and Social Justice*, *5*(5), 1–15.

Schlozman, K. A., Verba, S., and Brady, H. E. (2012). *The unheavenly chorus: Unequal political voice and the broken promise of American democracy*. Princeton, NJ: Princeton University Press.

Shirky, C. (2011). Political power of social media: Technology, the public sphere, and political change. *Foreign Affairs*, *90*(1), 28–41.

Singleton, H. W. (1980). Problems of democracy: The revisionist plan for social studies education. *Theory and Research in Social Education*, *8*(3), 89–103.

Sleeter, C. (2008). Teaching for democracy in an age of corporatocracy. *Teachers College Record*, *110*(1), 139–159.

Stoddard, J. (2014). The need for media education in democratic education. *Democracy and Education*, *22*(1), Article 4.

Sunstein, C. (2001). *Republic.com*. Princeton, NJ: Princeton University Press.

Thelwall, M. (2009). Homophily in MySpace. *Journal of the American Society for Information Science and Technology*, *60*(2), 219–231.

Thomas, D., and Brown, J. S. (2011). *A new culture of learning: Cultivating the imagination for a world of constant change*. Lexington, KY: CreateSpace.

Thornton, S. J. (2005). *Teaching social studies that matters: Curriculum for active learning*. New York: Teachers College Press.

Thorson, K. (2014). Facing an uncertain reception: Young citizens and political interaction on Facebook. *Information, Communication and Society*, *17*(2), 203–216.

Trottier, D. (2012). *Social media as surveillance: Rethinking visibility in a converging age*. Farnham, UK: Ashgate.

Tufekci, Z. (2013, June 1). Is there a social-media fueled protest style? An analysis from #jan25 to #gezipark. *Technosociology: Our tools, our selves*. [Blog]. Retrieved from http://technosociology.org/?p=1255.

Vlieghe, J., Vandermeersche, G., and Soetaert, R. (2014). Social media in literacy education: Exploring social reading with pre-service teachers. *New Media and Society*. Advance online publication.

Weinstein, E. C. (2014). The personal is political on social media: Online civic expression patterns and pathways among civically engaged youth. *International Journal of Communication*, *8*, 210–233.

Wellman, B., Quan-Haase, A., Boase, J., Chen, W., Hampton, K., Díaz, I., and Miyata, K. (2003). The social affordances of the Internet for networked individualism. *Journal of Computer Mediated Communication*, *8*(3), 0.

Westheimer, J., and Kahne, J. (2004). What kind of citizen? The politics of educating for democracy. *American Educational Research Journal, 41*(2), 237–269.

Wolfsfeld, G., Segev, E., and Sheafer, T. (2013). Social media and the Arab Spring: Politics comes first. *International Journal of Press/Politics, 18*(2), 115–137.

Xenos, M., Vromen, A., and Loader, B. D. (2014). The great equalizer? Patterns of social media use and youth political engagement in three advanced democracies. *Information, Communication and Society, 17*(2), 151–167.

Zuckerman, E. (2013). *Rewire: Digital cosmopolitans in the age of connection.* New York: W. W. Norton.

CONTRIBUTORS

Cory Wright-Maley is Assistant Professor of Education at St. Mary's University. He teaches elementary social studies education and pedagogy. His research interests include simulations, democratic education, and social studies teacher education. He taught history, civics, and economics in California prior to his doctoral studies and is dedicated to addressing economic disparity, particularly as it relates to democracy and democratic education.

Trent Davis is Associate Professor of Education at St. Mary's University. He teaches educational philosophy, educational history, and the philosophy of Catholic education. His research interests include ethics, existentialism, and pragmatism for democratic education. He has a growing interest in skepticism, as well as the relationship between epistemology and the problems of classroom life, and has written about civic virtue in democratic education.

Lauren Arend is Assistant Professor of Education at Saint Louis University. She teaches courses in school and community, action research, and research methods. She has worked as an independent program evaluator for non-profit programs including summer reading programs, arts integration programs, and youth leadership programs.

Jill Bass has worked in urban public education for over two decades. She taught high school social studies in Chicago and New York City, and was an instructional coach, curriculum writer, and teacher preparation consultant. At Mikva Challenge, she directs the Center for Action Civics, overseeing curriculum development, teacher professional development, and school partnerships.

Brooke Blevins is Assistant Professor of Social Studies Education at Baylor University. Her research interests include citizenship education in the digital age, critical historical thinking, and teacher education.

Jeffrey P. Carpenter is Assistant Professor in the School of Education at Elon University, and director of the Elon Teaching Fellows Program. He taught internationally and in U.S. public high schools and middle schools for ten years. His research interests include collaborative learning, social media, and pedagogical innovations.

Ryan Colwell is Assistant Professor of Childhood Education and Director of the Childhood Education Program in the Graduate School of Education and Allied Professions at Fairfield University. He previously served as a second and third grade teacher in two Connecticut public school districts.

Alexander Cuenca is Assistant Professor of Social Studies Education at Saint Louis University. His research examines social studies teaching and learning, democratic education, and the pedagogy of teacher education. He is co-editor of *Rethinking Social Studies Teacher Education for 21st Century Citizenship*, and his work has appeared in journals such as *Social Education* (focused on events in Ferguson), *Teaching and Teacher Education*, and *Critical Education*.

Jennifer E. Dolan is a Ph.D. candidate and Graduate Assistant in Curriculum and Instruction at the University of Connecticut. Her research interests include how culturally responsive teaching practices impact the development of young learners in the literacy curriculum. She is actively involved in many professional associations, presents at educational conferences, and is an expert reviewer for the *Journal of Literacy Research*.

Kathryn E. Engebretson is Assistant Professor at Indiana University in Bloomington, with research interests in teacher education, social studies, controversial issues, and gender. She teaches elementary social studies methods, multicultural education, and curriculum discourse classes and holds a particular interest in feminist pedagogies.

Henry A. Giroux is Visiting Distinguished Professor at Ryerson University. His scholarship focuses on critical and public pedagogy, youth studies, higher education, cultural studies, and other areas. He has published more than 50 books and nearly 300 articles and is a vociferous critic of neoliberalism and a defender of democratic education. His latest book is *The Violence of Organized Forgetting*.

James M. M. Hartwick is Professor of Curriculum and Instruction. His research interests include social studies education, cultural studies, teacher education, and theology. He has published several articles on the topic of teaching about big money in the U.S. political process for practicing teachers.

Alexandria Hollett is pursuing her doctorate in the School of Education at Indiana University. She leads workshops on intersectional approaches to activism and queer issues in schools for university students, educators, and community members. She teaches courses on multicultural education for preservice teachers, with specific attention to antiracist pedagogy, queer theory, feminist theory, labor politics, and gender studies.

Tara Hyland-Russell is Vice-President Academic and Dean at St. Mary's University, where she teaches in the Radical Humanities program, focused on social justice and self-empowerment for marginalized adults. She specializes in narrative, transformative learning, life writing, and twentieth-century literature. Her recent publications focus on reflective journaling and aboriginal novels.

Mark Edward Johnson is Assistant Professor of Education at Abraham Baldwin Agricultural College in Tifton, Georgia, where he teaches foundations of education. His current scholarship concerns rural education and conceptual histories of field-defining notions such as democratic and transformative education and *Bildung*, and how these ideas have been understood through emancipatory and pluralist approaches to educational theorizing.

Wayne Journell is Assistant Professor at the University of North Carolina at Greensboro. He has over 40 peer-reviewed publications and is currently an associate editor for *Theory and Research in Social Education*, the premier research journal in the field. In 2014, he won the Exemplary Research in Social Studies Award from the National Council for the Social Studies (NCSS) and the Early Career Award from the College and University Faculty Assembly of NCSS.

Douglas Kaufman is Associate Professor of Curriculum and Instruction, and University Teaching Fellow, at the University of Connecticut's Neag School of Education. His research interests include the nature of writing and writing instruction in schools, organization of literacy workshops, and teacher education, as well as issues of equity and social justice that pertain to all three.

Emma Kornfeld is earning her Master's in Social Work from the University of Michigan, concentrating in Community Organization and Community/ Social Systems. She worked at Mikva Challenge, directing their Issues to Action program, supporting the creation of nearly 240 community activism projects, co-directing youth policy-making councils advising the Mayor and the Cook County Board President, and overseeing a summer internship program placing students in the offices of local elected officials.

Daniel G. Krutka is Assistant Professor of Curriculum and Instruction at Texas Woman's University. His research interests include citizenship education and the role participatory media might play in cultivating more democratic educational experiences.

Karon LeCompte is Assistant Professor of Curriculum and Instruction at Baylor University. Her research interests include civic education, social justice education, and teacher education.

Brett L. M. Levy is Assistant Professor of Educational Theory and Practice. His research explores how educational programs can support civic and political engagement among youth and how such engagement can in turn foster academic and life skills. His dissertation won the 2012 Exemplary Dissertation Award from the National Council for the Social Studies, and he is currently conducting studies exploring students' experiences in discussion-based government courses at several high schools. He teaches courses on youth civic engagement, social studies education, research methods, and environmental education.

Joseph R. Nichols, Jr. is Assessment Coordinator and Assistant Professor of Education at Saint Louis University. His research interests include: teacher education assessment, accountability, and policy, and the politics of education; democracy and democratic theory; and schooling in global society. His recent works related to democracy education have focused on economic paradigms and their effects on citizenship and citizenship education, as well as teaching preservice teachers about democracy.

John Rogers is Professor or Education at UCLA's Graduate School of Education and Information Studies and Director of UCLA's Institute for Democracy, Education, and Access (IDEA). He studies the role of civic engagement in equity-focused school reform and civic renewal and the relationship between education and different forms of inequality. He is the co-author of *Learning Power: Organizing for Education and Justice* and co-editor of *Public Engagement for Public Education: Joining Forces to Revitalize Democracy and Equalize Schools*.

Tamara L. Sober is a Doctoral Fellow in the Virginia Commonwealth University's School of Education, where she is a Graduate Assistant for the Metropolitan Education Research Consortium. She is a former social studies teacher, and served the Virginia Education Association (VEA) as the Assistant Director of Government Relations and then as the Assistant Director of the Office of Teaching and Learning, She is the author of *Teaching Economics As If People Mattered*. Her professional experience, academic expertise, and research interests are in organizing, advocacy, and curriculum and instruction, with a focus on economics education and power analysis.

Corinne Syrnyk is Assistant Professor of Psychology at St Mary's University. She works in the fields of Psychology and Education across both the UK and Canada. Her research spans the spectrum to include studying the mechanisms of socio-educational opportunities for children with social, emotional, and behavioral disorders and for marginalized, non-traditional adult learners. Her recent publications have focused on teacher nurturance.

Joel Westheimer is Professor and University Research Chair in the Sociology of Education at the University of Ottawa. He has won multiple awards for his research, writing, and leadership in the field of democracy education. His publications on educating the "good citizen" are considered seminal in the field. He is the education columnist for CBC Ottawa's Morning Show and co-founder and executive director of Democratic Dialogue, a think-tank dedicated to considering democratic ideals in education.

INDEX